Reconstituting
AUTHORITY

Reconstituting
AUTHORITY

American Fiction in the Province of the Law, 1880–1920

William E. Moddelmog

UNIVERSITY OF IOWA PRESS

IOWA CITY

University of Iowa Press,
Iowa City 52242
Copyright © 2000 by the
University of Iowa Press
All rights reserved
Printed in the United States of America
http://www.uiowa.edu/~uipress
No part of this book may be reproduced or
used in any form or by any means, without
permission in writing from the publisher. All
reasonable steps have been taken to contact
copyright holders of material used in this book.
The publisher would be pleased to make
suitable arrangements with any whom it has
not been possible to reach.

The publication of this book was generously
supported by the University of Iowa
Foundation.

Printed on acid-free paper

Library of Congress
Cataloging-in-Publication Data
Moddelmog, William E., 1961–
Reconstituting authority: American fiction in the province of the
law, 1880–1920 / by William E.
Moddelmog.
    p.   cm.
Includes bibliographical references
(p.   ) and index.
ISBN 0-87745-736-0 (cloth)
1. Legal stories, American—History and criticism.   2. American
fiction—19th century—History
and criticism.   3. American
fiction—20th century—History
and criticism.   4. Law and literature—History—19th century.
5. Law and literature—
History—20th century.
6. Authority in literature.
7. Law in literature.   I. Title.

PS374.L34M63 2001
813'.409355—dc21
                00-044743

00 01 02 03 04 C 5 4 3 2 1

for Cecilia

CONTENTS

ACKNOWLEDGMENTS

This book would not have been possible without many and varied forms of support, influence, advice, and guidance. *Reconstituting Authority* began as a dissertation in the English Department at UCLA under the direction of Martha Banta. I am indebted to her not only for her wise counsel, but also for her unfailing encouragement and positive reinforcement throughout the dissertation stage and after. Eric Sundquist and Kenneth Karst also read the dissertation and provided invaluable comments and suggestions. My understanding of the issues involved in this work has developed over a long period of time and has benefited greatly from the challenging intellectual climate provided by my colleagues at UCLA, especially Luke Bresky, Martin Kevorkian, Kris Fresonke, Rebecca Anderson, Maurice Lee, Jayne Devens, and Stan Orr.

A Dissertation Year Fellowship from UCLA and an American Literatures and Cultures grant from the Department of English enabled me to complete the dissertation in a timely fashion. The advice and assistance of Chris Mott and Jeanette Gilkison throughout my career at UCLA helped me to balance my research and teaching duties. I also wish to thank my colleagues at UCLA Writing Programs for giving me the opportunity to teach while working on the book manuscript. I am especially grateful to Bruce Beiderwell for his example and influence before as well as after graduate school.

Special thanks must go to Michael Colacurcio, without whose inspired teaching I might never have realized the pleasures and rigors of American literary and intellectual history. He has also served as a mentor in matters both professional and personal, and his advice has helped me to negotiate the twists and turns of academic life with only an occasional sensation of vertigo.

Holly Carver at the University of Iowa Press has shown wonderful enthusiasm for the book from the start, and I appreciate her unflagging commitment to it. Lee Mitchell read the manuscript and provided comforting words of praise and thoughtful suggestions for improvement, and John Mulvihill's editing enhanced the quality of the final manuscript considerably.

The support of my family before, during, and after graduate school has been of immeasurable help to me. My mother and father, Lynn and Jim Moddelmog, have (perhaps with some perplexity) consistently encouraged me in my very long career as a student of both the law and literature. Debra Moddelmog has given me insight into professional matters at crucial junctures in my career, and Scott Cairns's advice and humor have helped me keep things in perspective. Finally, Cecilia Moddelmog's love, inspiration, and patience in the face of my academic obsessions have meant more to me than I can express.

Reconstituting
AUTHORITY

Professionalism in Law and Literature

Whenever the pulpit is usurped by a formalist, then is the worshipper defrauded and disconsolate. . . . I once heard a preacher who sorely tempted me to say, I would go to church no more. . . . The capital secret of his profession, namely, to convert life into truth, he had not learned. Not one fact in all his experience, had he yet imported into his doctrine.

    Ralph Waldo Emerson, "The Divinity School Address"

Those who are esteemed umpires of taste, are often persons who have acquired some knowledge of admired pictures or sculptures, and have an inclination for whatever is elegant. . . . Their knowledge of the fine arts is some study of rules and particulars, or some limited judgment of color or form, which is exercised for amusement or for show. It is a proof of the shallowness of the doctrine of beauty, as it lies in the minds of our amateurs, that men seem to have lost the perception of the instant dependence of form upon soul.

    Emerson, "The Poet"

What is the use of courts, if judges only quote authorities, and no judge exerts original jurisdiction, or recurs to first principles?

    Emerson, "Address to the Citizens of Concord"

M y epigraphs from Emerson may seem out of place in a book that concentrates on American fiction published between 1880 and 1920. Yet in attempting to describe the contours of legal and literary authority in American culture, I find myself formulating two narratives — one that ends with Emerson, and one that begins with him. The first of these stories is the subject of Robert A. Ferguson's *Law and Letters in American Culture*, a study that compellingly recounts the growth of a liaison between the legal and literary spheres in the United States beginning with the Revolution, and the decline of that configuration before the Civil War. Emerson figures prominently in the denouement of this story, not because he rejects any relationship between the legal and the literary, but because he identifies a developing formalism in the law that deprives it of its claim to authority. As my epigraphs indicate, Emerson decried the rise of this formalistic mode of thought in the religious and literary spheres as well as the legal, and his works stand largely for the proposition that an authority grounded in narrow specialization and professionalization — a kind of knowledge based on "rules and particulars" rather than on the "instant dependence of form upon soul" — is no authority at all.

Yet the label of "amateur" that Emerson pins on weak poets (clergymen and judges included) is telling. While he may be employing its Latin root ironically (with "lovers" like this, poetry needs no enemies), his usage also points to a conception of authority that is itself dependent upon some version of what it means to be "professional."[1] Thus, his rejection of formalism can be seen not as an end to a connection between literature and the law in the cultural geography of nineteenth-century America, but as a reformulation of that connection. If Emerson critiques the professions for their adherence to "rules and particulars," he does so in the name of defining the true professional as one who converts "life into truth." And this conception of professionalism makes possible a second narrative of legal and literary engagement, a narrative that begins with Emerson but whose primary development occurs in the late nineteenth and early twentieth centuries. In this story, the law's formal integrity — a formalism that once served to establish the law as a realm of independence and political neutrality — begins to give way to a more Emersonian conception of professionalism that requires it to be accountable to something like "experience." And at roughly the same moment in this narrative, writers of fiction are struggling to imagine their own authorship as a form of professional activity and to imbue it with an authority in the public sphere to which the professions — especially law — had historically laid claim. The result is not just a literary interest in legal issues (though that is part of what occurs), but an attempt by authors to create texts that exercise a measure of institutional power. Presenting themselves as official and thereby asserting a regulative (though not coercive) role in American public life, these works strive to redefine authority in such a way that their own narratives can be seen as simultaneously legal and literary. This is the story that *Reconstituting Authority* seeks to tell.

To begin, some clarification of what I mean by "authority" is in order. Let me first express what I do not mean. I do not mean "force." As Hannah Arendt notes, "Since authority always demands obedience, it is commonly mistaken for some form of power or violence. Yet authority precludes the use of external means of coercion; where force is used, authority itself has failed" (92–93). Authority, unlike coercion, is a kind of constraint to which one *willfully* submits.

This point also distinguishes authority from something like persuasion, which, as Stanley Fish argues, can be seen as a kind of force. For Fish, force is what we all engage in whenever we assert our beliefs, since those beliefs can never be "true" in any transcendent sense and can thus never claim to be "true" or even "good" for those we try to convince. As Fish succinctly puts it, "you can never get away from your beliefs, which means that you can never get away from force, from the pressure exerted by a partial, non-neutral, nonauthoritative, ungrounded point of view" (*Doing* 519). Beliefs are "nonauthoritative" precisely because they are merely beliefs, and not truths. Authority for him is simply the illusory quality that certain beliefs have obtained by virtue of having "won" — by having become dominant ways of viewing and thinking about the world — and such victories can come about only through a process that draws upon existing beliefs that have themselves become so institutionalized as to have attained the status of truths.

Fish's perspective, like most poststructuralist theory, is an "inside" one. It completely rejects such Emersonian concepts as "soul," "original jurisdiction," and "first principles," denying the possibility of grounding thought or action in anything "outside" of the present configuration of socially, culturally, and politically interested modes of perception and behavior. It even excludes recourse to a concept like "experience," at least as Emerson uses that term. Experience for Emerson serves to disrupt the rigidity of form and provides an "outside" perspective against which to test the adequacy of formal principles. Fish, however, implies that form is all we have, so that even when we think we are genuinely "experiencing" something we are actually interpreting it — an act that requires the use of formal rules already available to us, rules that in fact *constitute* us. But Fish dismisses authority a bit too easily, because his argument is persuasive only to the extent that it asserts a kind of latent authority — a power that stems from our own willful submission to the forms that it embodies. Those formal elements would include the particular logic and rhetorical structure the argument employs, its publication by a major university press, its connection with Fish's reputation in the academic community, and similar factors. Such elements make the argument seem either true or false — objectively and absolutely — even though the argument itself denies it asserts anything more than contingent, nonauthoritative belief. Although Fish would undoubtedly agree with this, he would also claim that the "truth" he asserts is still just a supposition and can therefore be influenced by persuasion.[2] But my point is simply that we can never engage in any type of communication that does not invoke some form of authority, and that even the claim that authority is illusory cannot escape that fact. Authority links our contingent, limited, formally bound claims and beliefs to something we imagine as substantive, permanent, universal. Although the "truths" upon which beliefs are founded may be illusory, the fact of authority is not. Without it, language, social life, and all other forms of order would be unthinkable.

The questions that need asking then are not whether authority does or should exist, but what shape it takes and how it is exercised.[3] By focusing on the relation of law and literature in the late nineteenth and early twentieth centuries, I hope to reveal a transformation in the way Americans thought about the relation of "inside" to "outside," and thus about authority itself. That transformation was intimately bound up with the rise of professionalism. Fish's "inside" view of authority (or rather, his attempt to replace authority with belief) is an important contemporary formulation of a problem that faced both legal and literary professionals in the nineteenth century and that made the definition of professionalism especially vexing. For if on one level being professional meant establishing a kind of independence from the merely contingent and contextual norms of social and political life — an independence that would make possible a direct and unmediated (or as Emerson puts it, "instant") relation to objective reality — on another it meant instituting a set of procedures, rules, and forms that would allow that independence to be exercised. And it is at this point that the ideology of professionalism begins to collapse in on itself. Since experience, by definition, cannot be codified, what forms would allow for the conversion of "life into truth" except ones that were not themselves "true"? Such forms would be nothing but "inside" versions of maps to an "outside" that must of necessity always remain "outside."

The problem of professionalism is simply one manifestation of the larger problem that plagues liberal-democratic ideology — a problem that might be phrased as follows: How can norms that are understood solely as the result of current standards, desires, or beliefs (enacted democratically) possess the authority to command willful obedience? Are norms authoritative only when their foundations can be connected to an "outside" that is imagined as absolute — "truth," "reality," "God," "reason," or perhaps "the Constitution" (imagined as a moral document)? Versions of this problem have dominated the work of such philosophers and theorists as Arendt, Richard Rorty, John Rawls, Ronald Dworkin, Jürgen Habermas, Pierre Bourdieu, and Fish, to name but a few. But if we are looking for an individual whose work best frames the issue, we might look no further than Max Weber. Weber drew distinctions between three types of authority — charismatic, traditional, and legal-rational — and posited the latter as the glue that holds the modern liberal state together. As opposed to charismatic authority (which emanates from individuals conceived in some way as seers or prophets) and traditional authority (which founds itself on a past hallowed by time itself), legal-rational authority relies upon no claim to transcendence. Instead, norms are legitimized through their enactment within a formal process that is purely positivistic in nature, and those norms command respect simply because they are legal. For Weber, systems grounded in legal-rational authority can also contain elements of the other forms of authority, thereby masking the constructed nature of the norms they generate. Nonetheless, he implies that legal-rational authority also makes possible real choice, because it looks to no "outside" source of compulsion to justify its normative structure.[4]

Weber's attempt to describe a strictly "inside" form of authority, however, still seems to presuppose values that lie "outside" of the system. As Anthony Kronman has indicated, Weber's perspective implicitly posits freedom itself as a kind of meta-norm that elevates legal-rational authority over the other forms Weber discusses (Kronman 95). That is to say, norms that are the products of a process fashioned purely by humans can possess authority only if the process is seen as increasing the potential for individual freedom — a value that is not itself a product of the process. This fact suggests that the concept of authority necessarily requires some conception of an "outside," even if it is tenuous and uncertain. In the absence of such a conception, norms are just "beliefs" in Fish's sense, and beliefs are necessarily "nonauthoritative." Contemporary critical theory has struggled mightily to find a way of acknowledging the limited and constructed nature of our norms, while nonetheless insisting that some form of authoritative critique is possible. Such attempts, however (as Fish himself has argued), have largely been futile.[5] What might be called the absent "outside" continues to haunt these efforts. Moreover, there is a sneaking suspicion among many who read and write about theory that beneath even the most stubborn forms of antifoundational-ism (such as Fish's) lurks an unacknowledged foundation.[6]

Although Weber does not adequately address the problem of founda-tions, we might nonetheless misread him in a way that sheds a different light on legal-rational authority, and thus on the ideology of profession-alism. Instead of embodying a strictly "inside" perspective, it is possible to argue that the formal properties of any legal-rational system always rest upon some meta-norm that lies beyond the system's own bounds, but that the formalism of such a system implies a mediated relationship between the "inside" form and the "outside" substance. In this sense, rules and procedures constitute a bridge to a remote and uncertain truth, and are thus always subject to revision depending on the conception of the meta-norms that give them authority. But the corollary to this argu-ment is that those meta-norms are cognizable only through the very au-thoritative structures that they seemingly authorize. If the "outside" serves as foundation for the "inside," it is nonetheless true that the "in-side" also constructs the "outside." The two terms, of course, have mean-ing only relative to each other, and this fact implies that whenever we are participating in an institutional mode of thought — one defined by for-mal rules and procedures (indeed, there may be no other kind) — we are not only relying upon a foundation that legitimates that mode, but help-ing to construct the foundation itself. For Fish, this delegitimates the very notion of a foundation, but it need not. It simply means that the au-thority of institutions and of professions is always subject to challenge *from within*. Every assertion that adheres to the conventions of its pro-fessional context (whether an argument in court or an interpretation of a novel in a literary journal) rests upon an unstated connection to a "truth" implied by those conventions, and this connection to a transcendent standard means that those conventions contain within them the seeds of their own destruction. Or revision, I should say, because whatever new relation of "inside" to "outside" might be proposed could be imagined only within the context of the formal principles that continue to define the profession.

Professionalism and Storytelling

I have attempted to define a particular model of authority — one in which form and substance serve as mutually constitutive concepts — because it is this model that begins to emerge in both legal and literary circles after the Civil War. Although few intellectuals in nineteenth-century America would have adopted the antifoundationalist premises of contemporary critical theory, that is not to say that they accepted without question the unmediated relationship between form and substance, inside and outside, upon which Emerson had insisted. Emerson's "dependence of form upon soul" does not identify a relationship of mutual dependence ("soul" does not depend upon "form"), and so it refuses to acknowledge the power of institutional or professional codes. By the late nineteenth century, however, the influence of such codes was inescapable and helped to effect an entirely new relation of "inside" to "outside." Thomas Bender has described this change as a gradual reformulation of the relationship between knower and known:

> The authority of disciplinary professionalism was linked to new perceptions of the nature of "reality." Representatives of urban culture — from Daniel Drake to P. T. Barnum — had assumed that reality was generally accessible to common observation. However democratic, this naïve empiricism was gradually rejected as inadequate. . . . Valid knowledge, formerly concretized in individual relationships to nature and society, now seemed to be defined in forms and processes one step removed from direct human experience. (13)

As a result of this epistemic shift, professional codes began to multiply in the late nineteenth century, partly fueled by the founding of associations geared toward marking off specific areas of cultural territory and thereby asserting an authoritative voice over those spheres. The American Bar Association, for instance, was founded in 1878 and the Modern Language Association in 1883.[7] But even though such disciplines were staking out their own professional claims, they were doing so in a way that also denied the very lines being drawn. What united these efforts at professional boundary-drawing was the ideology of professionalism itself — an ideology that made the project of defining disciplines inherently interdisciplinary.[8] And this is especially apparent with respect to the fields of law and literature.

One of the earliest attempts both to make use of and to revise the Emersonian "dependence of form upon soul" came from within the legal arena. In his series of lectures delivered at Harvard in 1880 (published the following year as *The Common Law*), Oliver Wendell Holmes Jr. invoked "experience" as an antiformalist principle, claiming that the law's rules and forms were bound up with such extralegal elements of thought as "the felt necessities of the time," "prevalent moral and political theories," "intuitions of public policy," and even the "prejudices" of judges (*Common* 1). Of course, these considerations are decidedly worldly; they lack the kind of transcendent authority with which Emerson had imbued the concept of experience. In some ways, they make Holmes a precursor of contemporary antifoundationalists, since they seem to construct the law as a realm of belief rather than truth, of politics instead of principles, and thus as an institution whose inside can be grounded only in another inside. Such an institution would seem to lack any claim to authority, at least in the Emersonian sense of a direct relation between a formal and contingent inside and a substantive and permanent outside. Yet Holmes was decidedly not an antifoundationalist. He insisted upon the law's claim to authority in American culture, even as he derided those who adhered to natural or higher law conceptions of its foundation, and those (like Christopher Langdell of Harvard) who thought law could be taught as a science.[9] Rather than imagining the law as a realm of fixed principles and moral absolutes, Holmes envisioned it as a kind of master narrative of a community's history, values, and beliefs:

> The law embodies the story of a nation's development through many centuries, and it cannot be dealt with as if it contained only the axioms and corollaries of a book of mathematics. In order to know what it is, we must know what it has been, and what it tends to become. . . . The substance of the law at any given time pretty nearly corresponds, so far as it goes, with what is then understood to be convenient; but its form and machinery, and the degree to which it is able to work out desired results, depend very much upon its past. (*Common* 1–2)

The distinction Holmes draws between the law's form and substance is a distinction between its responsiveness to extralegal elements such as politics and theories of morality, and its own inner logic — its precedents, traditions, and abiding rules of construction. The importance of such formal elements, however, does not deprive it of its authority, nor does its openness to experience endow it with a claim to transcendence. Instead, it is through the conflict between these two elements that the law gains its authority as *narrative*. Were it simply a way of enacting present policy objectives, it would not exist as a story because it would have no internal coherence — no relation of past to present. And were it an expression of enduring principles of nature or morality, it would remain fixed and static — it might be a poem (neoclassical perhaps), but it could not be a story. The model of narration bridges the gap between a conception of the law as an institutional structure defined by its formalistic rules and settled doctrines, and an Emersonian vision of the law as a realm of "original jurisdiction" and "first principles." The trick, for Holmes, is to understand how to read the law. If we read it just for its formal properties, it becomes ossified, nostalgic, unable to respond to changing circumstances and standards. If we read it only as rhetoric, on the other hand — as simply a method of instituting particular sets of contingent and self-interested beliefs — its lack of internal integrity would expose an absent foundation and deprive it of any claim to authority. If we read it as a "story," however, it possesses both a formal integrity and a responsiveness to change and revision. Thus, the metaphor of the story functions as a way of showing how the law's inner structure is compatible with its need to adapt to "outside" conditions (moral, political, economic, and so on).[10]

Although Holmes attempted to draw a sharp line between law and morality, he did so not to make the practice of law a strictly "inside" game, but to underscore the extent to which legal principles are always in some way moral principles (and political ones and economic ones, etc.). In entering the legal realm, we do not leave "experience" at the gate. Instead, we use it in employing the very formal concepts that would seem (theoretically) to prevent its use. The "dependence of form upon soul" remains in Holmes's configuration, but the dependence also moves in the other direction. If Holmes's view of "experience" strikes us as more contingent than Emerson's — more like Fish's "belief" than like Emerson's "soul" — it may be because such concepts as "politics," "felt necessities," and "theories of morality" are ways of emphasizing this state of mutual dependence. Furthermore, this dependence is no longer "instant," as it is for Emerson — the law's authority springs from a *mediated* relationship between its formal "inside" and an experiential "outside."

We might see Holmes's comparison of the law to a story as a way of redefining not only the law, but "stories" as well. Holmes, of course, chose to practice law rather than follow in his father's literary footsteps, and while that choice was on one level a rejection of literature, on another it was simply a way of doing a different kind of literary work. Consider this description of the law from an 1885 speech delivered by Holmes to a gathering of lawyers:

> To the lover of the law, how small a thing seem the novelist's tales of the loves and fates of Daphnis and Chloe! How pale a phantom even the Circe of poetry, transforming mankind with intoxicating dreams

of fiery ether, and the foam of summer seas, and glowing greensward, and the white arms of women! For him, no less a history will suffice than that of the moral history of his race. For him every text that he deciphers, every doubt that he resolves, adds a new feature to the unfolding panorama of man's destiny upon this earth. . . . When I think thus of the law, I see a princess mightier than she who once wrought at Bayeux, eternally weaving into her web dim figures of an ever-lengthening past — figures too dim to be noticed by the idle, too symbolic to be interpreted except by her pupils, but to the discerning eye disclosing every painful step and every world-shaking contest by which mankind has worked and fought its way from savage isolation to organic social life. ("Law" 26–27)

Although Holmes insists on drawing distinctions between law and literature in this passage, those distinctions nonetheless reveal a relation. The law is literary, he implies, since it occupies the space that literature has traditionally filled. But it is a kind of literature that is more valuable than the classical myths of Daphnis and Chloe, or Odysseus and Circe. Those stories operate like seductresses themselves; they are static tales of timeless encounters that draw attention away from a more vital form of storytelling — something more like "history." And this history can be told only because the law's formal integrity allows one to read it with comprehension, while its continual incorporation of new elements allows it to change. This tension creates its narrative.

A similar tension is present in literary manifestoes of the era as well, as in Henry James's "The Art of Fiction." James's essay attacks the formalism inherent in current definitions of literary genres, using "experience" as its sword. For James, experience cannot be institutionally constrained; it "is never limited, and it is never complete; it is an immense sensibility, a kind of huge spiderweb of the finest silken threads suspended in the chamber of consciousness, and catching every airborne particle in its tissue." Yet in the same essay, James asserts that "the novel is history" and that its subject matter is stored "in documents and records" — a very different manifestation of experience than that represented by "the chamber of consciousness" (82, 78). His effort to assert a form of literary freedom is delicately balanced against his desire to authorize literary work as a discipline and to define its substance in a way that both constrains and legitimates it. In the process, he does not assert the inherently "outside" character of fiction as much as he proposes an "outside" that will construct an institutional "inside"— a way to practice the art of fiction with a kind of mediated, or bounded, freedom. A way that looks much like Holmes's conception of the study and practice of law.

Laying Down the Law

I do not mean to suggest that legal thinkers such as Holmes defined the literary for novelists such as James, nor that authorial reconceptualizations of literature determined legal ideas or practices. Rather, I view the two spheres as engaged in internal debates over the nature of authority that largely paralleled each other, and those parallels allowed for an interdisciplinary way of thinking that made possible a conception of fiction as a form of law-making. Yet such a conception could emerge only in the context of reimagining the process of law-making itself. While there are obvious differences between a judicial opinion and a novel (the most important, of course, is that the judgments of the former are enforceable through the machinery of the state), it is nonetheless true that the law's dictates are mediated by the process of storytelling. The law's stories shape both the facts at hand and the meaning of the law to be applied, and these stories endow its judgments with an authority that does not depend solely on the threat of physical force. What if the articulation of stories, more than the rendering of judgments, were seen as the primary function of the law? If the law's fundamental purpose in American public life were to construct authoritative narratives — narratives that act as norms by regulating conduct and defining choices — would that not mean that authors might construct narratives of equal weight and power by presenting literature as an institution analogous to the law? [11]

These are the questions probed in the works of William Dean Howells, Helen Hunt Jackson, Pauline Hopkins, Charles Chesnutt, Edith Wharton, and Theodore Dreiser. I have chosen these authors not because they are the only ones in this era addressing legal issues (there are many more), but because all tell stories that reflect a sense of their own institutionality — an institutionality that they explicitly or implicitly present as "legal." It is worth noting that the authors in this list span the literary genres of realism, naturalism, and romance. The phenomenon I highlight crosses the bounds of these literary movements and alliances, and in fact undermines the solidity of those bounds. What these authors share is a common framework for asserting a public voice, and that framework draws upon a model of authority that developed gradually between the end of the Civil War and the beginning of the twentieth century. It not only helped to restructure the disciplines of literature and the law, but science, medicine, journalism, and newly emergent academic disciplines such as sociology and ethnography as well. The word that best sums up this model is "professionalization." Robert Ferguson's argument that literature and the law had ceased to inform one another by the end of the nineteenth century is grounded in the notion that the law's movement towards professionalization transformed "the grand style of the generalist" — a form of legal thought that made the lawyer "literary" — into a specialized and positivistic approach to the law (epitomized by Holmes) that discounted moral and philosophical speculation (Ferguson 287). But Ferguson overlooks the ways in which professionalization simply reoriented the legal paradigm that had produced an earlier generation of lawyers (Jefferson, Story, Webster, Choate). Later figures such as Holmes rejected the neoclassical foundations of concepts like nature, reason, and equity, but they did not thereby narrow the scope of issues with which lawyers and judges would be concerned — they redefined them. As we have seen, Holmes insisted upon the relevance of "experience" to the law, even while he was adamant about the line separating law from morality. If he argued for lawyers and judges to adhere to modes of analysis and forms of evidence that were "purely" legal, he did so because the "legal" for him was already moral, philosophical, social, and political.[12]

But Ferguson is correct in noting that legal practitioners in the late nineteenth century began to think of their own profession less and less in literary terms. This might be attributed to the decline of a republican conception of the lawyer as a public figure whose broad education and rhetorical skills made him seem uniquely qualified to assert a voice — both oratorical and literary — on matters of public concern. This version of republicanism was nearly dead by the end of the nineteenth century, although it feebly emerged every now and then in the form of mugwump social critiques. Professionalism was what replaced it. If the authority of the professional was more circumscribed than the authority of the republican lawyer or judge had been, it was nonetheless still a form of authority, and thus filled the holes in the fabric of American public life that the decline of figures such as Webster had initiated. The explosion of new "professions" during this era testifies to the power of the ideal. But while each profession claimed to assert an authoritative voice over a particular sphere of American life, none could lay claim to the public weight and influence that the law had traditionally been accorded. Thus, even though its status declined markedly after the Civil War, the law nonetheless continued to embody the ideal that there could be an arena within the public sphere that would be capable of resolving political and social conflicts by reference to "rules and particulars" that were independent of the conflicts themselves, an arena whose judgments, ultimately rooted in a foundational "outside," would be truly authoritative. The viability of the "rule of law" had not, and still has not, disappeared from the catalog of national ideals.[13]

All of the works I discuss use the new conception of the law's institutionally mediated norms to assert the legitimacy of an authorial voice in the public sphere. They do so in two ways. First, they operate not primarily as comments on the law from an alternative literary perspective, but as attempts to revise or reimagine legal principles from within the law's own structure and discursive parameters. In this sense, these works present themselves as "professional" and "institutional," for they adhere to a set of principles whose meanings have been methodically constructed through the disciplinary regime of legal case law and commentary. And in this way, the authors imbue their own writing with the authority that attaches to professional and institutional structures, even if they can do so only by denying the possibility of complete authorial freedom and creative license. As Louis Menand notes, "nothing in professional life is *ex nihilo*; professionalism is the art of precedent" (111). Consequently, one striking feature common to each of these works is restraint — each author's presentation of legal issues is moderated by the unstated desire (or even the need) to remain within the bounds of legally acceptable structures and formulae. None of these works either reflects or valorizes a transcendent plane from which those structures could be objectively confirmed or critiqued.

Yet this form of institutionality does not negate the possibility of proposing changes to the legal universes the works invoke. The second way in which authors assert the public authority of their own authorship is by highlighting the narrative bases for the law's standards and precepts. In so doing, they present those principles as inherently unstable, subject to challenge depending on the current state of "experience." Although the authors do not claim the privilege of inventing new narratives (thus placing the category of "narrative" in the transcendent position they deny access to), they do assert the authority to present narratives that the law has not validated — narratives that are already implicit parts of the law's formulations by virtue of having been rejected or compromised.

Such stories, in a sense, have already been authorized; their power lies dormant beneath the surface of dominant legal formulations. In other words, if one of the law's functions is to legitimate certain narratives by transforming them into abiding principles, then authors might engage versions of those narratives and thus view their own stories as legal arguments. "The law" in this sense may seem to spill over its institutional bounds, but in fact it does not because it cannot. Whether its authority is grounded in "nature" and "morality" or "experience" and "public policy," it requires a theoretical connection to an outside — a connection that gives the law an intrinsically volatile quality and interdisciplinary orientation (an interdisciplinarity that might be imagined as "the grand style of the generalist" or as the "legal-rational" structure common to the professions). The important consideration in analyzing literary representations of legal issues is not whether such representations come from outside the law (of course they do, since they are not judicial opinions, statutes, etc.), but whether the outside position they imagine themselves occupying is *an outside that is already implicitly recognized by the law's own inside (institutional) structure.* And when concepts such as "experience" and "narrative" begin to make a kind of legal sense, then those who conceive of their own practices in terms of such concepts — writers of fiction — can start viewing themselves as doing legal work.

The relation between law and literature that these works reflect thus involves both a faithfulness to and a reconceptualization of earlier definitions of "literature." In some ways, the version of authorship they embody is prophetic, in that it claims access to a reality unrecognized by current institutional structures. But their form of prophecy — unlike, say, Emerson's — is expressed in terms that make sense institutionally; the truths they find may challenge accepted legal formulae, but they do not elude legal understanding (a kind of understanding that structures thought outside as well as inside the legal profession). My understanding of this relation has been influenced by Pierre Bourdieu's concept of the "field" as a relatively autonomous sphere of culture in which values and judgments that are politically interested gain legitimacy and emerge as universalized norms within the field. Bourdieu builds upon the work of Weber by emphasizing the ways in which the formal elements of modern legal institutions (grounded in legal-rational authority) can disguise their positivism and thus deny their origins in free choice. In what Bourdieu terms the "juridical field," the process of universalization is especially powerful, affecting ideas and practices seemingly far removed from the legal sphere: "Law is the quintessential form of the symbolic power of naming that creates the things named, and creates social groups in particular. It confers upon the reality which arises from its classificatory operations the maximum permanence that any social entity has the power to confer upon another, the permanence which we attribute to objects" ("Force" 838). Yet precisely because of the extent of the law's "symbolic power," I would argue, its "reality" is vulnerable to challenge from outside its predefined bounds. Such challenges, however, must nevertheless accept at least a portion of that "reality"— otherwise they simply confirm their own impotence in the face of the law's institutional standing. As Bourdieu puts it,

> Symbolic power, in its prophetic, heretical, anti-institutional, subversive mode, must also be realistically adapted to the objective structures of the social world. . . . [T]he will to transform the world by transforming the words for naming it . . . can only succeed if the resulting prophecies, or creative evocations, are also, at least in part, well-founded *pre*-visions, anticipatory descriptions. These visions only call forth what they proclaim — whether new practices, new mores or especially new social groupings — because they announce what is in the process of developing. . . . By granting to historical realities or virtualities the recognition that is implicit in prophetic proclamation, they offer them the real possibility of achieving full reality — fully recognized, official existence — through the effect of legitimation, indeed of consecration, implied by publishing and officializing them. ("Force" 840)

This is roughly the process I see at work in much of the legally oriented fiction of the late nineteenth and early twentieth centuries. Seeking to transform the reality that the law constructs, the authors of such fiction also confirm significant elements of that reality to endow their narratives with legitimacy — to make them official. They do not seek to invent new legal principles as much as to "call forth" revisionist principles latent in the law's texts. Consequently, they both confirm and rewrite the legal logic inherent in such "fundamental" (and formalistic) principles as property, race, privacy, and nature, presenting literature as an authoritative arena of public norm-making.

Of course, the boundaries between the legal and literary are not and, indeed, could not be erased completely. While exposing the fragility of these boundaries, the writers in this study are also invested in maintaining them. "Literature" in their works slips between its newly institutional definition — one that emphasizes its constraints — and a more romantic version of the literary as a realm of freedom and unmediated representation (a position that has also been attributed to literary realism). The interdependence of the prophetic and the institutional, the experiential and the formal, implied in these works means that freedom is not the only (or even the primary) value they assert. This point is important in light of Brook Thomas's recent interpretation of American literary realism. Thomas emphasizes realism's foundation in contract ideology — an ideology that, he maintains, "promises an immanent, rather than a transcendental, ordering of society" and organizes relations along a "horizontal" rather than "vertical" axis (*American* 3). His work constitutes a valuable contribution to the study of literature's relationship to the law in the late nineteenth and early twentieth centuries and argues persuasively for the kind of interdisciplinary approach upon which my own analysis rests. But while I am convinced that Thomas is right about the influence of contract on the development of American literary realism, his assertion that immanent choices, rather than transcendental compulsions, lie at the heart of realism's engagement with contractual thought seems to leave room only for a Weberian conception of realism's (and contract's) authority; it is legal-rational by virtue of its constructed nature. In Thomas's version of contract, we honor our promises not because it is "wrong" to break them, but because they constitute the only meaning available to us — a meaning we create and that helps constitute the very self that engages in acts of promising. His analysis, therefore, does not explicitly identify the "outside" value that authorizes the otherwise "immanent" exchanges he describes — namely, the value of freedom itself. Such a principle of authority can stem only from some form of hierarchy, or verticality — not necessarily among persons, but at least among principles. Freedom is also the value that remains unstated in Weber's description of legal-rational authority; both Thomas's and Weber's versions of authority imply a connection to a transcendent standard that cannot, by definition, be institutionalized. A "purely immanent" social order would be one in which no particular actions (promissory or otherwise) were authorized over others, and it is difficult to imagine such a world containing a "social order" at all.

I also want to emphasize the ways in which my model of legal and literary interaction at the turn of the century both draws upon and diverges from those employed in other studies within what might be called the "law and literature" movement. Such studies tend to break down into two categories: as Paul Gewirtz puts it, "law and literature includes the study of both law *in* literature and law *as* literature" (Brooks and Gewirtz 3). The first of these models focuses on representations of the law in literary works and the second involves reading and interpreting legal texts by making use of the tools of literary analysis. My discussion of literary and legal texts in this study makes use of both these approaches, but it also proposes a third model: literature as law. Scholarship that emphasizes the literary nature of the law often imbues the category of "literature" with an explanatory force that it cannot sustain. Attempts to excavate the legal sources of literary works, on the other hand, frequently lead down one of two roads: a conclusion about the law's hegemonic control over literary production, or an overly romantic conception of literary resistance to authority.[14] But to view "literature" as a professionally constructed category along with the law is to suggest a form of overlap; neither is fully "outside" the other. This way of looking at literature presupposes a certain fluidity in the bounds that separate it from institutions such as the law — a fluidity that arises from the structure of professional authority itself. I take this to be, in part, what J. Hillis Miller means when he asserts that literature can be seen as a kind of law-making, that it can and does "lay down the law" (80). While contemporary critical theory has given us the tools to imagine such forms of interpenetration, it is also possible that similar perspectives were available to writers and other intellectuals during the formative era of professionalism's credo, especially in light of the historical connections between law and literature in the United States. And when we look closely at literary and legal texts of that era, this hypothesis appears to be borne out.

Representing Professionalism: Melville vs. Twain

I contend that the particular relation between the immanent and the transcendent expressed in the works I have chosen reflects a distinct break with earlier ways of imagining that relation. I want to illustrate that break by looking briefly at two of the most "legalistic" texts of the late nineteenth century — Herman Melville's *Billy Budd* and Mark Twain's *Pudd'nhead Wilson*. Both works, of course, raise issues related to guilt and innocence, legal judgment, evidence, and punishment — themes that have been explored in a number of analyses dealing with literary representations of the law. My purposes here, however, are more limited — I want to look at how each author invokes professionalism as a key term in thinking about the relation between law and literature. The ways in which the two authors tell their stories are especially revealing in this regard, for in narrating stories about the law they implicitly make arguments about the relationship between the literary and legal arenas. And those arguments turn out to be very different.

Melville's story, written between 1886 and 1891 (and left in manuscript at his death), highlights the disjunction between literary and professional modes of thought. Captain Vere is the consummate professional: he is "thoroughly versed in the science of his profession" and he "disinterestedly" opposes the radicalism of the French Revolution because it seems "insusceptible of embodiment in lasting institutions" (Melville 60, 63). Melville equates this professional credo with the practice of law when he has Vere serve as both witness and, in effect, prosecutor in Billy's court-martial.[15] Vere cautions the members of the drumhead court against considering any matters not explicitly authorized by the terms of the Mutiny Act, making no effort to justify that act by endowing it with transcendent significance. Perhaps the most chilling example of Vere's professionalism, however, lies in his reliance on "forms, measured forms." Billy's execution is a testament to the power of those forms not only to suppress dissent, but to compel assent as well; the sailors reflexively echo Billy's final words of "God bless Captain Vere!" (123, 128). The description of Claggart's particular form of madness applies equally to Vere, and to the nature of the professional mind:

> Though the man's even temper and discreet bearing would seem to intimate a mind peculiarly subject to the law of reason, not the less in heart he would seem to riot in complete exemption from that law, having apparently little to do with reason further than to employ it as an ambidexter implement for effecting the irrational. That is to say: Toward the accomplishment of an aim which in wantonness of atrocity would seem to partake of the insane, he will direct a cool judgment sagacious and sound. These men are madmen, and of the most dangerous sort, for their lunacy is not continuous, but occasional, evoked by some special object; it is protectively secretive, which is as much to say it is self-contained, so that when, moreover, most active it is to the average mind not distinguishable from sanity, and for the reason above suggested: that whatever its aims may be — and the aim is never declared — the method and the outward proceeding are always perfectly rational. (76)

The passage, of course, does not describe Vere completely; his professional demeanor gives way to excited and confused exclamations immediately after Claggart's death. But that demeanor reasserts itself and controls his subsequent behavior. The "method" of Billy's trial and execution serves to disguise the insanity that lies at its heart. Melville subtitles his work "an inside narrative," and so it is with respect to the "self-contained" legal logic that dominates Vere's consciousness and relegates the "natural" acts of Billy to the status of crimes.

But the subtitle is also misleading, for if Vere's thought conforms to a purely "inside" version of professionalism, the perspective conveyed by the story's narrator decidedly does not. Again and again, the narrator asserts the privilege of violating rules and crossing disciplinary and generic lines. He tells us that his story is "no romance" because it violates romantic conventions, and he takes pleasure in committing a "literary sin" by momentarily diverging from his plot (53, 56). In explaining the character of Claggart, he affirms the need to "cross 'the deadly space between'"— a space that results from the drawing of literary boundaries — and this crossing means that he will bring together realistic and romantic literary practices that a strict formalism would preclude. Thus, Claggart's inexplicable antipathy to Billy is "in its very realism as much charged with that prime element of Radcliffian romance, the mysterious, as any that the ingenuity of the author of *The Mysteries of Udolpho* could devise" (74). These assertions of literary freedom contrast with the disciplinary constraint to which Vere subjects himself, and suggest that the narrator's story lies "outside" of Vere's legalism. Consequently, the narrator presents his story as authoritative precisely because it lacks "symmetry of form"; its "ragged edges" endow it with the authority of experience, as opposed to the nonauthoritative "brute force" associated with Vere's "measured forms" (128, 122, 1425). The two realms — literature and the law — have nothing to say to one another in Melville's story; the line between "inside" and "outside" narratives is absolute, impregnable. *Billy Budd* has been interpreted as Melville's "testament of acceptance."[16] It is anything but. The story constitutes a dogged and unflinching protest against the institutional processes that curtail the exercise of free will — processes whose expansion and proliferation were redefining the American cultural landscape during the final years of Melville's life.

Pudd'nhead Wilson was published only three years after Melville's death, and it responds to the same conditions that lie at the heart of *Billy Budd*'s despair. But while Twain's novel is in many ways as bleak as Melville's, it registers a form of protest that accepts, in part, the structure that it criticizes. The events take place before the Civil War, but like many readers I take it to have more to do with the 1890s than with the 1830s.[17] The work's "hero" (a problematic word, I admit) is David Wilson, a lawyer who, like Vere, seems to embody the new professionalism. He was trained at "an Eastern law school," a form of professional education that did not come into vogue until later in the nineteenth century and that exemplified a version of the law as a specialized discipline rather than a neoclassical arena of reason and breadth (Twain 8). His occupation as a surveyor also conveys his association with line drawing, and the implication is that the lines are professional as well as physical. Above all, however, his methodical practice of taking the fingerprints of everyone in town and storing the information in his "records" exposes a bureaucratic mentality rooted in regularity and process — Vere's "measured forms." Yet Wilson, unlike Vere, is not presented as an "insider"; his professionalism lies outside the bounds of the town's understanding and remains a dormant form of authority until the end of the novel, when it is finally vindicated. The ironic calendar entries that precede each chapter serve to remind us of his outsider status and to present a kind of sophisticated wit that relies on doubleness — a wit not possessed by the narrow and limited simpletons who constitute the "insiders" of Dawson's Landing. Thus, Twain depicts the professional as someone whose specialized knowledge and emphasis on rational process carries the potential to liberate individuals from the confines of convention and ignorance.

That potential seems to be realized when Wilson's "records" vindicate Luigi and expose Tom Driscoll as a murderer. The victory, however, is also a defeat; for convention and ignorance reassert their sway when Tom Driscoll is sold into slavery. This result stems from Wilson's lawyering, but Twain does not present it as a natural or inevitable consequence of that professional activity; in fact, Wilson disappears from the novel at the point when the town's tragically absurd decision is made. Thus, the narrow-minded and self-interested racial ideology that the decision reflects can be seen as a defeat for Wilson's more objective and detached approach to the law. Twain deliberately leaves Wilson in limbo; he is both insider and outsider at the novel's conclusion, and this state embodies the doubleness that forms an essential part of his identity.

And that doubleness permeates Twain's voice as well. On one level, Twain's novel clearly intends to critique legal definitions of race grounded in a "one-drop" ideology, and perhaps all biological conceptions of racial difference. In the context of the 1890s, it is difficult not to interpret his critique as directed against the legal system of Jim Crow as well, which relied upon those conceptions. Nonetheless, Twain's narrative voice, unlike Melville's, does not speak from a position that is purely "outside" the system it represents. The preface makes this clear. Titled "A Whisper to the Reader," it facetiously describes the process by which the book's legal chapters were subjected to review by a "trained barrister" — a stable boy in Italy who had briefly studied law thirty-five years earlier. As Twain puts it, "He was a little rusty on his law, but he rubbed it up for this book, and those two or three legal chapters are right and straight now. He told me so himself" (3). The reference seems to mock the notion of consulting a professional for literary guidance and instead asserts the authorial license to represent legal matters in whatever way a writer sees fit. But it does so, like Wilson's calendar entries, ironically. Its form recognizes the authority of legal professionals, while its substance mocks their claims to expertise. This doubleness is even more apparent in the preface's final paragraph. Beginning with a legal formality — "Given under my hand this second day of January, 1893" — it then deteriorates into a rambling account of the view from the author's Italian villa and his desire to connect his family lineage with that of the villa's past residents. Once again, the official is disrupted by the unofficial. Twain's posture is not of someone who is removed from the law's "inside" structure, but of someone whose relation to it is that of an amateur, an innocent, a "pudd'nhead." It is worth noting that this is also the way he imagines his relation to a kind of literary professionalism. In the afterword to "Those Extraordinary Twins" in which he describes his struggle to reconcile the story's plot with that of *Pudd'nhead Wilson*, he concludes, "The reader already knew how the expert works; he knows now how the other kind do it" (209). Twain's double-edged invocation of professionalism decries the self-contained autonomy of professional structures, while simultaneously acknowledging his own placement within those structures. If he brings an amateurish "outsider" perspective to these professional arenas, it is only to reestablish a form of professional authority by critiquing practices that have become solely inside games. The posture he assumes might be described as that of the amateur professional.

This is where *Billy Budd* and *Pudd'nhead Wilson* diverge. Melville insists on a kind of literary freedom that cannot be reconciled with the formal and institutional structure being adopted by the law in the late nineteenth century. Twain, however, signifies upon the law, using its own forms to underscore a necessary relation between form and substance. The type of substance Twain proposes remains as elusive as it is for Melville, and it might even be said to be present in the novel only through absence. But by representing Wilson's legal performance as both a triumph and a failure and by refusing to posit a "free" authorial point of reference, Twain adheres to the structure of the law in a way that suggests the incompleteness of that structure. His discursive restraint (his use of irony rather than Melville's bold assertions of freedom) allows his readers to ask what is missing, and thus to question the authority of the very discourse that makes that questioning possible. How can a discourse undo itself? The question is the same as asking how the law or the standards of literary representation can change. They can change because the only way their forms exercise sway over their fields is by possessing authority, and authority requires that immanent standards be legitimized by transcendent ones, thus making those immanent standards subject to constant revision.

Narrative Re-Visions

The dialogic relations I see in Twain's novel — between form and substance, inside and outside, law and literature — are made possible by the reconception of authority inherent in the logic of professionalism. And the works I focus on in *Reconstituting Authority* embrace that logic. This is not to say that each of these works exercises that logic in the same way, or expresses it in relation to the same set of legal or literary concerns. In fact, they vary widely with respect to the specific legal matters they address and the uses to which they put the legal and literary dialogue they employ. What ties them together is their willingness to trade freedom for authority, to place literature on the same institutional plane as the law, and thus to engage the law on its own terms — terms that are never *just* legal, but also moral, political, and cultural. In each of these works, stories operate as tenuous links between "inside" forms and "outside" truths — links without which the very notion of authority would disappear. By performing this function, the authors both confirm an existing order grounded in liberal conceptions of the rule of law and challenge that order by exposing its failure to adhere to the very principles it promotes. Their texts are not revolutionary. They are, however, revisionary.

Two central concepts structure the ways in which authors engaged legal issues at the turn of the century — the ideal of the rule of law and the foundational role of property in American jurisprudence. Accordingly, the two parts of *Reconstituting Authority* address the ways in which authors dealt with these specific principles. Much of the legally oriented fiction of this period constitutes a sustained jeremiad about the decline of a republican vision of the polity grounded in the rule of law (Henry Adams's *Democracy*, for instance), but an alternative perspective was also being voiced by authors who accepted, and even promoted, a revised understanding of authority. The "rule of law" in the early republic had meant that, when politics and social upheaval made the resolution of conflict impossible in the wider arena of American public life, there was an authoritative realm to which the public could appeal — a realm that was authoritative precisely because it was above the fray. The series of legal failings that led to the Civil War, however, dashed this image of the law's bounded integrity. If the "rule of law" was to continue as a central ideal in American public life, it would have to do so on new terms. Part I of this study focuses on authors whose works expose a breakdown in the traditional boundary separating the law from other aspects of political, social, and cultural life. The works of Howells, Jackson, and Hopkins reimagine the law in ways that destroy its former bounds; the law, they suggest, is made and enforced by newspapers and novels as much as it is by courts and legislators. But they do not thereby deconstruct the concept of the "rule of law" entirely. Instead, they rely upon a new model of authority — the mediated and institutionally grounded authority of professionalism — to reconceptualize the law and to suggest that authors, as literary professionals, can relate stories that operate in a legal manner. Their novels suggest that literature (as a profession) may allow its practitioners to harness the chaos of competing politically interested narratives that dominate the public sphere, and tell them in a more principled way by grounding them in such established legal concepts as sovereignty, citizenship, and due process. If the meanings of those terms should not be determined solely by legal precedents, documents, and processes, these authors suggest, neither should they be subject to the uncontrolled whims of the American media or the arena of politics. Chapter 1 looks at Howells's attempt to put a Holmesian model of the law to use in reconfiguring the literary landscape along professional lines. In so doing, Howells carves out a prominent space for authorship in a public sphere dominated by storytelling, suggesting that the authority of the "rule of law" requires a narrative bridge between the law's fixed principles and the ever-changing standards of a social world in flux. Chapters 2 and 3 examine the literary attempts of Helen Hunt Jackson and Pauline Hopkins to expose the law's abandonment of principle in its treatment of American Indians and African Americans, respectively. Although both authors call attention to legally sanctioned abuses and inequities, both also tell stories that highlight alternative perspectives contained *within* the law's own formulations — alternatives that their own works seek to reawaken. Jackson and Hopkins thus redeem the ideal of the rule of law by offering narrative re-visions of its most fundamental principles.

Part II of this book concentrates on the issue of property. More than any other legal concept in the late nineteenth and early twentieth centuries, property defined the ideological content of American jurisprudence. Even the principle of contract, cited by Thomas as the dominant legal principle of the era, was ultimately dependent upon a conception of freedom grounded in Lockean self-ownership. Property's pervasive influence caused it to show up in legal, literary, and other cultural texts in ways that were often subtle, and thus all the more powerful. Chesnutt, Wharton, and Dreiser all address issues of ownership in their works in ways that recognize the force of this idea, but they also seek to expose the contingent and politically interested uses to which the concept of property is put. In this way, they both affirm its centrality in American public life and simultaneously undermine its authority as a fixed and immutable foundation capable of regulating all aspects of social existence. Chesnutt and Wharton each underscore how property serves as a vehicle of political power — Chesnutt by emphasizing the connection between whiteness and property, and Wharton by highlighting the gendered conception of ownership that lies at the heart of domestic ideology and prevalent notions of privacy. Dreiser, conversely, celebrates the ideal of property as a natural and philosophically transcendent foundation for social relations, but paradoxically consigns the ideal to the past. By presenting property as a subject for nostalgia, Dreiser legitimates the kind of economic revisionism being promoted by prominent progressives of the time — a revisionism focused on controlling the growing power of the corporation and trust. None of these authors takes the socialistic position that private property should be abolished. Instead, each emphasizes the extent to which property's authority is tied to narratives in a way that makes it subject to revision.

My study ends at the opening of the decade that saw the rise of high modernism in fiction and poetry and the emergence of the New Criticism in literary studies. These developments constitute the apex of the process of professionalization that began in the late nineteenth century —

a process that by the 1920s was so complete that literary professionalism no longer had to be modeled on a field such as the law. For writers like T. S. Eliot, literary activity is self-referential; it possesses its own rules and forms that stem from its past and guide its future. In "Tradition and the Individual Talent," published in 1920, Eliot proposed the now famous model of literary production that he termed "depersonalization," which he defined as the process by which authors "surrender" themselves to a larger tradition. Something like experience still matters, but only that form of experience already recognized by the literary tradition. As Eliot put it, "Impressions and experiences which are important for the man may take no place in the poetry, and those which become important in the poetry may play quite a negligible part in the man, the personality" (56). Eliot's version of literary creativity is similar to Holmes's version of legal change and to the dialogic relation between form and substance present in a work like *Puddn'head Wilson*. What separates Eliot from these earlier figures is his unwillingness to acknowledge his own model as part of a professional credo, or I should say a professional credo that extends beyond the bounds of the literary. As Menand notes, Eliot was willing to identify what he did as a form of "literary professionalism," but that meant sharply delineating its objects of interest (literary tradition) and pursuing literature with "singleness of purpose" (Menand 125). In a 1918 essay Eliot titled "Professional, Or . . . ," he described the distinctly unprofessional practices of the Victorians:

> The opposite of the professional is not the dilettante, the elegant amateur, the dabbler who in fact only attests the existence of the specialist. The opposite of the professional, the enemy, is the man of mixed motives. Conspicuously the Victorian epoch is anti-professional; Carlyle as an historian, Ruskin as an economist; Thackeray who could write such good prose as the Steyne episode, and considered himself a kindly but penetrating satirist; George Eliot who could write *Amos Barton* and steadily degenerate. Decadence in art is caused by mixed motives. The art of the Victorians is spoiled by mixed motives, and Oscar Wilde finally added ingredients to the mixture which made it a ludicrous emetic. (61)

Eliot's narrow sense of professionalism as a concept that excludes boundary crossing ("mixed motives") causes him to miss the relation that his literary theory and practice bear to a larger political and social context.[18] The same complaint, of course, can be lodged against the New Criticism, whose insistence that interpretation should rely on nothing outside the text itself fails to incorporate the sense of the "outside" that always informs the "inside" structure of any institutional system.[19] My intent, however, is not to beat an already dead critical horse, but to underscore the relevance of the texts I have chosen to examine. For in proposing an institutional and disciplinary definition of literature that associates it with the law, these works point the way to a conception of disciplines that is of necessity interdisciplinary. And this conception makes it possible to invoke morality, truth, culture, public policy, God, or whatever other transcendent standard we might rely upon in a work of literature or literary criticism without insisting on absolute authorial or critical freedom. In fact, it is precisely because we are not free, the texts suggest, that we can understand and incorporate principles gleaned from disciplines and professions other than our own (in a way, they too are ours), and to debate those foundational principles to which we willfully submit when we adhere to professional rules and forms.

In an era in which the humanities are increasingly criticized for their emphasis on specialization and professional expertise, this seems like an important point to make both to those of us "inside" the various disciplines and to those critics on the "outside" (who are often "insiders" as well). As Bruce Robbins argues, "professions — even the notoriously unworldly literary theory — are not self-enclosed and self-sustaining, however much they would sometimes like to believe it. The outside constitutes the inside, and vice versa" (166). If the "inside" is not "self-sustaining," however, it is no less true that the "outside" is not as far outside as it might think; its critique of professionalization is just a way of proposing a different foundation for professional activity. Professional conceptions of authority have so permeated our culture that we cannot propose an "outside" that is truly antiprofessional. But that is not to be lamented, for we can still change professional configurations by invoking those "outside" values that already make sense within the logic of professionalism. To be sure, this is what we do already — what we cannot *not* do — but the more we understand the ways in which institutions, professions, and disciplines feed off one another, the more we can place our own professional activity in a larger context and the better we can communicate that activity's relevance. This is the "work" these texts can do.

And this is why my own narrative had to begin with Emerson. Reaching back to a "transcendental" foundation, I have sought to connect my story to a figure who resists all disciplinary limitations on his own thought. Since this study is really more about a certain kind of freedom than it is about constraint, Emerson grounds it in a foundation that stands elusively "outside" the circumscribed disciplinary realms from which these authors (and I) speak. My narrative, however, seeks to bridge the gap by drawing the "outside" in. Consequently, I have incorporated Emerson into a narrative of which he surely would have disapproved, for I have turned him into the professional par excellence: only someone who implicitly understood his own confinement within the prisonhouse of disciplinary discourse could make such a sustained and powerful case for interdisciplinary freedom.

I

The (Mis)Rule of Law

CHAPTER I

The "Official" Narratives
of William Dean Howells

What a subject is . . . this abstraction called the Law, wherein, as in a
magic mirror, we see reflected, not only our own lives, but the lives of
all men that have been.
   Oliver Wendell Holmes, Jr., "The Law"

I n an essay entitled "Police Report" that appeared in the January 1882 edition of the *Atlantic*, William Dean Howells describes paying two visits to what he calls a "police court" — a Boston court that summarily disposed of minor criminal offenses. Howells does not specify the dates of his attendance, stating only that the first occurred during summer and the second took place "nearly a year later" ("Police" 12). It seems likely, however, that he visited the courtroom either shortly before or during his work on *A Modern Instance* — most of which he wrote in 1881 — and the novel's legal concerns seem to link it closely to the short piece in the *Atlantic*. The essay manifests Howells's qualms about the emerging relationship between law and literature — a relationship that he would explore in much of his subsequent fiction. The opening paragraph of "Police Report" is particularly revealing:

One day in summer, when people whom I had been urging to behave in some degree like human beings persisted in acting more like the poor creatures who pass for men and women in most stage-plays, I shut my manuscript in a drawer, and the next morning took an early train into the city. I do not remember just what whim it was that led me to visit the police court: perhaps I went because it was in the dead vast and middle of summer, and the town afforded little other amusement; perhaps it was because, in my revolt against unreality, I was in the humor to see life whose reality asserts itself every day in the newspapers with indisputable force. If the latter, I was fated to a measure of disappointment, for when the court opened this reality often appeared no more substantial than the fiction with which I had lost my patience at home. But I am bound to say that it was much more entertaining, and that it was, so to speak, much more artistically treated. It resolved itself into melodrama, or romantic tragedy, having a prevailing comic interest, with moments of intensity, and with effects so thrilling that I came away with a sense of the highest theatrical illusion. (1)

Howells's lighthearted treatment of his visit grows darker during the course of the essay as he ruminates further on the "genre" of the police trial. Even in this relatively cheerful opening, however, he characterizes the experience as one of "disappointment." Having gone to the court for a dose of "reality," he finds only another version of the "fiction" — albeit more "artistically treated" — from which he had sought refuge. Although he expresses outrage over the public degradation suffered by the witnesses and defendants involved in the trials, he also makes it clear that the law fails him as an author almost as much as it does the hapless souls more directly subjected to its inadequacies.

Beneath the wryly cynical tone of "Police Report" lies a troubled concern about the erasure of distinctions between law and narrative — an erasure that threatens the integrity of the rule of law. Howells's visit was motivated by a belief in a privileged legal space within American society and culture — a space in which "the real" remains uncorrupted by "the fictional." What he finds within the Boston courtroom, however, is an incestuous conglomeration of legal standards and cultural stories. By seeing through the lenses of popular fiction and the theater, the law weakens its claim to authority and participates in the proliferation of social fictions. The rule of law in the United States had always meant that law and culture were distinguishable — although the law (in theory) reflected the popular will, it did so in a way that remained true to its history, precedents, and foundational principles ("nature," "reason," and the substantive rights and duties articulated in the Constitution). Under this conception, legal forums that simply indulge the political, economic, or cultural whims of the moment would lose their claim to legitimacy and become nothing more than public stages — hence, Howells's disillusionment at the police court. But while he finds that the law is no longer worthy of its privileged status in American life, the author nonetheless uses its failings to create the essay itself. Exposing the false assumptions that lie beneath the legal system's claim to authority, he offers his own authorship as a kind of legal proxy by revealing the "reality" of the law's capitulation to "illusion."

Yet if Howells's essay suggests the possibility of a literary redemption of the legal, it also worries that the same forces that have breached the self-contained integrity of the law have transformed the nature of literary authority as well. "Police Report" notes that the "reality" of the justice system is asserted "with indisputable force" in the newspapers, thereby implicitly accusing journalism, along with popular culture, of usurping literature's epistemological claim upon the "real." Locating the legal and the literary in the same relative position within American public life, Howells identifies a common threat to their claims of authority. Wai Chee Dimock's observation that the law "was spacialized in the nineteenth century; it had a specific locale and a specific set of boundaries," might be said of literature as well, and Howells expresses considerable anxiety about the integrity of the borders of both institutions (Dimock, *Residues* 23). We might view those borders as the remnants of a version of professionalism that was rapidly passing away — a version dependent upon the assumption that the true professional could uphold the rule of law by distinguishing such absolutes as reason, nature, and morality from the merely expedient and contingent norms of society. Although Howells seems to lament this passing, he also posits the existence of a new professionalism: one that acknowledges the blurred boundaries between a legal realm of ordered reason and a more contingent and volatile social sphere; a mode of representation that grounds its authority not in the self-contained operation of timeless ideals, but in a cultural meeting place of law, literature, and such popular modes of storytelling as the theater and journalism.

This meeting place becomes the central concern of *A Modern Instance*. The tension between Squire Gaylord and Bartley Hubbard is, in part, a struggle between differing conceptions of legal authority — one grounded in a republican conception of the law as a bastion of order amid the chaos of politics and self-interest, and the other based upon the institutional form of legal positivism embodied in the views of Oliver Wendell Holmes Jr. Howells was hard at work on his novel when Holmes published his now famous collection of lectures, *The Common Law* (1881), in which he presented a view of law not as moral guidepost but as social product, authored by forces beyond its control. Much of what Bartley has to say about journalism mirrors Holmes's legal philosophy. Yet Howells's juxtaposition of law and journalism also expands the terms of Holmes's discussion, identifying a newly constituted realm of public discourse in which the legal, the journalistic, and the literary merge. Howells's realism attempts to come to grips with Bartley's legalism, and thereby acknowledges that the terms of literary authority have been transfigured. Rejecting the philosophical idealism that underwrites the domestic novel of marriage, the realistic novel of divorce that Howells seeks to create looks to the shifting public norms of American culture for its material rather than to the private convictions (reached subjectively through reason or intuition) of the author. In so doing, he calls upon a form of "experience" connected to the chaotic and often contradictory standards conveyed on the pages of the daily newspaper. But Howells also suggests that normative universes need interpreters — individuals who can plumb the depths of socially constructed values and reveal the "truths" on which those values tacitly rely. This is the job of the new literary professional.

The title of Howells's novel comes from the speech by Jacques on the seven ages of man in Shakespeare's *As You Like It*. Cynically delineating the various "parts" played by men at different stages of life, Jacques defines the fifth age as that of "the justice," who is "Full of wise saws and modern instances" (II, vii, 153–56).[1] Shakespeare uses "modern" to mean "commonplace," an archaic usage that Howells undoubtedly intends to invoke in addition to the denotation it now possesses. The relationship between Bartley and Marcia calls upon both meanings, constituting a small example of the larger transformations working at the end of the century to undermine older and more conventional conceptions of legal and literary authority. While Howells attempts, in part, to make a case against Bartley and his ilk — to act as both lawyer and judge in his exposure of Bartley's fictions — Jacques's irony is not lost on him, and he finds himself as author resisting the role of "justice" more than playing it. He would return to similar legal (and Shakespearean) ground in his 1892 novel, *The Quality of Mercy*, once again exploring the possibility of an authorial function removed from the demands of a Bartleyan public sphere. But the literary redemption of the legal that Howells implicitly calls for in "Police Report" seems nostalgic and quixotic within the logic of the novels, leading him toward a conception of the author as someone who can lay down the law only by learning to interpret the voice of the people.

The Holmesian Rule of Law

The rule of law has always been one of the most deeply cherished and ill-defined ideals in American culture. From the very inception of the republic, its imprecise meaning has been the source — either explicit or implicit — of countless controversies involving the role of the judiciary in regulating national affairs. The problem has stemmed in part from the notion that the United States government ultimately derives its authority from popular sovereignty — the law speaks for "the people," in their corporate capacity. Nonetheless, the rule of law also means that the legal order cannot be manipulated for political ends — it is responsive to the will of "the people," but not to that of individual persons. Supreme Court Justice Joseph Story noted in 1829 that "our government is emphatically a government of the people, in all its departments. It purports to be a government of law, and not of men; and yet, beyond all others, it is subject to the control and influence of public opinion" (quoted in Kammen 116). Story, however, would later chastise his brethren on the bench for succumbing to the pressure of public opinion and thus disregarding the law.[2] In other words, belief in popular sovereignty has never meant that the law is obliged to bend utterly to the vicissitudes of a fickle popular will. Jeffersonian Republicans in the early national era sought to make law amenable to rapid change when the public sentiment seemed to demand it, but Jefferson lost that issue to the Federalists, who insisted that the judiciary serve as a buffer between "the people" and the foundational principles of the nation that "the people" might otherwise be too willing to ignore.[3]

This, more than any other, is the message behind Chief Justice John Marshall's vindication of judicial review in *Marbury v. Madison* (1803). Marshall opened his famous decision with the assertion that the Constitution is "designed to be permanent," by which he seems to have meant not only the *language* of the document, but the *interpretations* of that language as well. As Paul W. Kahn notes, the Constitution can hardly be said to be permanent if new meanings are ascribed to it every time public opinion changes:

A critical element of our belief in the rule of law is that the future of the political order should be the same as its past. Law's rule is an exercise in the maintenance of political meanings already achieved. It links the future to the past. So the problem of law's rule in *Marbury* appears to the Court as a problem of maintaining the Constitution in the face of political innovations created by the other two branches of government. To abandon the problem of interpretation of meanings already present in the legal order, and to ask only how we can best order the future, is to abandon the rule of law. (19)

The rule of law thus embodies a delicate balance between acknowledging the legitimating force of popular sovereignty and adhering to an interpretive tradition that operates as a check on that sovereignty. Moreover, requiring submission to an interpretive tradition suggests the existence of a "truth" by which to judge that tradition — the "truth" cannot be determined by the public will alone.

This conception of the rule of law helps to explain the metaphor of the "story" used by Oliver Wendell Holmes Jr. Holmes sought to free legal thought from a rigid formalism grounded in a pre–Civil War past — a past that, by the 1880s, seemed to offer little guidance to the present. Yet Holmes also insisted that legal transformation must make a kind of narrative sense — that the vision of the present and future it posits must incorporate the meanings generated by the law's past. Thus, even for Holmes, the law is anchored in some form of stable meaning; objective criteria exist by which we can judge whether changes demanded by the public would either continue the "story" or disrupt it.

Although a later generation of "legal realists" in America would look back upon *The Common Law* as a revolutionary text, Holmes's approach to the law can be viewed as part of a long legal struggle to reconcile the conflicts intrinsic to the very notion of the rule of law. Moreover, much of the book's approach accorded with legal theories that were rapidly gaining acceptance in both England and the United States.[4] Since the publication of Sir Henry Maine's *Ancient Law* in 1861, many historians and legal scholars had adopted a reflective theory of law in which legal principles figured as expressions of societal values and customs, as mirrors of the community's norms that did not significantly influence their social environment. Holmes agreed with Maine that the law was an instrument in the hands of society rather than an autonomous and independent sphere of public life that could guide social change. Maine's assertion that "social necessities and social opinion are always more or less in advance of Law" was reformulated in *The Common Law* to express the same idea even more bluntly: "The life of the law has not been logic: it has been experience. The felt necessities of the time, the prevalent moral and political theories, intuitions of public policy, avowed or unconscious, even the prejudices which judges share with their fellow-men, have had a good deal more to do than the syllogism in determining the rules by which men should be governed" (20, 1).[5] For both Maine and Holmes, the Enlightenment model of law as the enactment of universal truths gleaned from reason and nature — and made accessible through the sub-jective operation of conscience — was no longer viable, and both empha-sized the need for legal rules to change with the times. As one reviewer of Holmes's book noted, "The entire work is written from the stand-point of the new philosophy, and those hackneyed terms *natural justice* and *equity* are excluded from it" (quoted in G. Edward White 184).

The "new philosophy" expressed in the book also incorporated an ar-gument about the disjunction between the law's form and content — be-tween its moral language and its policy objectives. Specifically, Holmes sought to prove that, "while the law does still and always, in a certain sense, measure legal liability by moral standards, it nevertheless . . . is continually transmuting those moral standards into objective or external ones, from which the actual guilt of the party concerned is wholly elim-inated" (38). "Actual guilt" is precisely the kind of transcendent standard, based largely upon an individual's state of mind, which Holmes consid-ered legally irrelevant. He argued that the law's "terminology of morals" serves to hide the fact that legal precepts originate in the "generally ac-cepted" standards of the community — standards that, in effect, ignore individual subjectivity in order to implement the community's sense of "expediency" and "public policy" (38, 44, 35). For Holmes, the commu-nity acts as sovereign, and its perception is filtered through the lens of public opinion. One of the radical implications of this position is that it seems to envision law as nothing more than a convenient fiction by which the public enacts its will while declaring it to be sanctioned by some higher authority. His perspective deprives the law of its majesty, decon-structing its claim to occupy a privileged position outside the battlefield of social, cultural, and political strife. And even more important, it sug-gests a redefinition of the very meaning of "law." If law is nothing more than a reflection of "generally accepted" community standards, then its bounds seem to disappear entirely, for other forms of public expression could also articulate those standards and thus operate in a way that is just as "legal" as the law. The function of serving as social "mirror" could be performed by any form of public discourse that gives voice to public opinion. The law, in this model, possesses no more authority than the opinion page of the newspaper, or the journalistic stories that both articulate and shape community norms in less visible ways.

Yet the combination of these intellectual strains in *The Common Law* creates what G. Edward White has called an "epistemological tension" (181). Despite the radical implications of his argument, Holmes did not believe that connecting law to the public will destroyed the law's claim to authority. In fact, his position assumed the existence of empirical standards by which the community's norms might be understood, interpreted, and measured. "Policy" and "public opinion" are not necessarily synonymous in his work; he sometimes treats "policy" as simply one aspect of "experience," but at other times he appeals to it as something more stable — "the secret root from which the law draws all the juices of life" (*Common* 35).[6] And while the law's fictions suggest comparison to other "stories" that manifest public sentiment, Holmes nonetheless implies that legal stories are privileged — that they reflect a deeper version of the public will than that embodied in the shifting and whimsical manifestations of public opinion. The rule of law had genuine significance for Holmes; although it did not mean that law was the repository of timeless absolutes discernible through the operation of conscience, it did mean that the application of "generally accepted" norms would be governed by a principled form of interpretation. His notion of law as a "story" seems to allow for a way to bridge the gap between the contingency of community norms and the universality of something like "truth."[7]

Thus, beneath Holmes's emphasis on "fictionality" — on the law's contingency and the facade of its "moral terminology" — lies an appeal to some version of "reality," a content that transcends the illusion of form. Yet at the same time, the bounds of that "reality" are dangerously unstable; verging on collapse, they threaten to expose law as nothing more than one genre of public speech and to authorize other "stories" to operate in a way that is just as "legal" as the law. Nonetheless, Holmes suggests, there is a difference between stories; if we can tell the right one, we can potentially reconcile the public will with something more permanent and foundational. The lawyer or judge must be more than a *mere* storyteller; he must be a professional one — one whose discipline and attention to form enables him to see the "growth" and "development" in the seemingly chaotic parade of social and legal transformations, and thus to connect the law's form to the "secret root" of its substance. This is what

Holmes attempts to do in *The Common Law*. And Howells struggles with a similar model of storytelling in *A Modern Instance*.

Bartley's Legal Narratives

Howells's decision to address the convergence of law and fiction in "Police Report," as well as in *A Modern Instance*, may have as much to do with the series of lectures that Holmes delivered at the Lowell Institute in 1880 (lectures that would be published as *The Common Law* the following year) as it does with his own observations of American culture inside and outside the Boston courtroom. Howells and Holmes had been youthful friends; they met at the house of Holmes's famous father in 1860 and established a correspondence in which they exchanged poems and philosophical essays. The correspondence, however, ceased with the Civil War, which Holmes attended as a soldier and which Howells, significantly, did not.[8] The friendship failed to resume when the fighting ceased, as Howells seemed to seek the company of others — such as Henry James and Mark Twain — who had "missed out" on the war experience.[9] Yet both Howells and Holmes were prominent Boston residents, and the former was undoubtedly aware of the latter's book. *The Common Law* appeared just as Howells's own interest in legal matters was at a peak; not only was he preparing his "Police Report" piece for the *Atlantic*, but he had also attended a divorce proceeding in Crawfordsville, Indiana, to gather material for *A Modern Instance*.

Howells's treatment of the uneasy relationship between Squire Gaylord and Bartley Hubbard in the novel mirrors the conflict between a conception of legal authority grounded in reason, nature, and justice, and a positivistic model based on expediency and community standards. Gaylord is the leading lawyer and most influential citizen in the town of Equity, a name that associates him with natural law principles and with the system of courts that originated in England as a counterpart to the more rule-bound courts of law. Just as the system of equity was gradually disappearing in the nineteenth century, and just as "equity" constituted a "hackneyed term" within the "new philosophy" articulated by Holmes, everything about Gaylord is outmoded, from his title as "squire" to his "old-fashioned deistical opinions." Nonetheless, he continues to function as Equity's voice of authority, acting as "the censor of morals and religion" (33, 241). Gaylord lives in a kind of active isolation; he watches over the town while secluding himself in a house "on the border of the village," and even separates himself from his family in an office detached from the rest of the residence (49). The privacy he covets suggests the subjective nature of his epistemology, but it is a form of subjectivity tempered by a stark sense of determinism. Like the "old Puritanic discipline" that he defends, and like the beliefs of such Enlightenment figures as Hume and Gibbon whom he still reads, his model of the mind is rooted in reason and nature — terms that connect it to an objective reality and that make the concept of justice intelligible. Gaylord's authority is premised upon the kind of republican virtue championed by individuals such as John Adams in the period following the Revolution; it is precisely because Gaylord *cannot* be influenced by social whims that he can claim to define "the good." [10]

Gaylord's outdatedness contrasts with Bartley's modernity, an attitude that entails not only wearing "city-cut clothes" and remaining spiritually uncommitted, but also relying upon norms gleaned from public discourse rather than private reflection. Bartley's approach to journalism mirrors Holmes's legal philosophy; he sees newspapers as entities that must reflect, but not guide, social standards. Thus, he tells his friend Ricker, "I don't believe that a newspaper is obliged to be superior in tone to the community," and that "if the community is full of vice and crime, a newspaper can't do better than reflect its condition" (17, 264). Howells gives Bartley's opinions on journalism decidedly legal implications by locating him in a professional limbo between the careers of newspaperman and lawyer, and by taking pains to emphasize that, even though he never practices law, his perspective is the most legalistic one in the novel: the opening scene has him playfully writing a contract in which Marcia will agree to go sleigh-riding with him; when their marriage begins to disintegrate, it is Bartley who mentions the fact that not all of the legal requirements were met by the minister who married them; and Bartley interprets his contract with Witherby, the editor of the Boston *Events*, in a narrow manner that emphasizes his legal — as opposed to his gentlemanly — obligations. The distinctly Holmesian shape of Bartley's character, however, does more than identify a journalistic corruption of the legal sphere. It also voices the unstated implications of Holmes's theory by suggesting that newspapers, in their "modern" incarnation as the mouthpieces of public opinion, are more "legal" than the law itself. Expressing the "generally accepted" norms of the community (albeit without the narrative discipline Holmes calls for), Bartley, it turns out, is practicing law by practicing journalism.

The novel's distinctly unflattering portrait of Gaylord suggests that Howells was not particularly nostalgic about a bygone era in which moral determinacy and legal prominence went hand in hand. Yet the alternative that Bartley offers is, of course, unsettling in its own right. Howells's ambivalence about these stark options leads Brook Thomas to conclude that he offers his readers a third model of the public sphere — one grounded neither in the natural foundations of equity nor in the positivistic shifting of legal and political norms, but in what Thomas terms "the promise of contract." For Thomas, works of realism such as *A Modern Instance* express the hope that society will order itself on such a contractual basis, thus transferring the seat of authority from God or nature and locating it in individuals defined through acts of promising. While this argument explains much about realism's vision of individual freedom and responsibility, it does not account for the concern that *A Modern Instance* expresses about the effect of the public sphere on individual choices and values. Journalism, Howells suggests, stands for a kind of social power that is able to construct the terms of reality itself, and that mere individual will cannot combat. Howells's concern with the problem of moral agency stems from an awareness that agency operates on a social as well as individual level, that the community is an agent that expresses its will through such institutions as law and journalism. Consequently, he asks not only how social relations can be reconstructed on the basis of a radical individualism, but also how public stories shape the kinds of transactions in which individuals choose to engage. Since some form of authority will invariably affect the public consciousness, Howells struggles to frame Bartley's world of journalistic (and legal) narratives in a way that reaches the "secret root" of those narratives — a way that expresses norms that the community itself may not have known it had.[11]

The newspaper notice of Bartley's divorce action against Marcia crystallizes Howells's concerns about the institutional establishment of a public sphere in which "the law" is no longer recognizable as such — an arena over which "stories" and those who write them preside with the community's full consent. The notice is simultaneously legal and journalistic, factual and fictional. But while on one level it can be read as a critique of both law and journalism, on another it seems to embody a discursive mode that, in combining the legal and journalistic, creates something entirely new.[12] The divorce notice appears as a kind of fracture in Howells's text; he interrupts his narration to transcribe its details onto the pages of the novel — even indicating the exact spot where the clerk's seal would appear — thereby imbuing it with an aura of insistent officiality. The feeling it creates is distinct from the truth of the claims it asserts. The reader knows these claims are inaccurate, yet the notice's form provides them with a legitimacy they would not otherwise have; it normalizes them by placing them within a framework that has distinctly legal meaning. The sudden appearance of this document within the novel, along with its foreign quality, forces us to reexamine Bartley's journalistic career in its light, to look for clues as to whether it conforms with what we already know about the nature of his publications.

In fact, the notice seems a kind of extension of Bartley's journalistic career. The power he wields as a reporter is directly connected to the normative nature of what he publishes. This is particularly true of his exposé on lodgings in Boston, written shortly after he and Marcia arrive in the city. In its "alarming" treatment of the subject, the article bears no relation to his own recent experience of renting an apartment — an experience in which his own landlady lowered the price of her rooms out of sympathy for the couple. Bartley leaves out this "fact," but in so doing he simply articulates the "facts" relevant to the community's version of reality. Howells makes it clear that, far from hurting the success of his story, such an omission actually helps it:

> There is nothing the public enjoys so much as an *exposé*; it seems to be made in the reader's own interest; it somehow constitutes him a party to the attack upon the abuse, and its effectiveness redounds to the credit of all the newspaper's subscribers. After a week's stay in Boston, Bartley was able to assume the feelings of a native who sees his city falling into decay through the rapacity of its landladies. (169)

Ultimately, Howells implies, the article seeks not to present "facts" as much as to enlist support, and it does so by telling a story that has, in effect, already been written by the "natives" of Boston. Its normative quality springs largely from the sense it provides of being authored by the community itself rather than by an individual with personal experiences and convictions. By bringing the newspaper's readers together in their outrage over the alleged abuse, it gives voice to the community's norms and, at the same time, valorizes them. Thus, its purpose is not primarily to inform, but to codify.

Pierre Bourdieu's analyses of the law and of the juridical operation of nonlegal codes shed light upon the nature of Bartley's reportage. For Bourdieu, codification is a kind of legal practice not limited to a self-contained legal realm, but extending to all acts that operate to normalize actions in a way that makes them "official." It constitutes, he asserts, "an operation of symbolic ordering" that seeks to "minimize ambiguity and vagueness" by objectifying reality and establishing an "explicit normativity" (*In Other* 80, 79). Bourdieu's description of the process by which such objectification becomes "official" is particularly relevant to Bartley's form of journalism:

> To objectify is . . . to bring out into the open, to make visible, public, known to all, published. An *author* in the proper sense of the word is someone who makes public things which everyone felt in a confused sort of way; someone who possesses a special capacity, that of publishing the implicit, the tacit; someone who performs a real task of creation. A certain number of acts become official as soon as they are public, published (such as marriage bans). Publication is the act of officialization *par excellence*. The official is what can and must be made public, displayed, proclaimed before everyone's eyes, in front of everyone, as opposed to what is unofficial, or even secret and shameful; with official publication . . . everyone is both invited to be a witness and called upon to check, ratify and sanction, and he or she ratifies or sanctions even by staying silent. (*In Other* 82)

Bartley's article participates in the process Bourdieu describes. It objectifies the feelings already present in the community and, in so doing, provides them with a new validity — a form of public recognition and endorsement. Each reader "ratifies and sanctions" the image of the "rapacious landlady" by reading the article and by assuming a portion of the "credit" for it, and the exposé thereby serves as the medium through which subjective impressions become objective facts and communal assumptions become "official" narratives. Of course, something is also lost in this translation. Bartley eliminates "vagueness and indeterminacy" from his presentation of reality only by ignoring his own experience in renting lodgings, endowing his article with an "essential cheapness" that Howells cannot refrain from noting (170).

Bourdieu's reference to marriage banns is particularly relevant to Howells's analysis of what might be termed a culture of "the official." When Bartley and Marcia are married, Bartley realizes that the somewhat flustered minister has forgotten a portion of the ceremony. After the two begin experiencing marital problems, he reveals that the minister had neglected to ask them if they had declared their intention to marry — a requirement, known as "publishing the banns," usually fulfilled by an announcement made in church on three successive occasions. Having married on a whim, of course, the couple had never declared their intentions publicly. Bartley correctly notes that such an omission does not invalidate their marriage, but he concludes that it deprives the relationship of any "sacred" content (322). On one level, his interpretation indicates the extent to which the authority of the church has declined and points toward the transformation of marriage from a sacrament into a primarily contractual arrangement.[13] On another level, however, it exposes a distinction between legality and officiality, the former being a function of explicit rules laid down by the polity and the latter constituting a separate — and higher — form of authority premised upon acts of publication.

Notices of divorce, like marriage banns, become "official" as soon as they are published, regardless of whether they reach the attention of the party involved. Howells makes it clear that the function of this particular one is not, in fact, to notify at all, for he takes pains to emphasize that it falls into Marcia's hands only by chance and that under normal circumstances she would never have become aware of it. Failing in most instances to perform their ostensible function, such notices, Howells suggests, are directed more to the collective consciousness of society than to the consciousness of any individual. Their real purpose, rather than to notify, is to enlist the support of the community in the process of dissolving the marriage — a function they fulfill by showing that an effort (however ineffectual) has been made to contact the person involved and, even more important, by publishing the grounds for the divorce. Exposing his allegations to the public, Bartley's notice sets forth a sketchy narrative that the community will fill in with appropriate details and, in the absence of any counternarrative, ratify accordingly.

The inaccuracies contained within the notice of Bartley's action for divorce suggest that Howells was concerned about the fictionality of the "official" narratives that, he felt, were beginning to dominate public life. Yet the subsequent trial in Indiana is clearly an inadequate means of recouping what is lost in this new paradigm. The "old" legal model reasserts itself in Squire Gaylord's invocation of "God's right and the everlasting truth," but the courtroom in which he waxes eloquent no longer operates under the principles he embodies. Howells returns to the terms he had employed in "Police Report," noting that the "spectators," who appeared to have been watching "an interesting affair," adopted Marcia and her supporters "as a necessary element of the scene" (437). The courtroom is more theater than seat of justice. Thus, while Gaylord's old-fashioned oratory succeeds in resolving the question of who divorces whom, it cannot determine the moral question of Bartley's culpability, and the latter's escape indicates that he had never really lost control of the proceedings. As Marcia's group of friends and family approach the courthouse before the trial, Flavia, the daughter of the soon-to-be-divorced couple asks impishly, "Is this the house where papa lives?" (437). Yes, Howells seems to reply to this reincarnation of Hawthorne's Pearl; Bartley has occupied Gaylord's house and made it his own.

Howells and Professionalism

The conflict between Bartley and Gaylord, as little Flavia's comment suggests, is largely territorial, and the public space over which they fight relates both to the legal function they wish to perform and to the professional status they achieve as a result. Besides highlighting the legal nature of his journalism, Bartley's uncertain state of occupational limbo also invokes the changing meaning of the term "profession" at the time Howells was writing his novel. At the beginning of the century, the word was applied primarily to the fields of law, medicine, divinity, and education. As Bruce A. Kimball has noted, the law was preeminent among this list and, as a result, "the meaning of 'profession' was informed by certain jurisprudential characteristics" (199). While the concept was never sharply defined, for most people the practice of a "profession" involved an independence from pecuniary concerns and other forms of worldly pressure, an ethic of service, an elevated status in the public's esteem, and, in the case of lawyers, a corresponding level of influence in public affairs (Kimball 105ff.). The end of the century, however, saw a decline in the status of the law and an expanded use of "profession" to signify "occupation." Lawyers after the Civil War found themselves frequently attempting to defend the term's antebellum connotations, especially in response to public scandals involving judicial corruption and the perception that the allure of corporate law was turning legal practice into a purely mercenary career.[14] As one prominent New York attorney asserted, the purpose in founding the New York City Bar Association in 1870 was "to make ourselves once more a *profession*" (James Emmott, quoted in Keller 352). But if lawyers sought a return to a nostalgic version of professionalism, journalists attempted to broaden the concept to incorporate their own occupation. For instance, an editor of the *Philadelphia Times* told an audience in 1888 that teaching journalism as a distinct subject would help raise it "from a trade . . . to the dignity of the learned profession that it ought to be" (Eugene Camp, quoted in Marzolf 14).[15]

Howells's good friend Charles Dudley Warner expressed this uncertainty about the status of journalism in a speech that was published in book form in 1881, while Howells was working on *A Modern Instance*. In *The American Newspaper*, Warner wondered about the "moral effect upon a community" of reading about "murders and abnormal crimes" year after year, and criticized newspapers for encouraging a "hunger for publicity" (63, 39). Although he acknowledged that "the newspaper is a private enterprise," he insisted that its editor has a public duty: "It is scarcely necessary to say . . . that the editor who has no high ideals, no intention of benefiting his fellow-men by his newspaper, and uses it unscrupulously as a means of money-making only, sinks to the level of the physician and the lawyer who have no higher conception of their callings than that they offer opportunities for getting money by appeals to credulity, and by assisting in evasions of the law" (7–8). By comparing the unscrupulous editor to the lawyer who helps his client escape legal consequences, Warner implicitly acknowledged the public function of journalism. He endowed it with the status of a profession — nostalgically defined — thereby emphasizing its need for pecuniary independence and "high ideals." The newspaper has a responsibility to do more than reflect the values of its readership, he suggested; it must seek to influence them for the better. Oddly enough, however, he concluded that the distinctly Holmesian aspects of journalistic practice that he decried throughout the book are not serious problems after all, asserting that "the moral tone of the American newspaper is higher, as a rule, than that of the community in which it is published" (69). His book reveals the tension inherent in the growth of journalism's public power; having issued a plea for it to function with the "high ideals" of a profession, he sought to manage its potential threat by constructing it as already "professionalized."

The very slipperiness of the term "profession" in the late nineteenth century evidences the redefinition of authority with which writers such as Howells and Warner were concerned. In *A Modern Instance*, Howells notes the increasing social elevation of journalists by describing the "distinguished and honorary recognition from the public" that they receive in the form of free meals, hotel bills, and other forms of privilege. Although Marcia does not consider it "comparable to the law in dignity," Bartley speaks to his friends of "the sovereign character of journalism" and increasingly views it as an acceptable alternative to the practice of law

(177). His characterization inflects "sovereignty" with Holmesian meaning; the "sovereign character of journalism" endows it not with the authority to command or even to lead, but with the authority to express that which already exists — to articulate the "generally accepted" norms of the community. When Gaylord visits Boston, he expresses disdain for the editor of Bartley's paper, but enjoys the company of the prominent lawyer Eustace Atherton, "who was of a man's profession" (237). Implicitly discrediting other "professions" by feminizing them, Gaylord's backward-looking views seek to protect a concept that has already been redefined.

The "professional" conflict between Bartley and Gaylord is mediated, in part, by Ricker, who edits the *Chronicle-Abstract*. Responding to Bartley's assertion that "A newspaper is a private enterprise," Ricker states, "It's private property, but it isn't a private enterprise." For him, a newspaper has "certain distinct duties to the public" and is "sacredly bound not to do anything to deprave or debauch its readers" (262, 263). Like Warner, he tries to manage the tensions inherent in journalism's public role, and he voices Warner's concern with the "moral tone" of newspapers. Agreeing with Bartley that a newspaper is not "obliged to be superior in tone to the community," Ricker nonetheless maintains that "There are several tones in every community" and that a newspaper can "mirror" those it considers more virtuous (264–65). His opinions at once accept Bartley's communitarian construction of professionalism while leaving room within that construction for the exercise of moral agency and influence. Ricker, however, is a minor character who is later duped by Bartley into violating his own ethics; the balance he tries to walk is too fine. Howells clearly sympathizes with the editor's attempt to resolve the conflict between reflecting and molding community norms, but Ricker's version of professionalism is still mired in an outworn and elitist ideal of republican virtue. The novel's ongoing dialogue on the nature of professionalism reveals the way in which such a concept could establish a life of its own, serving as a means of endowing the practice of journalism with the authority of law while, at the same time, redefining the very meaning of that authority.

Howells's invocation of "professionalism" suggests that he was concerned not simply with law and journalism, but with the new configuration of the public sphere in which they coincided. As "Police Report" reveals, this space was also literary, at least to the extent that it incorporated the conventions of popular fiction and drama.[16] But by relating fiction to both law and journalism, Howells puts his own public status at issue.

Both Daniel Borus and Amy Kaplan have discussed American realism in ways that highlight its "professional" self-image, identifying it as a literary mode that attempted to control and modify the terms of public discourse. Arguing that realism sought to resurrect the belles-lettristic conception of the author as "independent intellectual," Borus maintains that "Realists . . . saw themselves as conciliators, revealing to contending parties their shared characteristics. Because of their ostensible neutrality and burgeoning professionalism, realists felt themselves admirably suited for the task" (173).[17] Kaplan asserts a similar view, arguing that "realists engaged in the construction of a new kind of public sphere" and that they sought to enact "a strategy for containing social difference and controlling social conflict within a cohesive common ground" (13, 23). These positions, while noting realism's engagement with a newly expansive and authoritative public sphere, also characterize it as a kind of "professional" creed that bases its legitimacy on its spatial separation from the discursive realm it seeks to change. In this respect, both implicitly agree with Donald Pizer's assertion that realism is defined largely by its "ethical idealism" (*Realism* 8).

But Bartley's form of professionalism — and Howells's recognition of it — challenges the perspective that Borus, Kaplan, and Pizer attribute to American realists, suggesting that Howells did not identify with the nostalgic definition of the term. Neither Gaylord nor Atherton (to whom I will return later in this chapter) are able to offer significant challenges to the terms of Bartley's power. Unwilling to equate the author with the lawyer of an earlier era, whose moral authority endowed him with considerable influence over American public discourse, Howells emphasizes the impotence of such a figure in the "modern" world. Thus, while Bartley's journalistic ethic is also a kind of legal one, it nevertheless renders him curiously immune to the law's disciplinary mechanisms; he is able to evade all attempts to judge him. Having physically assaulted Henry Bird in the offices of the Equity Free Press, he manages to escape any legal repercussions, asserting when all danger has passed, "I didn't believe from the first that the law could touch me" (88). He repeats this phrase after eluding prosecution for perjury in the wake of the divorce proceedings in Indiana. In fact, Howells suggests, Bartley is correct; the law really can't "touch" him, not because he is somehow above the law, but because, in effect, he *is* the law. As the voice of the community, he stands at the very source of the law's reconstituted authority and is therefore impervious to judgment on anything other than communitarian grounds. His escape from the courtroom in Tecumseh while Gaylord lies prostrate on the floor completes his authoritative ascendance. Gaylord had intended to show Bartley that "there is a God in Israel yet," but his Old Testament conception of justice connects him with a kind of "professionalism" that can neither control the terms of public discourse nor serve as a model for the author who wishes to do so.

"Untouched" by the law, Bartley's primary concern after the proceedings, as he tells Ben Halleck, is not with legal consequences but with the "popular feeling" of the townspeople (447). His concern, of course, is warranted. Although he moves to a new community — Whited Sepulchre, Arizona — he cannot escape a form of communal "justice," as he is murdered by a "leading citizen" of the town for printing a story on the citizen's presumably questionable "domestic relations" (451, 450).[18] On one level, Howells suggests that Bartley gets what he deserves. On another, however, he deliberately deprives the incident of any moral content. The "leading citizen" clearly acts not as a paragon of virtue authorized to impose judgment upon a sinner, but as a representative of the community, and his social prominence makes his own self-interest look like the town's. Howells thus saves Bartley from legal punishment only to have him regulated out of existence by society's mechanisms of self-preservation. As Holmes had asserted, "no society has ever admitted that it could not sacrifice individual welfare to its own existence," and Bartley therefore perishes at the hands of the model of authority he helped to construct (*Common* 44). By the novel's conclusion, Howells has defined a Holmesian social universe governed by official narratives rather than moral absolutes and presided over by the new professionals who are able to articulate the will of the community rather than by the old ones who seek to influence it.[19]

The Realist as Interpreter

Influence, of course, is precisely what Howells had as editor of the *Atlantic* from 1871 to 1881, and his decision to resign his position and to throw himself upon the mercy of the literary marketplace bears heavily on *A Modern Instance*'s concern with authority. Although he was to return to a similarly "influential" position with *Harper's* in 1886, his experiment as a writer without an institutional voice constitutes an exploration of the terms by which literature might command authority in a changed social environment. The *Atlantic* had served as the bastion of the Boston literary establishment and the guardian of literary tastes for three decades when Howells relinquished his position. To leave such a post was either a renunciation of power altogether or a tacit acknowledgement that the terms of his influence as editor were no longer those that mattered. *A Modern Instance* points towards the latter explanation. Bartley's challenge to an image of the legal sphere premised upon its independence from and its influence over social norms also threatens the very form of literary professionalism on which the *Atlantic*'s conception of authorship was based.

Richard Brodhead notes this threat and argues that Howells seeks to disarm it in *A Modern Instance*. He asserts that the novel "describes a culture whose previously rigid communal codes — domestic, ethical, religious, professional — have recently lost the force of their social authority," and that the author seeks to replace that loss with the authority of literature. Noting that Howells began writing at a time that coincided with the "demarcation and institutional reinforcement of a separate, prestigious sphere of high or literary writing, in the 1850s and 1860s," Brodhead claims that Howells views literature as a kind of public institution and realism as "a moral reconstruction program." Thus, he reads Atherton's judgmental pronouncements as examples of the function of the realistic novel: "that of strengthening the public's enfeebled mechanisms of moral judgment, of shoring up and clarifying the structures of moral perception that Howells fears contemporary experience is blurring and eroding." But he also claims that Howells's uncertainty about his moral vision is present in the voice of Halleck, and that the author "never loses a certain skepticism toward his own project" (Brodhead 101, 103).

Brodhead's argument insightfully locates *A Modern Instance* within a cultural environment that is undergoing profound and disruptive transformation. Yet his sense that the novel makes use of the "prestige" of the literary sphere to engage in a kind of "reconstruction" of authority implies that Howells simply seeks to redefine and reinstitute the terms of authorial influence that formed the ideology of the *Atlantic*. What he refers to as Howells's "skepticism" is, I would contend, a model of authority that competes with the moralistic perspective of Atherton and, by extension, the literary version of that perspective. Halleck's dispute with Atherton over his right to pursue Marcia is, at least in part, a dispute over whether Halleck may rely upon the communal norms embodied in divorce legislation or whether he must act upon a private sense of duty — the duty to serve as an "example" to the community and to influence it for the better. Atherton's assertion that Halleck's marriage to Marcia would constitute a "lapse from the ideal" identifies him with the New England literary tradition of the mid-nineteenth century, and Halleck's exclamation to him that "Character is a wretched fetish" invokes the specter of Emerson, among others.[20] But for Howells such "idealism" has begun to look suspiciously sentimental.[21]

What Rodney D. Olsen calls "the middle class ideal of 'influence'" dominates Atherton's form of "idealism" and forms the ideological foundation of the relationship between Bartley and Marcia (Olsen 252). As Howells well knew, this notion was also at the center of the sentimental literary tradition in the United States, especially the domestic fiction of the mid-nineteenth century. Harriet Beecher Stowe's *Uncle Tom's Cabin*, for instance, had exercised its "influence" by revealing the impact of slavery on marriages and families, both black and white, and by emphasizing the role of women in the process of "moral suasion" needed to abolish slavery. Such novels celebrated and sought to strengthen the influence exerted on men by women, and on the political and social sphere by the domestic one. This ideological proposition forms a cornerstone of the way in which both Bartley and Marcia view their marriage. Thus, in telling Marcia of "the processes by which he had formed his own character," Bartley recurs not only to a lecture he had heard on the subject, but to the ideology of sentimentalism as well: "Of all the women I have known, Marcia . . . I believe you have had the strongest influence upon me. I believe you could make me do anything; your influence upon me has been ennobling and elevating" (13). By exposing the failure of this perspective and its issuance in divorce, Howells was staking out a distinctly antisentimental position.[22] But sentimentalism, for Howells, has legal as well as literary meaning; if "influence" fails in its literary manifestation, it fails equally in its legal one, and Atherton's reliance upon it is ultimately shown to be as "sentimental" as the fiction he claims to reject.

Atherton's prominence as a lawyer, along with his Brahmin credentials, makes him the most "influential" character in the novel. Insisting that Halleck not give in to his feelings for Marcia because of the damage that would result to the fabric of society, he seems at first glance to possess a Holmesian concern for public policy. His admonitions, however, take on the pious and moralistic quality of the novel of seduction: "You don't *look* like one of those scoundrels who lure women from their duty, ruin homes, and destroy society — not in the old libertine fashion in which the seducer had at least the grace to risk his life, but safely, smoothly, under the shelter of our infamous laws" (397). The lawyer's judgments embody the same problems that motivate Howells's criticism of the criminal justice system in "Police Report": they ultimately resolve themselves into "melodrama, or romantic tragedy"—genres that allow for moral judgment only by sacrificing "reality."[23] On one level, Atherton seems to take control of the novel as the marriage of Bartley and Marcia disintegrates and as Halleck's ethical dilemma becomes more acute. On another, however, his assumption of authority constitutes a feeble attempt to manage a set of circumstances that no longer responds to the terms he deploys.

Those terms mimic not only popular fiction, but also alarmist treatments of the consequences likely to result from the new availability of divorce. The title of one such account, published in the *Journal of Social Science* in 1881, encapsulates its author's perspective; calling his paper "The Effect of Lax Divorce Legislation Upon the Stability of American Institutions," the Reverend Samuel W. Dike — a leader in the movement to stem the rising tide of divorce after the Civil War — argued that a "lax system" of divorce "*lessens the power of the family and home over the individual*" and that "a part of this weakened influence of the family . . . is, and will be, seen in a diminished influence of woman as such" (157, 158, emphasis in original). Furthermore, his concern with "influence" extended to the law's obligation to limit the availability of divorce: "the true legal system . . . will hasten on the steps of an imperfect society towards the desired rule by its forms of procedure, and diligent culture of public opinion" (163). For Dike, the legal system stands in the same relation to society and public opinion as the family does to the individual and as woman does to man. Each of these institutions (including the institution of "woman as such") rests on moral ground and thereby has a duty to elevate, rather than reflect, the values of the community. His piece reveals the cultural affinity between a moralistic conception of legal authority and a sentimental version of literature's function, and suggests that Howells's antisentimentalism in *A Modern Instance* constitutes, in part, an implicit rejection of Atherton's legal paradigm.

At the novel's conclusion, Atherton is in a quandary over how to respond in writing to a letter from Halleck. Howells's invocation of authorship reveals the extent to which Atherton's position is literary as well as legal, and its literary nature partakes not only of the "low culture" of sentimentalism, but of the "high culture" of the *Atlantic* as well. In fact, Atherton operates as a legal surrogate for Howells's own recently vacated editorial position. Thus, Atherton cautions Halleck against relying upon popular fiction for his impressions of human nature, telling him that his own legal practice has provided him with "a glimpse of realities" that conflict with what he reads in novels. His moral advice, supposedly grounded in such "realities," forms a counterpart to Howells's editorial efforts to deflect literary tastes away from the unreality of popular fiction and toward a more "truthful" and socially responsible form of writing. But Howells now sees his own former position within the Boston literary establishment as "sentimental," premised as it was upon a kind of professional influence that was more nostalgic than "modern."[24] Atherton's concern with private judgment makes him unfit to serve as the model for either the new legal professional or, it seems, the realistic author. For Howells, to be a realist is to be both "legal" and "modern," and it is clear that Atherton's legalism is not quite "modern" enough.

In fact, the paralysis evident in Atherton's final "I don't know! I don't know!" contrasts with Bartley's linguistic presence at the end of the novel. The article describing Bartley's murder treats it with "cynical lightness," and Howells tells us that "the parenthetical truth in the closing statement, that 'Mr. Hubbard leaves a (divorced) wife and child somewhere in the East,' was quite in Bartley's own manner" (451). In its "spicy" exposure of his marital status, Bartley's obituary belies the fact of his death by paradoxically announcing the continued vitality of his writing. It also acts as Howells's acknowledgment that his own novel springs from the same sources as Bartley's journalism; the fact that Bartley was "(divorced)" is precisely *A Modern Instance*'s voyeuristic and scandalous subject.[25] Bartley's resilience underscores both the triumph of his form of professionalism and Howells's concession to the literary version of it. Unable to inspire an "influential" letter to Halleck on his public duty, Atherton's professionalism leads to a loss of authority that also puts him at a loss for words. The lawyer's loss, however, is Howells's gain; his completion of the novel at Atherton's expense reveals that it is Bartley's voice that inspires his own fiction.

Repudiating a conception of authorship grounded in republican virtue and moral influence, Howells simultaneously renounces one kind of power and gains another. By foregoing any claims to moral authority, he reinvents himself as spokesman for community norms and author of "official" narratives. Yet the "epistemological tension" that exists in Holmes's thought is present in Howells's novel as well. Resorting to the kind of melodrama characteristic of dime novel tales of the Wild West, Howells plays Jacques's "justice" by authoring a fitting punishment for his protagonist. Nonetheless, he will not interpret Bartley's death for us, calling it "consequence or penalty, as we choose to think it" (451). If that death expresses Howells's reluctance to relinquish an ethical conception of authorship — and the "influence" that goes along with it — his unwillingness to interpret it as a "penalty" reveals an equal distaste for such a conception. Howells recognizes the ascendance of Bartley's "philosophy," but at the same time he fears the utter dispersal — even denial — of authority that it implies. By "killing" Bartley, he reasserts some form of control over the processes that threaten to overwhelm his own story.

Exposing both the power and the weakness of Bartley's legal and journalistic fictions, and throwing his own literary one into the cultural mix, Howells suggests the possibility of drawing meaningful distinctions between the public narratives available for consumption. Like Holmes, he grounds narrative in a version of "experience" that bears some relation to an objective reality — a space outside the socially constructed norms of "modern" society. Bartley's stories are "inside" narratives — they look only to the ever-shifting norms of the community for their legitimacy, never explicitly applying an "outside" value to structure their representations of social patterns and principles. Such representations, in the final analysis, are unable to command the willful submission of the community (Bartley cannot even sustain a marriage). Although Howells's narratives, like his character's, spring from a public rather than private sphere, they seek to narrativize the narratives — that is, to place the socially produced standards embodied in journalistic representations in a context that underscores the values they rely upon, but never articulate. By delving *beneath* the kinds of fictions produced by society's Bartleys — by connecting them to the "truths" they tacitly claim to embody — Howells's fiction asserts a claim to the kind of authority that makes the "rule of law" meaningful.

A Modern Instance finally vindicates the concept of popular sovereignty. It does so, however, only after moving authorship from its seat of ethical prominence and placing it in the midst of the mob — a position from which authors can both listen to the voice of the populace, and interpret its meanings back to it. Howellsian professional authors are not Emersonian seers, but they are figures of power nonetheless. They may lack the warrant of a Lycurgus, Justinian, or Napoleon to inaugurate new legal paradigms, but they are as close as we can come to "modern" incarnations of lawgivers.

A Return to the Law: The Quality of Mercy

Howells's increasing commitment to values rooted in Christianity in the ten years following the publication of *A Modern Instance* — a commitment manifested in his Tolstoyan concept of "complicity" — never led him far from a this-worldly concern with the law. In fact, the most important event for him as an author and public figure during this period was a legal one: the trial and execution of the Haymarket anarchists. Howells protested their sentences vehemently in an 1887 letter to the New York *Tribune*, asking "all those who believe that it would be either injustice or impolicy to put them to death" to demand that the governor of Illinois — "whose prerogative [was] now the supreme law in their case" — mitigate their punishment (*Selected* 199). In a letter that he wrote after the executions and decided not to send to the paper, he employed the terms of critique he had used in his "Police Report" essay, asserting that the state prosecutor, Julius Grinnell, had "shown gifts of imagination that would perhaps fit him better for the functions of a romantic novelist than for the duties of official advocate in a free commonwealth," and that the trial "[had] not been a trial by justice, but a trial by passion, by terror, by prejudice, by hate, by newspaper" (*Selected* 202). His uncertainty about the grounds of his protest — "injustice or impolicy" — reveals the extent to which questions of legal authority continued to vex him throughout this period. While the second letter is more sure of the distinction between morality and public opinion — between "trial by justice" and "trial by newspaper" — his decision not to send it may signal a certain discomfort with the terms he employs.

The issues involved in the Haymarket affair manage to work their way into much of Howells's fiction of the late 1880s and early 1890s. While *A Hazard of New Fortunes* is now the novel most frequently associated with it, *The Quality of Mercy* (1892) confronts the legal conflicts raised by the case more directly and, in so doing, revisits the ground covered in *A Modern Instance*.[26] Taking its title — like the latter novel — from a Shakespearean legal reference, it wonders if a communitarian conception of the law must inevitably embody the cruelty of Shylock's insistence upon "justice," or if "the quality of mercy" may drop "as the gentle rain from Heaven" from the pen of the author and, hence, into the consciousness of the community. The novel was the only one that Howells ever serialized in the newspapers — it appeared originally in the New York *Sun* and was subsequently syndicated by S. S. McClure in eight other papers. Its concern with the relationship among law, journalism, and literature, and its appearance in the very engines of public sentiment that Howells criticized in his unpublished Haymarket letter, make the novel an important addendum to *A Modern Instance*.

Bartley Hubbard does not appear as a character in *The Quality of Mercy*, but he is nonetheless present in spirit. The novel centers around John Milton Northwick, an embezzler from Hatboro', Massachussetts, who runs off to Canada with funds from the Ponkwasset Mills Corporation. Bartley's former newspaper, the Boston *Events*, sends a reporter named Pinney to cover the story, and Pinney's job is to carry on Bartley's legacy. Howells tells us that some years earlier, "the *Events* had been in the management of a journalist once well-known in Boston, a certain Bartley Hubbard, who had risen from the ranks of the reporters, and who had thoroughly reporterized it in the worst sense," turning it into "a journal without principles and convictions, but with interests only" (118–19). Following in the Holmesian footsteps of his predecessor, Pinney attempts to capture "The Consensus of Public Feeling" regarding the embezzler, and he writes a "space-man's masterpiece" in which "all scruples and reluctances became fused in a devotion to the interests of the *Events* and its readers." Opposed to Pinney's superficially populist treatment, however, is a more "literary" article written by a reporter named Maxwell for the *Abstract* (formerly the *Chronicle-Abstract*), which is still run by Ricker and still reflects "his ideal of a conscience in journalism" (117, 119). Maxwell is an aspiring poet and dramatist who had been working on a play about defaulters — a play meant "to appeal rather to the compassion than to the justice of the theatre"— that he simply adapts for the purposes of his article. While Pinney's piece condemns Northwick and gives voice to the community's righteous anger, Maxwell's argues that "it behooved society to consider how far it was itself responsible" for such actions (125–26). Howells leaves little doubt about which version he condones.

Oddly enough, however, Maxwell eventually disappears from the novel, as his reporting career falters and he decides to focus more upon poetry. Pinney, on the other hand, becomes not just the leading reporter covering the story, but a detective as well. He concocts a scheme to track down Northwick in Canada and, through "moral suasion," to convince him to return and face his punishment (302). In so doing, he would not only solidify his career as a journalist, but possibly open up a new career as a detective as well. His plans change slightly when Northwick's family hires him to find the fugitive, for they want only to communicate with him about the money he still possesses and not to bring him to justice. Pinney's ambiguous status as journalist/detective and his uncertainty about his public/private function are central to the novel's concern with the narrative productions of journalism and their quasilegal effects. When preparing his initial story on Northwick, he meets Northwick's daughter and tries to repress a strange pang of guilt about the story he is working on: "Pinney was not going to punish him, he was merely going to publish him; but all the same, for that moment, it seemed to him that he was Northwick's persecutor and was hunting him down, running him to earth" (96). The passage foreshadows the fact that the reporter literally will "hunt him down" later in the novel and suggests that "publishing" and "punishing" bear more relation than Pinney would like to believe.

Howells's treatment of Pinney implies that the post–Civil War transformation of journalism has endowed it with a disciplinary function, reconfiguring it as an arm of a newly broadened and decentered legal realm. In this sense, the novel instantiates Michel Foucault's thesis that, since the adoption in the West of the "new penal system" in the eighteenth and nineteenth centuries, "the power of judging has been transferred, in part, to other authorities than the judges of the offence," and that "the whole penal operation has taken on extra-juridical elements and personnel" (Foucault, *Language* 22). For Foucault, such "extra-juridical elements" are primarily medical and psychological, but Howells's novel suggests that we redefine the penal system even more broadly to encompass all those who participate in the production and enforcement of "official" narratives. The president of the board of the Ponkwasset Mills, Eben Hilary, begins to understand his own role in this process upon reading Pinney's "masterpiece." Although the story makes him "sick," he concludes that "there was really nothing more to blame in the attitude of the papers than in that of the directors who gave the case to the detectives and set the machinery of publicity at work. Both were acting quite within their rights; both were fulfilling an official duty." Hilary's "growing sympathy" for Northwick conflicts with his "official duty," and this fact (along with his son's amorous relationship with Northwick's daughter) causes him to resign his position and offer his own funds as compensation for the corporation's losses (127). His authority within the company paradoxically deprives him of the power to act as a moral agent, constituting him instead as a part of the "machinery" by which the community regulates its norms and disciplines its members. His resignation, therefore, signals both his discomfort with the disciplinary nature of his duty to publish and his corresponding rejection of judgment in favor of "sympathy."

Hilary's uneasiness with "the official" contrasts with Pinney's embrace of it. Pinney's career as a detective is simply an extension of his reporting, and Hilary's son points out that "the two things run together" (291). But detection provides conflicts of its own; Pinney goes to Canada with a warrant for Northwick's arrest while under instructions from Northwick's family to simply locate him so that they might resolve the problem privately. His wife cautions him about confusing private and public functions, telling him, "if you go as a detective, *go* as a detective; and if you go as their friend, to help them and serve them, then go that way. But don't you try to carry water on both shoulders" (302). Pinney, however, disregards her advice and employs "moral suasion" to convince Northwick to return with him. Although he sees no conflict of interest as long as Northwick returns of his own free will and not by dint of the warrant he possesses, his skill at manipulating narratives gives his "moral suasion" the force of law. Earlier in the novel, Howells had suggested that newspapers have replaced preachers as the nation's "moralists," but Pinney's bad faith reveals that their "morality" simply disguises a self-serving ambition to achieve institutional status as the official guardians of public norms.

Nonetheless, what appears to be a triumph of both journalism and detection for Pinney ends up backfiring. As the two begin their journey back to Hatboro', Pinney notes a "spiritual peace" in Northwick's face and states, "anybody to see us would think *you* were taking *me* back." The reversal is complete when, after crossing the border, reviewing the warrant for his arrest, and demanding that Pinney place him in handcuffs, Northwick quietly dies and the "loosened handcuffs" fall from his wrists (353, 355). While Howells clearly wishes us to view Northwick's death as a challenge to Pinney's seemingly vast authority, the basis of that challenge remains unclear. Is it an act of God that deprives Pinney of his power? A chance occurrence? A final assertion of moral force by Northwick after struggling throughout the novel in a kind of moral paralysis? The command that the embezzler exerts at the end of the novel suggests that Howells wishes us to view his death, at least in part, as self-willed, but the strength he needs to free himself from Pinney's control seems to spring paradoxically from his submission to that control. The novel's lawyer, Putney, asserts that "Justice herself couldn't have her way with Northwick," and suggests that he was "a mere creature of circumstance" whose death came at the hands of "Fate." When Dr. Morrell asks, "Why not call it Law?" Putney replies that he will "split the difference . . . and call it Mercy" (359). Their attempts to find transcendent meaning in Northwick's death, however, ring hollow. If "mercy" is involved, Howells implies, it emanates from a source other than God.

"Mercy," for Howells, is as much a literary as a theological term. If in the New England tradition mercy is a manifestation of God's sovereignty — of the belief that the deity is more powerful than any law by which the concept of justice might operate — then Howells's use of it within a novel troubled by the legal nature of publication suggests the possibility that authorship might, like God, transcend the rule of its own being. In this reading of the ending, Northwick's evasion of Pinney's legal authority models the manner by which Howells hopes to assert his own form of sovereignty. Howells might be said to hold out hope for a kind of authorial "influence" that takes its cue not from the law, but from standards immanent in the very conception of authorship. Howells may have been moving in the direction of a form of literary professionalism that was more insulated — a disciplinarity that was less interdisciplinary. In *Criticism and Fiction* — the collection of essays he had written for *Harper's* and which, like *The Quality of Mercy*, appeared as a book in 1892 — he maintained that novelists should not feel fettered by criticism, for "the original mind cannot conform to models; it has its norm within itself; it can work only in its own way, and by its self-given laws" (27). If the "laws" of criticism reflect the norms of the community, then Howells's assertion might also be read as a declaration of independence from the kind of Holmesian legalism he had embraced in *A Modern Instance*; the "laws" he refers to, apparently, are "purely" literary. Howells might here be said to anticipate the conception of literary professionalism later articulated by modernists such as T. S. Eliot.

But the "mercy" that Howells shows toward Northwick at the end of the novel is not necessarily the reflection of authorial sovereignty that it initially seems. Although Howells is less comfortable with a communitarian theory of fiction by the time he writes his 1892 novel, he cannot ultimately abandon the concept of realism's legal engagement in favor of a version of literature grounded only in "self-given laws." Thus, the novel suggests that "mercy," like "judgment," may exist in the mind of the social body as well as in the mind of the author. In Canada, for instance, Pinney discovers that many of the American defaulters are "in society," and that the Canadians "judged them by their known intentions and their exigencies, as the justice they had fled from could not judge them" (303). Furthermore, following its initial outrage, a significant portion of the community of Hatboro' had evidenced a willingness to show Northwick the sort of "mercy" that the author does. Even his former enemy, Putney — who, prior to Northwick's flight, had almost been run over by Northwick's carriage and had shouted at him, "You can't drive over the Law" — is ready by the end of the novel to defend him on the grounds of insanity. Such views do not represent those of the entire community; yet they are prevalent enough within the bounds of Howells's narrative to suggest that his own decision to dispense grace in the form of mercy is a function of, and legitimated by, a similar social impulse. In fact, it is this impulse that brings the residents of Hatboro' together as the novel concludes. "Mercy" rather than "justice" ultimately springs from the public will.[27]

Both Bartley's death in *A Modern Instance* and Northwick's in *The Quality of Mercy* are subject to conflicting interpretations: one that manifests a romantic belief in the privileged state of the authorship, and another in which authorship is itself "authored" by larger social forces. But it is precisely this tension that makes Howells's works the very embodiments of literary professionalism. The sense of constraint imposed by the need to conform to a predetermined normative universe (community standards) is balanced by Howells's invocation of an "outside" — a foundation that makes his own narrativization of those standards "true," "good," "ethical" — in other words, authoritative. Howells's novels never claim direct access to the foundational principles they rely upon — those principles are always mediated — yet they operate throughout his fiction as objects of desire. As *The Quality of Mercy* demonstrates, that desire becomes more acute in the wake of the social disruptions of the 1880s and early 1890s. Thus, while Maxwell's disappearance from the novel — along with his ethical and literary approach to journalism — signals his inability to compete with the Bartleyan power of Pinney, it also keeps his perspective alive; his banishment allows him to exist in an ideal space outside the text, writing poetry and appealing to "the tribunal that searches hearts and judges motives rather than acts" (141).[28] Howells's later utopian novels would seek to represent this locale explicitly, to posit the possibility of a seamless concurrence of internal and external norms. But the "outside" here is also an "inside" — Maxwell's presence, and the privileged form of judgment he represents, hover over *The Quality of Mercy* as a kind of ghostly, extralegal presence.

At the end of "Police Report," Howells describes seeing the Black

Maria driving away from the courthouse after receiving "its dead" — the convicted criminals it is transporting to prison. He notes that, in contrast to the police trials, "it was fulfilling its function with merciful privacy" ("Police" 16). But the thought he then articulates, in its subjective and distinctly irrational quality, reveals his desire for a form of "privacy" that is not legally sanctioned, that confirms the sovereignty of his own consciousness:

> I could not help thinking — or perhaps the thought only occurs to me now — that for all reasonable hope as to the future of its inmates the Black Maria might as well have been fitted with one of those ingenious pieces of mechanism by which some of our adoptive citizens propose to disable English commerce, and driven out to some wide, open space where the explosion could do no harm to the vicinity, and so when the horses and driver had removed to a safe distance —
>
> But this is perhaps pessimism. ("Police" 16)

Howells's thought does not express a desire for execution — the convicts, after all, are already "dead" — as much as it indulges a fantasy of authorial illegality.[29] Disappointed by the operation of the criminal justice system and anxious about the relationship between the literary and legal spheres, he imagines himself a kind of anarchist, mercifully freeing himself and others from the handcuffs of a legal environment grown oppressively public. Yet by catching his "pessimism" before it goes too far, he brings himself back into the legal and professional fold.

While Howells acknowledges that such thoughts are ultimately no more than passing fancies — dreams of authorial influence and "self-given laws" — his revolt against the new order, like the more muted protests registered in his novels, ends up affirming it.

It also, however, exposes the instability of that order, its vulnerability to the very fancies it helps to construct. Holmes, of course, recognized the same thing; the law's vulnerability — the tension between its responsiveness to public opinion and its dedication to foundational principles — is precisely what allows it to "grow," "develop," and thus serve as a coherent "story." And in that sense, Howells and Holmes continued their intellectual alliance, even in the wake of their broken friendship.

CHAPTER 2

Helen Hunt Jackson and the Romance of Indian Nationhood

If I could write a story that would do for the Indian a thousandth part of what
Uncle Tom's Cabin did for the Negro, I would be thankful the rest of my life.
Helen Hunt Jackson, letter to Thomas Bailey Aldrich, 4 May 1883

Using Harriet Beecher Stowe's wildly popular and politically momentous condemnation of slavery as a touchstone for the success of her work-in-progress on American Indian victimization, Helen Hunt Jackson set perhaps an overly ambitious standard for the novel that would eventually become *Ramona*. This was not because the reform climate of the 1880s had lost the fervor of the abolitionist era. In fact, movements for social reform proliferated in the post–Civil War years, and the sentiment in favor of Indian "uplift" became especially strong in the late 1870s and early 1880s, particularly in Jackson's native New England; the crucible of reform in the United States was as strong as ever. What had changed were the terms of reform — terms that literary works advocating social positions were now obliged to incorporate. In the wake of the postbellum wave of civil rights legislation, reformist literature could no longer speak effectively (as Stowe had done) from a space wholly outside of the established modes of institutional discourse; the law, the Constitution, and the federal government now stood (at least theoretically) for the principles of racial justice and equality, and any arguments invoking those principles had to account for their legal meanings and applications. Criticism of the law was certainly possible, but only by reference to ideals that were written into the fabric of legal reasoning and precedent. If Howells theorized about the legal dimensions of storytelling, Jackson was faced with the task of putting that theory to practice in the specific context of Indian reform. Originally titled

"In the Name of the Law," *Ramona* reflected the challenges posed by this new legal and literary environment.

And it was precisely the novel's legality — its adherence to positions that had been sanctioned by federal judges, legislators, and administrators — that made the novel something of a disappointment by comparison to *Uncle Tom's Cabin*. *Ramona* was almost as popular — it stands today as one of the most widely read American novels of all time — but its popularity has hinged on its love story and its romantic evocation of a pristine, precommercial southern California rather than on the outrage it expresses about the treatment of American Indian tribes.[1] Moreover, by today's standards the novel suffers much the same fate as that of Stowe's work — both *Uncle Tom's Cabin* and *Ramona* are widely viewed as doing almost as much (if not more) harm than good. Although the two works address serious matters of oppression and injustice, they do so in ways that confirm stereotypes about the childlike helplessness of their respective objects of pity, calling for an enlightened white paternalism toward African Americans and Native Americans. Michael Dorris, for instance, notes that *Ramona* "cashed in on every positive stereotype in the cultural repertoire" and "failed to reflect the complicated aspirations of particular tribes for sovereignty, self-government, and maintenance of treaty accords" (xvii). And Carl Gutierrez-Jones accuses Jackson of "a romanticism that ultimately denies the very issues [she] hoped to enliven" (58).[2]

Such criticisms are justified, but reveal little about the ideological assumptions behind the novel's romanticism. Neither Jackson nor a substantial number of nineteenth-century critics and readers viewed her work as an artistic failure, and our understanding of it should account for the climate that produced both the author's intentions and the responses of her contemporaries. That climate was defined by an official Indian policy that was in the process of shifting directions and by a new interest in Indian affairs on the part of philanthropists and religious groups. Together, these developments led to a concord between reformers and government officials on a general approach to U.S.-Indian relations, although the two groups frequently disagreed on specific applications. After the end of the Civil War and the beginning of President Grant's "peace policy" (and following a series of Indian massacres by U.S. troops in the Great Plains), there was substantial agreement among the country's white population that the policy of treaty-making with Indian tribes should stop and that every effort should be made to encourage (or force) Indians to assimilate into mainstream American society.[3]

The word most often used to describe the consensus approach was "civilization." The hierarchy inherent in the terms "civilized" and "savage" infused the rhetoric of Anglo-Saxonism and American expansion throughout the nineteenth century, but in the 1870s and 1880s that hierarchy was being used not to emphasize racial or ethnic difference, as it had earlier in the century. During Andrew Jackson's presidency, the official policy had been to separate American Indians from whites as much as possible through both treaty-making and forced removal, under the rationale that Indians were an alien race incapable of successfully integrating into white American society. Beginning with the Grant administration, however, the "savagery" of Indian tribes was emphasized to *promote* integration. The temporary outrage over Little Big Horn notwithstanding, Indians were portrayed by both government agents and reform-minded citizens as essentially childlike, dependent, and in need of Anglo guidance. Their "savagery" conveyed a form of difference that did not mandate separation, but rather an enlightened parental tutelage.

The white advocates of Indian rights during this period, including Helen Hunt Jackson, disagreed with many of the specific actions taken by the federal government with respect to Indian tribes, but there was little disagreement as to the general nature of the relationship. *Ramona* was written from a reformer's perspective and takes issue with a number of the government's official and unofficial practices, but the novel also sprang out of Jackson's work as an official commissioner appointed by the government to investigate the plight of California's Mission Indians. As a result, her novel's critique of governmental policy never strays far from the model of U.S.-Indian relations that lay behind *both* the government's and the reformers' agendas. The issue for Jackson was not whether to "civilize" the Indians, but how best to do it.

What is most striking about the novel, however, is the way in which it diverges from its own clear intentions. While much of Jackson's work is devoted to chronicling the repeated dispossessions suffered by the half-blooded Indian, Ramona, and her full-blooded husband, Alessandro — a narrative that calls attention to the government's failure to protect the interests of its Indian wards and its ineffective attempts to encourage their adoption of white standards — the story also highlights the persistent "Indianness" of its main characters. That is to say, by establishing the fact that their love is grounded largely in a shared Indian identity, Jackson commits herself to a literary logic grounded in the conventions of the domestic romance that requires an endorsement — even a celebration—of this identity. And this is where the novel articulates a vision of U.S.-Indian relations based not on a paternalistic hierarchy of "civilized" and "savage," nor on the notion of an unbridgeable gap between the two, but on a sense of coequal and self-contained nationhood. Although Jackson presents both Ramona and Alessandro as already "civilized," neither chooses to be fully Americanized (by affiliating themselves with either the United States or Mexico), and their ability to exercise a kind of self-sovereignty in this respect mirrors the position taken by many Indians in the nineteenth century (and the twentieth) that their tribes constituted sovereign nations. Jackson's representation of Indian identity as a national identity accords it a weight that the discourse of "civilization" and "savagery" does not, entitling the possessor of national membership to certain rights by virtue of what has traditionally been called the "law of nations." Jackson had repeatedly invoked the "law of nations" in her first work on Indian issues, the nonfictional *A Century of Dishonor* (1880), and the reemergence of an argument grounded in tribal sovereignty in *Ramona*— even though it conflicts with the terms of her reformism — indicates how problematic the tenacity of this concept was to those who wished to envision U.S.-Indian relations as familial, paternalistic, and hierarchical.

Thus, the representations of Indian subjection and dependence that run through *Ramona* are not the only story to tell about the novel, nor are such representations the only story to tell about the "official Indian" of political and legal discourse. Although Jackson's evocations of Indian nationhood work against the established governmental policy of the time — a policy that federal courts were generally eager to support — the uncanny persistence of the concept of Indian sovereignty within the law indicates the extent to which her novel reflects a larger unresolved tension over the definition of nationhood within both the legal system and American popular culture (indeed, the two reflect each other). Ever since Chief Justice John Marshall declared Indian tribes "domestic dependent nations" in 1831, American legal and political figures had struggled over how much those tribes should be considered "domestic" and "dependent" on the one hand, and how much they should be treated as "nations" on the other. No clear policy had emerged with respect to that issue until the Congress and President Grant attempted to regulate away all remnants of tribal sovereignty as a means of forcing Indian assimilation into mainstream American culture. But although that policy continued well into the twentieth century, the repressed residue of Marshall's famous phrase refused to disappear — a survival due in part to the law's emphasis on precedent and continuity, but even more to the persistence of Indian tribal identities in the face of all efforts to eradicate them. If Indian tribes were no longer to be considered sovereign nations, apparently someone had forgotten to tell the tribes' members. Because of this persistence, the doctrine of tribal sovereignty continued to rear its head within the law in ways that cast serious doubt on the wisdom and viability of the government's assimilation policy.

And it also reared its head within American popular culture, even in works like *Ramona* that were written from an assimilationist perspective. In fact, it would be surprising if this were not the case, since Jackson's novel essentially constitutes a kind of extended legal brief. Jackson may have aspired to become a latter-day Harriet Beecher Stowe, but by the time she had finished serving as a special commissioner for the Office of Indian Affairs she could no longer claim to be writing solely from the exalted moral position of political outsider. Her novel, published only two years after *A Modern Instance*, follows in Howells's footsteps. Although *Ramona* partakes more of romance than of realism, it nonetheless exemplifies an approach to Indian reform that is thoroughly professional — it conforms to a logic about Indian identity that had been written into both political and legal discourse by the early 1880s and seeks to expose official failings by recourse to that logic. But Jackson's professionalism also leads her inexorably "outside" that discursive territory to examine the foundations of her argument, and it is this process that repeatedly draws her back to a conception of Indian identity grounded in nationhood. Her Indian characters exert self-sovereignty not by losing their "Indianness," but by retaining it, and in making their individual freedom and self-determination the core of her romance Jackson promotes a recognition of tribal sovereignty that undercuts assimilationist policies. In so doing, *Ramona* not only exposes the fissure at the heart of official representations of Indian identity in the nineteenth century, but also anticipates and even encourages the turn toward a legal recognition of tribal sovereignty that has occurred in the twentieth.

Sovereignty and Indian Nationhood

The very concept of sovereignty — applied to either the individual or the nation — is grounded in a Western philosophical tradition that would seem inapplicable to American Indians or their tribal groups. And if we regard some conception of sovereignty as a distinct attribute of nationhood, then Indian tribes might well be excluded from the category of "nations" altogether. By defining "the nation" as a political community that is "imagined as both inherently limited and sovereign," for instance, Benedict Anderson limits nationhood to a European model grounded in the growth of Enlightenment conceptions of the self and the community. For Anderson, the nation replaces the form of political community based on a divinely ordained social order, and represents a mode of organization defined not by a sense of duty to a higher power, but by a secular version of freedom; "the gage and emblem of this freedom," he argues, "is the sovereign state" (6, 7). The more sacralized communities formed by American Indians would seem not to qualify for nationhood under this definition. Yet as Cheryl Walker has noted, American Indian conceptions of their own communities began to change upon contact with Europeans, and the Western concepts of sovereignty and nationhood began to inflect their sense of themselves as members of tribes and of a larger "people." Walker also points out the ways in which Indians modified those concepts, thus offering alternative nationalisms that employed Western discourses in the service of a more indigenous sense of self and community. While Indian identity was closely connected to tribes and specific bands, such associations did not preclude a pan-Indianism that accommodated a larger version of Indian nationhood. George Copway, for instance, protested the manner in which the "American government has addressed us like different nations, instead of addressing us as an Indian nation, and as one family" (quoted in Walker 104). Tribal affiliations in the nineteenth century increasingly served as a means of forming national connections between Indian groups that might earlier have been mortal enemies.

Moreover, Western powers in the New World implicitly acknowledged Indian claims to nationhood by entering into treaties with tribes just as they would have with any foreign power. Continuing that practice upon achieving independence from Britain, the United States also recognized the national status of the tribes within its borders, accepting the freedom of each tribe to enter into contractual relations on a communal basis. Of course, this practice also raised the disturbing specter of what one federal Indian agent called an "*imperium in imperio*" — a nation within a nation — thus posing a threat to the United States's conception of its own national sovereignty. Such concern makes it all the more surprising that Americans continued to imagine Indians as members of separate nations, even when expansionist impulses and hostility from individual tribes made that conception politically and economically inconvenient. One of the most antagonistic periods of U.S.-Indian relations in the early nineteenth century was the presidency of Andrew Jackson, in which the forced removal of thousands of Indians in the South resulted in innumerable deaths along what has come to be known as the Trail of Tears. Yet this was also the era in which the Supreme Court officially recognized the national status of Indian tribes, albeit with qualifications. And during the 1870s and 1880s, when white America was almost united in demanding that Indians abandon their traditional ways and tribal affiliations in favor of "Americanization," both the law and American culture at large continued to identify Indians as members of nations that possessed some form of sovereignty. The discourse of nationhood in nineteenth-century America was fraught with ambivalence, as Americans insisted upon the inevitable triumph of their form of "civilization" over Indian "savagery" yet also imbued the term "Indian" with meanings connected to the assertion of freedom, resistance to coercion, and a strong sense of national identity — qualities they also associated with being American.[4]

The doubleness that plagued "official" versions of "the Indian" also infected the rhetoric of America in the nineteenth century, as the nation made sense as a unified whole only if it could also be imagined as a house divided. While it can certainly be argued that the country's fractured sense of itself sprang from its birth in revolution and its consequent distrust of centralized authority (resulting in a constitutional separation of powers and a federal system grounded in *both* state and national sovereignty), the problems presented by Indian nationhood also suggest that the fractures had something to do with the United States's status as a colonial power. Viewed from this angle, we might see the internal contradictions of official Indian policy as examples of what Homi Bhabha terms "colonial mimicry" — "the desire for a reformed, recognizable Other, *as a subject of difference that is almost the same, but not quite*" (86). For Bhabha, mimicry is a central element in colonial discourse, as it turns a subjected people into a fit object of representation by a dominant one and thus renders the subjected group susceptible to the mastery implied in such representation. But Bhabha also notes that "the *ambivalence* of mimicry (almost the same, *but not quite*) . . . becomes transformed into an uncertainty which fixes the colonial subject as a 'partial' presence":

> The *menace* of mimicry is its *double* vision which in disclosing the ambivalence of colonial discourse also disrupts its authority. And it is a

double vision that is a result of what I've described as the partial representation/recognition of the colonial object. . . . [Mimicry] is a desire that reverses 'in part' the colonial appropriation by now producing a partial vision of the colonizer's presence; a gaze of otherness, that shares the acuity of the genealogical gaze which, as Foucault describes it, liberates marginal elements and shatters the unity of man's being through which he extends his sovereignty. (86, 88–89)

Bhabha's language captures the doubleness inherent in the official discourse of U.S.-Indian relations. Asserting a sovereign right to control its own territory as a unified whole, the United States designated Indian tribes as its "wards" and sought to justify its assertions of power by imagining itself a paternalistic "guardian" ready to conduct its charge further along the scale of civilization. But in promoting this model, the country also implicitly recognized Indian tribes as lesser versions of itself — partial presences who were capable of exercising some form of national sovereignty as well. And even more important, it began to connect the integrity of its own nationhood to the existence of Indian nationhood, so that the persistence of tribal identities in the face of all attempts to erase them came to symbolize the freedom that lay at the heart of the United States's self-conception.

This ambivalence troubles the representation of Indians in "unofficial" texts, such as Jackson's *Ramona*, as well as in the "official" texts of American law and politics. In fact, the similarities between the two categories suggest that we read Jackson's work as part of the same constellation of "official" texts that includes legal opinions and government regulations; *Ramona* is in essence an extended legal argument about the government's approach to Indian relations and employs a logic that incorporates the law's attempts to define Indian nationhood and rights. Written immediately following Jackson's service as a special commissioner for the Office of Indian Affairs — an appointment that she actively sought and that resulted in a report suggesting a number of specific legal and policy solutions to the problems confronting California's Mission Indians — the novel springs from the same professional spirit with which she approached her government appointment. Like the "official" report Jackson wrote, *Ramona* argues for changes in the government's Indian policy by recourse to the government's own legal standards, and thus uncovers meanings hidden within the law's texts that legal and governmental authorities would themselves repress. The novel, however, also shows us why those meanings continued to vex American Indian policy. The existence of Indian nations may have threatened to fracture the territorial sovereignty of the United States, but to reject Indian nationhood altogether would have been to do even more damage; it would destroy an important symbol of the kind of sovereignty that transcended territorial boundaries — that served as the glue holding together such concepts at the heart of American identity as "the people" and "the rule of law."

Although the love between Alessandro Assis and Ramona Gonzalez lies at the center of Jackson's novel, the shape that love takes and the consequences to which it leads are determined less by the two lovers themselves than by the strained relationship between Ramona and her legal guardian, the Señora Moreno. It is the Señora's outrage at Ramona's engagement to an Indian that results in the lovers' flight from the otherwise idyllic Moreno ranch and the state of exile they subsequently endure. Jackson saves her harshest criticism for the American settlers who forcibly eject individual Indians and entire tribes from their ancestral lands, but Ramona and Alessandro become subject to American rapaciousness only because they cannot rely upon the Señora's benevolent protection. Jackson distinguishes between the grasping selfishness of the new American residents of California and the more genteel Californios who have remained after the American triumph in the Mexican War; the latter exhibit a concern for Indian well-being completely abjured by the former. In this respect, however, the Señora Moreno is something of an anomaly among the characters associated with Mexican culture, such as Father Salvierderra and the Señora's son, Felipe; she professes a nostalgia for the glory days of the Mission era — a time that Jackson (wrongly) depicts as a golden age for the California Indian tribes — but the Señora's personal disdain for Indians and her lack of affection for the half-Indian Ramona associate her with an American disregard for Indian welfare. In her role as legal guardian, the Señora is more "American" than "Mexican."

The authorial decision to make Ramona a ward of the Señora, the placement of this legal relation in such a prominent position with respect to the novel's action, and the indifference that the Señora shows for Ramona's best interests, suggest that Jackson was attempting, at least in part, to invoke the legal relationship between the United States and the Indian tribes. That relationship had been defined, albeit indistinctly, by the Supreme Court opinions written by Chief Justice John Marshall in what have come to be known as the "Cherokee Cases." In the first of these decisions, *Cherokee Nation v. State of Georgia* (1831), Marshall had ruled that the Cherokee tribe did not constitute a "foreign state" within the meaning of the Constitution, and that the Supreme Court therefore did not have jurisdiction to render a decision in the tribe's suit against the state of Georgia for seeking to apply state laws on tribal territory. Marshall's opinion for the Court walked a fine line between acknowledging the sovereignty of Indian tribes and maintaining the power of the federal government to intervene, at least in a limited way, in their affairs. Citing "the numerous treaties made with the Cherokees by the United States," he concluded that "the acts of our government plainly recognize the Cherokee Nation as a State, and the courts are bound by those acts" (*Cherokee* 16). But he also found that "the condition of the Indians in relation to the United States is perhaps unlike that of any other two people in existence," and that this relation simply could not be defined as that existing between nations wholly foreign to one another (17). As a result, he denominated Indian tribes as "domestic dependent nations," asserting that "they are so completely under the sovereignity [sic] and dominion of the United States" that their relation to it was "that of a ward to his guardian" (17).[5]

Marshall's opinion inaugurated a legal tradition of emphasizing the anomalous character of U.S.-Indian relations. Time and again following *Cherokee Nation*, federal courts would return to this refrain, noting how strange and unprecedented these relations were and how little legal guidance was available. In Marshall's case, that sense of anomie led to an opinion that alternately affirmed and denied the Cherokees' national sovereignty, constructing the oxymoronic category of "domestic dependent nation" that, when applied to almost any set of circumstances, could lead to radically different legal results. The concurring opinion of Justice William Johnson in *Cherokee Nation* recognized the ambiguity and sought to dispel it by denying the status of statehood to the Cherokee tribe: "I cannot but think that there are strong reasons for doubting the applicability of the epithet 'State,' to a people so low in the grade of organized society as our Indian tribes most generally are" (21). But even Johnson was forced to qualify his view to account for the integrity of Indian national identities: "I believe, in one view and in one only, if at all, they are or may be deemed a State, though not a sovereign state, at least while they occupy a country within our limits. Their condition is something like that of the Israelites when inhabiting the deserts. Though without land that they can call theirs in the sense of property, their right of personal self-government has never been taken from them, and such a form of government may exist though the land occupied be in fact that of another" (25).

By comparing Indian tribes to the ancient Israelites (oddly casting the United States in the role of the Philistines), Johnson recognized their claim to nationhood, even while he invoked their alleged primitiveness to deny their entitlement to such a status. For both Johnson and Marshall, a full recognition of Indian national identity posed a threat to the authority of the federal government, yet each was forced to acknowledge the justice of Indian claims to nationhood — claims that were recognized in part because Indians themselves continued to assert them in innumerable ways. As Johnson noted in discussing the savage state of Indian society, the attempt "to incorporate [Indians] into our respective governments" was "a policy which their inveterate habits and deep seated enmity has [*sic*] altogether baffled" (24). Those "inveterate habits" were precisely what "baffled" the Court itself and required it to formulate a relation between the tribes and the federal government that was even more indistinct than that existing between the federal government and the states.

But Johnson's insistence on applying some conception of nationhood to Indian tribes might also have sprung from the law's implicit claim to represent definitively the subjects of its judgments. As the law's spokesman, Johnson needed to define the otherness of Indian identity. Yet he could do so only by presenting Indians as distorted versions of Americans — distortions that reflected "the menace of mimicry." Indians were "almost, but not quite" members of the same family as white Americans, and it was this partial presence that made it difficult to dismiss Indian claims to nationhood altogether, for the national unity Johnson sought to affirm depended to some extent on the creation of an Other that defied incorporation into it. And by its very resistance to incorporation, that Other was endowed with a freedom and communal integrity that came to resemble sovereignty and nationhood.[6]

Johnson's opinion is telling not only for its failure to clarify the terms of Indian nationhood, but also for the kinship metaphor it employs to describe the relationship between sovereign nations. Questioning whether the Cherokees had advanced enough for "admission into the family of nations," Johnson asserted that the United States must guard against a too hasty form of adoption: "Others have a right to be consulted on the admission of new States to the national family" (*Cherokee* 21, 27). For Johnson, national status confers certain rights and imposes certain obligations on those who possess it — rights and obligations that spring from a sense of commonality — and care must therefore be exercised in the construction of this extended "family." The danger he seems to have perceived is that legitimate members would suffer if illegitimate ones were admitted: "Where is the rule to stop? Must every petty kraal of Indians, designating themselves a tribe or nation, and having a few hundred acres of land to hunt on exclusively, be recognized as a State? We should indeed force into the family of nations a very numerous and very heterogeneous progeny" (25). "Family" in Justice Johnson's usage is a category of homogeneity; whether his terms refer to race or not is left unclear, but at the least homogeneity requires a similar rank on the scale from "savagery" to "civilization." The metaphor would seem to exclude the relationship between guardian and ward — although such a relationship might involve blood ties, it might just as easily not. Johnson, therefore, imagines Indians as wards, but not as family members; they are subject to the power of their guardian, yet the guardian's actions are regulated by no feeling of affection derived from a sense of shared heritage. Moreover, granting wards the status of family members threatens the common bonds that unite those family members in the first place.

In granting Indian tribes the status of "nations" but not of "foreign nations," does Marshall admit or exclude them from Johnson's "family of nations"? The question is important (if unanswerable) because embedded within the concepts of guardianship and kinship are assumptions about right and wrong conduct — norms of behavior that govern individual and collective action even more strongly than legal duties and prohibitions. Michael Grossberg notes that the republican version of family that rose to prominence in the early national era was one in which members were expected to respect one another's autonomy, and to encourage its exercise. The patriarchal model of the family in which the father's authority was absolute and unquestionable was no longer the recognized norm. As one state court put it in 1838, "children do not become the property of the parents. As soon as a child is born, he becomes a member of the human family, and is invested with all the rights of humanity" (*The Etna*, 1 Ware 474 [Me.], quoted in Grossberg 264). Thus, the Court in the Cherokee Cases was doing more than defining legal relationships when it employed domestic terminology; it was proposing narratives that would either legitimate Indian claims to sovereignty and self-determination or authorize a relationship between the government and Indian tribes grounded in the unrestrained exercise of power. Those narratives provided alternative yardsticks by which to measure the differences between Indians and white Americans. Ironically, the more Indians were seen to resemble whites (i.e., the more they could be imagined as family members), the more they were entitled to exert the privileges of national sovereignty. As unrelated wards, on the other hand, their differences from whites would render them unfit for anything but obedience.

Although the Cherokee Cases leave both options open, by the 1870s it was the guardianship rather than the kinship narrative that had gained ascendance in the minds of judges, government officials, and the majority of white Americans. Previous recognitions of tribal sovereignty and treaty rights increasingly began to look like dead letters. In 1871, Congress transformed U.S.-Indian relations by forbidding the government to enter into any further treaties with the tribes. The act that accomplished this metamorphosis specified that "hereafter no Indian nation or tribe within the territory of the United States shall be acknowledged or recognized as an independent nation, tribe or power with whom the United States may contract by treaty."[7] For Justice Marshall, the fact that Indian tribes were considered capable of making treaties had justified their claim to nationhood; the new policy, therefore, constituted an attempt to revoke that status by denying Indians the right to contract as sovereign communal entities. The 1870s and 1880s also saw a judicial emphasis on Congress's "plenary power" to regulate all aspects of Indian life in its own role as "guardian"; courts increasingly refused to intervene in any governmental attempt to impose its own assimilationist policies on Indian tribes, even when those policies explicitly violated treaties already in force.[8] This was a period of transition in white attitudes towards Indian national identity; the nebulous balance that Marshall had sought to strike — between legitimating government power over Indian relations and recognizing tribal claims to sovereignty — strained beneath the weight of its own inconsistency as well as from the pressure exerted by a white population growing more and more impatient with Indian attempts to frustrate its own expansionist impulses. The label of "domestic dependent nations" began to mean primarily "domestic" and "dependent," as the "inveterate habits" of Indian tribalism came to signify not a claim to statehood, but an incapacity for the assertion of true national sovereignty.[9]

What is surprising about this second phase of U.S.-Indian relations, however, is the extent to which both the law and American culture continued to acknowledge Indian nationhood in spite of this changed environment. Having been officially certified and woven into the fabric of the public consciousness, the concept of tribal sovereignty could not be easily erased. As a result, it continued to lurk beneath the surface of texts otherwise intended to establish the complete dependence of Indian tribes on the federal government and the consequent power of the government to regulate their affairs. For instance, in *Elk v. Wilkins* (1884), the Supreme Court ruled that an Indian who had separated himself from his tribe and taken up residence in a white community did not thereby become a United States citizen. In order to justify its exclusion of Indians from citizenship, the Court had to recur to the now repressed narrative of Indian national identity, asserting that Indian tribes were "alien nations, distinct political communities" and that the "members of those tribes owed immediate allegiance to their several tribes" (*Elk* 99). Just as Congress had the power to determine the qualifications for naturalizing foreign nationals, the Court reasoned, it must also have that power with respect to American Indians. Thus, upholding the power of the federal government to regulate Indian affairs in this instance meant acknowledging the validity of Indian national identity.

In the controversial case of *Ex Parte Crow Dog* (1883) the Supreme Court held that a Sioux Indian accused of murdering another Sioux in Indian territory was subject only to the tribal justice system and not to prosecution by the federal government. The United States, citing its treaty obligations, had argued that it had a duty to secure an orderly government for the Sioux, which included an American code of laws and system of justice. But in an opinion written by Justice Stanley Matthews, the Court ruled that "among the arts of civilized life, which it was the very purpose of all these arrangements to introduce and naturalize among [the Sioux], was the highest and best of all, that of self-government; the regulation by themselves of their own domestic affairs" (*Crow Dog* 568). The Court's reasoning constitutes an amalgamation of the discourse of "civilization" and "savagery" that was used to justify unrestrained federal power over Indian tribes, and the discourse of tribal integrity and national identity that remained a part of the law's "official Indian":

[This] is a case where [the law] is sought to be extended over aliens and strangers; over the members of a community separated by race, by tradition, by the instincts of a free though savage life, from the authority and power which seeks to impose upon them the restraints of an external and unknown code, and to subject them to the responsibilities of civil conduct, according to rules and penalties of which they could have no previous warning; which judges them by a standard made by others and not for them; which takes no account of the conditions which should except them from its exactions, and makes no allowance for their inability to understand it. It tries them, not by their peers, nor by the customs of their people, nor the law of their land, but by superiors of a different race, according to the law of a social state of which they have an imperfect conception, and which is opposed to the traditions of their history, to the habits of their lives, to the strongest prejudices of their savage nature; one which measures the red man's revenge by the maxims of the white man's morality. (*Crow Dog* 571)

Matthews's language clearly reflects the hierarchical distinctions between whites and Indians that were being used to justify the governmental policy of forced assimilation. But in simultaneously invoking such things as "the customs of their people," "the law of their land," and "the traditions of their history," Matthews also presents Indians as members of political communities with claims to national status and thus, national sovereignty. The language of racial and cultural difference in the decision results in both paternalism and, surprisingly, a measure of respect.[10]

The decision in *Crow Dog* outraged many whites, including those who considered themselves "friends of the Indian," and led Congress to pass the Major Crimes Act, which allowed the federal government to exert jurisdiction over certain enumerated crimes (such as murder) that took place in Indian territory. That act was upheld in *U.S. v. Kagama* (1885), and the Court — almost as an act of contrition — felt obliged in its decision to reaffirm the guardian/ward language that *Crow Dog*'s limited respect for Indian traditions had called into question: "These Indian tribes *are* wards of the nation. They are communities *dependent* on the United States" (*U.S. v. Kagama* 384, emphasis in original). But the Court's emphases only underscore the extent to which the problem of Indian nationhood remained — an indelible legacy of the Cherokee Cases, the symbolic meanings attached to "Indianness," and the "inveterate" adherence to tribal customs and identities shown by Indians themselves. The more the government asserted its right to engage in a policy of forced assimilation, the more that policy revealed its own weakness. The United States failed to eradicate Indian national identity within the tribes themselves, and it likewise failed to destroy the recognition of that identity within American law and culture. To be sure, Americans wanted Indian lands and resources. But they also wanted what the Indian had come to represent; in creating "dependent nations," they had also created lesser versions of their own nation, and they thus inadvertently linked their own national self-conception to the existence of the very Indian identities they professed to disdain.

Rights and Indian Reform: Jackson's Nonfiction

For examples of the hold that conceptions of Indian sovereignty had on the popular mind, one need look no further than Jackson's *A Century of Dishonor* and her report on California's Mission Indians. Jackson wrote the former to protest what she considered to be abuses of trust committed by the federal government in its treatment of Indian tribes. In so doing, she adhered to a melodramatic logic that led her consistently to portray Indians as innocent, good-hearted, and pure, and the U.S. government as inherently corrupt and wicked. For instance, her description of the government's relations with the Sioux — one of the more aggressive tribes both in its resistance to the United States and in its relations with surrounding tribes — begins by citing the Sioux's "simple hospitality, their unstinted invitations, and their guileless expressions of desire for a greater knowledge of the white man's ways" (Jackson, *Century* 136–37). Attempting to call attention to Indian victimization, Jackson feminizes the tribes in a way that makes use of the melodramatic gestures inherent in the novel of seduction. This perspective on U.S.-Indian relations, of course, was perfectly in keeping with the views of most white reformers at the time — views grounded in the need to exhibit Christian charity toward an essentially helpless race rather than in a respect for Indian culture or identity.

Yet Jackson's *Century of Dishonor* also undermines its own paternalistic depiction of Indians. Most of the individual chapters concentrate on the breaking of treaties by the United States — an emphasis that underscores contractual relations between the two groups rather than the duty of a powerful superior to care for a helpless inferior. This perspective dominates Jackson's introduction, which struggles to articulate a legal critique of U.S.-Indian relations without explicitly endorsing tribal claims to nationhood. But the only way Jackson can chastise the government for failing to adhere to its treaties is by invoking the "law of nations" — the doctrine that nations exist in a state of nature with respect to one another and are thereby bound by the moral precepts that govern natural law. Jackson cites such natural law theorists as Grotius, Vattel, and Hobbes in support of her argument that a moral obligation attaches to the terms of treaties, and that "the United States Government's repeated violations of faith with the Indians . . . convicts us, as a nation, . . . of having outraged the principles of justice, which are the basis of international law" (29). Although Jackson also states that Indians have accepted their position as "wards" of the government and have thereby lost "their right to be treated with as nations," the crux of her legal argument nonetheless assumes their status as national entities; the government is obliged to honor its treaties with them because the Indian tribes have been authorized by international law to enter into those treaties (27). Attempting to affirm the guardian/ward model of U.S.-Indian relations and to take the government to task for its uncaring form of guardianship, Jackson ends up going further; she admits Indian tribes into the "family of nations." Jackson's (and the law's) confusion over the proper model is really an uncertainty over the nature of Indian agency. On an individual level, Indians were widely seen as unable to govern their own affairs, leading to government limits on their ability to sell land and purchase alcohol, among other restrictions. On a group level, they were increasingly viewed as lacking the sovereign status needed to enter into treaties. But classical formulations of the law of nations (and of nature) start from the premise that the act of contracting is an expression of moral agency, and that there is a moral imperative to respect such expressions of agency. By critiquing the government for failing to adhere to its treaties, Jackson was affirming the free will, and hence the sovereignty, of the tribes who negotiated those treaties.

Jackson's desire to exert an influence on Indian relations that would be legally effective led her to lobby for a position as a special agent of Indian affairs — an appointment she received in 1882. The Commissioner of Indian Affairs, Hiram Price, directed her to investigate and report on the condition of California's Mission Indians, and the report that she and her fellow agent, Abbot Kinney, filed with the commissioner was dominated by a sense of the responsibilities of guardianship — it stressed the abject condition of the Mission Indians and advocated steps that would allow them to assimilate more quickly into white American society. Arguing that "our Government received by the treaty of Guadalupe Hidalgo a legacy of a singularly helpless race in a singularly anomalous position," the report emphasized the need to secure them in their property rights by creating new reservations and firmly establishing the bounds of existing ones (Jackson, *Report* 463). But the reservation system was seen both by the government and by Jackson herself as a mere way station on the road to full Indian assimilation — a place in which to wean Indians from their tribal allegiances. Thus, Jackson and Kinney recommended reservations only until the land could be allotted to Indians on an individual basis, when they should prove themselves ready for it.

The notion of allotting "in severalty" lands that had been granted to tribes on a communal basis would gain strength shortly after Jackson's death, when Congress passed the Dawes Act in 1887. The theory behind allotment was that, as Indians assumed the burdens and reaped the benefits of individual landownership, they would come to recognize the superiority of an American political and economic system grounded in private property, thus discarding their tribal identities. Jackson wholeheartedly supported this approach, as did most reformers interested in Indian affairs at the time. The report she and Kinney filed reveals the extent to which a political "outsider" such as Jackson could step seamlessly into the role of government bureaucrat. Although she had ruthlessly criticized the federal government's treatment of Indian tribes in *Century of Dishonor*, the assumptions behind her critique had not differed greatly from the government's view of its own responsibilities. In both cases, the guardian/ward model of relations predominated, with a more subversive sense of Indian sovereignty leaking into the rhetoric subtly and almost imperceptibly.

In fact, Jackson's appointment as a special agent was in keeping with the new strategy of Indian relations being pursued by the government across the country. The position of Indian agent had traditionally been one of political patronage, and agents were largely uninformed about Indian issues, uninterested in them, and notoriously corrupt. But part of President Grant's "peace policy" had involved allowing religious groups to recommend Indian agents, and such groups assumed the de facto power of making appointments (usually appointing members of their own sects). The policy began with the Quakers, but soon other religious denominations became involved in the selection of Indian agents. The new agents were representatives of both the government and of the religious faiths — their roles were simultaneously of a regulatory and missionary nature. But the dual capacities in which they served presented no real conflict of interest, since both the government and the organized faiths maintained the same hierarchical conception of Indians' relations to white America. Christianity, like property ownership, was simply another tool in the arsenal of weapons being deployed to destroy the existence of tribal identities. Jackson was not a reservation agent, nor was she strongly affiliated with a particular religious group. Nonetheless, her appointment reveals the strong links between the ideology of Indian reform and the government's attempts to resolve the "Indian problem" once and for all.[11]

The report filed by Jackson and Kinney, however, placed the law, not Christian faith, at the center of its reformist proposals. The authors stressed the extent to which the Mission Indians had been deprived of the protection of the law by being ejected from land to which they had a legal claim. To support this argument, Jackson and Kinney hired a Los Angeles law firm to prepare an opinion as to the legality of the federal government's practice of making land grants of property being occupied by Indians, and they attached the opinion as an appendix to their report. The opinion argues that, under the terms of most land grants made by the Mexican government, Indians were entitled to remain on the land they already occupied. When the United States took control of California under the Treaty of Guadalupe Hidalgo, it was legally required to respect the property rights of all the present inhabitants of California, including the Indians' possessory rights. Thus, the opinion concludes, Indians have a legal basis on which to challenge their own forced removal. Jackson and Kinney relied heavily on this opinion in making their case for the federal government's duty to protect Mission Indians currently threatened with ejectment, and to create new reservations for those already displaced.

But the discourse of rights they employ conflicts with the paternalistic assumptions behind the guardianship model on which they otherwise rely, supplying another instance of the doubleness that pervaded the Indian reform movement. The possession of rights implies the existence of a free will that cannot lawfully be intruded upon — a zone in which the exercise of agency is immune from interference by the state. The Indian rights raised by the report are communal rights rather than individual ones — they attach to groups of Indians possessing land in common. Thus, what Jackson and Kinney were ultimately defending were rights of self-determination that were akin to those possessed by sovereign nations. The "protection of law" to which Indians are entitled comes to mean two very different things within their report. On one hand, the authors suggest that the law can serve as a means of showing mercy and goodwill toward an essentially helpless and childlike race, thereby encouraging their development along civilized lines. On the other, however, the law endows Indians with rights that presuppose choice and agency, and it is thus conceivable that Indians might choose to exercise their freedom by *refusing* to become "civilized," holding on to their sense of national identity by asserting a sovereign right *not* to assimilate.

This was the tension at the heart of the "law for the Indian" movement in the late nineteenth century, of which the Jackson/Kinney report supplies a good example. Many well-intentioned white reformers viewed Indian reluctance to assimilate as a direct result of the government's unwillingness to grant them standing before the law — most Indians were barred from bringing legal actions in both state and federal courts. Asserting that "law is the solution for the Indian problem," one commentator writing in the *North American Review* argued that "the difficulties in the control of the Indian tribes . . . can never be removed until the protection of our law is accorded to the red men" and that "law has always availed to settle and civilize society" (Harsha 272, 274, 278). The law, from this perspective, comprises an element of "civilization" that, when extended to a more "savage" group, inevitably uplifts it. Yet what this position failed to acknowledge was the extent to which the very notion of the rule of law in the United States was grounded in the law's limits — in its inability to regulate a certain ill-defined but nonetheless critical zone of free will and self-determination. By advocating an extension of the law's reach to cover Indians, therefore, Jackson and Kinney were not only invoking the law's power to encourage the adoption of American cultural values; they were also proposing a recognition of Indians as rights-holders — a status that implied the freedom and capacity to choose an entirely different set of cultural norms, and even an entirely different national identity.

Thus, the Jackson/Kinney report on the Mission Indians reflected the same unresolved tension that had first appeared in the Cherokee Cases fifty years earlier. Although the federal government and reform-minded whites alike had ostensibly concluded that Indian tribes were more "domestic" and "dependent" than they were "nations," the sense of an indelible core of "Indianness" that stemmed from the maintenance of tribal affiliations continued to undermine perspectives based on a benevolent guardianship. Moreover, the unacknowledged recognition of Indian tribes as national entities inflected U.S.-Indian relations with familial undertones, as it seemed to accept Indians as more intimate members of a "family of nations" than did the guardian/ward model. But a "family" that included such a "heterogeneous progeny" was perhaps not a "family" at all; at stake in the United States' relations with Indian tribes was its conception of its own national identity and the extent to which its existence as a unified and sovereign entity could be squared with the principles implicit in the rule of law. *Ramona* ultimately confronts this tension in a way that exposes the latent conflicts at the heart of American Indian policy.

Celebrating "Indianness": Ramona

If the familial relations in Jackson's novel mirror the terms present in legal conceptions of U.S.-Indian relations, they do so in a way that incorporates the law's fractured response to Indian nationhood. Jackson wrote her romance to popularize the perspective set forth in her report on the Mission Indians and to promote a reform agenda that was, at bottom, identical to that being advanced by the federal government. Thus, her uncertainty about the representation of Indian identity should not surprise us. But in seeking to appeal to the "heart and conscience of the American people," *Ramona* reinvigorates the repressed narrative of Indian national sovereignty, presenting its Indian characters as noble and sympathetic precisely *because* they have resisted full membership in American and Mexican society (*Century* 30). Although Jackson's romanticization of Ramona and Alessandro is in keeping with a "noble savage" tradition of Indian representation, she uses this myth to highlight the free will of her characters and to insist that their exercise of agency be respected. Jackson seems to have recognized that an appeal to the need for Indians to assimilate would not ultimately reach the hearts and consciences of her readers; just as Stowe had appealed to a spiritual plane to garner support for her abolitionist message, Jackson attempts to find the transcendent basis in which to ground her own attempt at literary reformism. What she uncovers within the pages of her work, however, is the power of a legal narrative that white America could not quite discard, for rejecting the notion of tribal sovereignty would cast doubt on the existence of the very zone of free will that lay beneath the United States' own sense of national identity.

The family relations Jackson depicts in *Ramona* might be assigned to three distinct categories: the guardian/ward relationship between the Señora Moreno and Ramona, the sibling relationship between Ramona and Felipe (as well as the "brotherhood" of Felipe and Alessandro), and the spousal relationship of Ramona and Alessandro. Jackson clearly criticizes the Señora's form of guardianship, but she does not necessarily criticize the guardian/ward model itself. Rather, she takes issue with the exercise of guardianship powers untempered by familial affection. The problem with the Señora's treatment of Ramona is not that the Señora acts as a figure of authority and guidance, but that she does so in way that disregards Ramona's preferences and choices. Since the inherently hierarchical nature of family relations can lead to the exercise of unbounded power and authoritarian control, the true family for Jackson is one in which affection mediates parental power by creating a respect for family members as independent agents. This republican conception of the family transforms the absolutism of paternalistic authority into something approaching what Brook Thomas calls "the promise of contract"— a horizontal rather than vertical ordering of power that requires a recognition of the need for individual self-determination.[12] The Señora's failings as a guardian stem from her inability (or unwillingness) to feel the kind of familial connection to Ramona that would unleash a respect for her ward's autonomy.

The entire story is set in motion by a set of promises both broken and kept. The original Ramona (the Señora's elder sister) had broken a promise to marry Angus Phail, the father of the younger Ramona, and Jackson strongly suggests that it is partially regret over that broken promise (in addition to her own childlessness) that causes the Señora's sister to take in Phail's half-Indian daughter and raise her as her own. Before the elder Ramona dies, she exacts a promise from the Señora to care for the adopted child — a contractual obligation that the Señora takes quite seriously: "She had promised to be a mother to her; and with all of the inalienable staunchness of her nature she fulfilled the letter of her promise" (*Ramona* 24). But while the Señora professes a respect for the act of promising, she refuses to recognize the validity of Ramona's promise of marriage to Alessandro. Ramona, however, shows her own respect for contractual relations by telling the Señora that she cannot break faith with Alessandro: "I have promised, and I shall keep my word" (129). The difference between the two women's respect for Ramona's promise of marriage mirrors the difference between Mexican and American attitudes toward promises made to the Mission Indians. Alessandro asks if the "promises" made by Mexican landowners to the Indians regarding land rights must not be acknowledged by Americans, but Father Salvierderra replies that "They possess the country, and can make what laws they please" (67). The Señora's defects are precisely those of the American legal system; both profess a respect for contractual relations, but neither is willing to recognize the validity of contracts that imply Indian agency and self-determination. For the Señora as well as for the American government, guardianship does not involve an acceptance of Indians as members of a republican family — members who would possess inherent rights to autonomy and independence and whose contracts would be presumptively valid.

Unlike the relationship between the Señora and Ramona, that existing between Felipe and Ramona is grounded in mutual respect. Although Felipe loves Ramona himself, he also realizes the need to validate Ramona's decision to marry Alessandro, and he argues with his domineering mother over the acceptability of the engagement. Felipe fills the role of brother in a way that disavows the vertical power relations of the guardian/ward model, supplanting them with a more horizontal sense of equality and hence an implicit respect for Ramona's self-sovereignty. Of course, Felipe is also a relatively weak character, incapable of resisting his mother's imperious rule. He may be the titular head of the family, but it is clear that he abjures the power that goes with such a status. Along with that disavowal, however, comes a willingness to place himself on the same plane as Ramona — he fully accepts her membership in the family, and that acceptance leads to a recognition of her moral agency.

Yet Felipe's familial affection also slides toward romantic love, and it is in this slippage that Jackson exposes her own fears about admitting Indians into the "family of nations." Felipe's love for Ramona threatens to radically destabilize the hierarchical distance between "civilized" and "savage," thus undercutting the assimilationist position with respect to Indians altogether. Jackson wishes to acknowledge Indian claims to freedom and self-determination, but she also wants them to exercise that freedom in ways that involve rejecting tribal affiliations. The incestuous implications of Felipe's love represent a discomfort with relations that are perhaps too close.[13] Like most reformers of her era, Jackson did not believe that Indians should be accorded United States citizenship until they had already been "Americanized." To do so too early would be to valorize the tribal identities that Indians still held — to suggest that those identities were compatible with being American.[14] Rather than "Americanizing" Indians, the premature "marriage" involved in the granting of citizenship might mean "Indianizing" America, disrupting the terms of national identification and allegiance in the United States to the point of incoherence. Felipe cannot marry Ramona until she has been purged of her "Indianness." When he looks longingly into Ramona's eyes early in the narrative, he is met with "an abstracted sort of intensity which profoundly puzzled" him, keeping him from declaring himself and causing him to wonder, "What is it she thinks when she looks in my eyes so?" (40, 41). This unfathomable quality stems from Ramona's Indian heritage, and makes a true meeting of the minds between the adoptive brother and sister impossible. Under these conditions, the sibling bond between the two — and the coequal (but distant) relations that inhere in that bond — is the only appropriate familial connection Jackson can imagine.

But what keeps Felipe and Ramona apart is precisely what brings Ramona and Alessandro together. Jackson presents the relationship between the two lovers as a mystical connection that emanates from an indefinable source, but given the characters' ancestry the author invites us to posit their common Indian heritage as the origin of their attraction. Ramona is distant, mysterious, unknowable to Felipe, and that quality keeps him from declaring his love. Yet Alessandro's mysterious qualities are what draw Ramona to him; hearing him sing, Ramona thinks "this was from another world, this sound" (50). One reason she does not fully understand her own love is that she does not know of her own Indian ancestry. Jackson tells us that Ramona "would have found it hard to tell why she thus loved Alessandro; how it began or by what it grew," but she adds that "the sudden knowledge of the fact of her own Indian descent seemed to her like a revelation, pointing out the path in which destiny called her to walk" (162). Throughout the novel, consciousness is defined by national associations, and the common ancestry that makes possible an intersubjective understanding among Indians also sets up a wall between Indians and whites. If Alessandro walks right out of "another world," his marriage to Ramona either signifies a renunciation of that world or Ramona's acceptance of it. And since the two lovers flee deeper and deeper into territory occupied by Indians, ending up high in the hills near the Cahuillas — the most "wild" of the southern California Indians — Jackson strongly suggests that the terms of their marriage are defined by their "Indianness" rather than by any connection to Mexican or American nationality.

Jackson's strategy in *Ramona* is to highlight the differences between Indians and whites as a way of insisting upon Indians' self-sovereignty — their status as independent agents capable of exercising free will. By presenting her Indian characters in this light, she also seeks to present them as legal subjects, thus valorizing their entitlement to rights under the rule of law. But since law for Jackson is a means of inducing "Americanization," the differences she underscores also pose a threat because they are *national* rather than racial in nature. Race (i.e., "blood") does not separate whites from Indians in the novel; the mixed-race Ramona is herself the best evidence for Jackson's view that Indian genealogy does not degrade its possessors or render them unfit for association with whites. What separates the two groups is national affiliation; being Indian means maintaining an allegiance to a group that is ultimately incompatible with assuming an American identity. Jackson must argue both for and against Indian nationhood — she must present her Indians as simultaneously sovereign and dependent, domestic and foreign. Their "foreignness" ironically draws them into the legal fold, making them a part of the "family of nations" and validating their claims to agency and self-determination. But it also casts doubt on the very assimilationist ideology that Jackson wishes to promote.

The marriage of Ramona and Alessandro is an expression of the freedom and self-sovereignty Jackson would recognize in Indians. The two choose to affirm their engagement in spite of the Señora's adamant opposition, thus honoring their mutual "promises" and, in the process, asserting their own autonomy and independence. Of course, their marriage also results in their expulsion from the white community represented by the Señora's ranch, and thus their association with various bands of Mission Indians. The assertion of freedom and the assumption of Indian identity would seem to go hand in hand in the novel — a configuration that undercuts the notion that Indians, if allowed, would freely choose assimilation into American culture over continued tribal affiliations. But Jackson makes it clear that the two lovers choose to live as Indians only because they have been denied the option of living as whites. Both Alessandro and Ramona are depicted as figures on the cusp of Indianness and whiteness — Ramona because of her mixed ancestry and Alessandro because of his acculturation within Mexico's mission system — and they are consequently capable of moving in either direction. In fact, Alessandro initially imagines that his marriage to Ramona will result in his dissociation from the Temecula band of Luiseño Indians. Although Ramona recognizes he is "held to Temecula by bonds that would be hard to break," Alessandro believes that "for her sake he must leave his people" (122, 117). If not for the Señora's interference, in other words, Alessandro would have the requisite incentive to leave his Indian identity behind him and adopt the values and lifestyle of whites. Thus, Jackson presents the lovers' decision to live among Indian communities as, at least in part, a consequence of the Señora's absolutism and her ineffectual exercise of guardianship; they choose Indian affiliations only because they are denied the chance to choose white ones.

For Jackson, the Franciscan missionaries — embodied in the person of

Father Salvierderra — represent a more enlightened form of guardianship. By recognizing the integrity and sovereignty of Indian communities while at the same time promoting white cultural practices, they allow for Indians to freely adopt those practices and therefore gradually lose their "Indianness." Jackson, of course, romanticizes the Mission era, but she does so to highlight the failure of American policy. Mexico's missions embody the form of guardianship that acknowledges the ward's autonomy, while the Señora and the American squatters in the novel reflect the failures of a policy of forced assimilation. Given the Señora's demands, the only way Ramona and Alessandro can exert their self-sovereignty is by choosing to be Indian.

Jackson's argument attempts to account for what Justice Johnson had termed the "inveterate habits" of Indians — their intransigence in the face of all efforts to "Americanize" them. The problem, Jackson suggests, lies not in a deeply rooted Indian national identity, but in the defective manner in which the process of "Americanization" has been carried out. In this sense, *Ramona* falls firmly within the bounds of the reformist perspective prevalent at the time — a perspective that saw no conflict between, on the one hand, recognizing Indians as sovereign legal subjects and, on the other, promoting policies such as allotment that were calculated to encourage assimilation. But the very notion that assimilation cannot be forced — that it must, somehow, be chosen — requires an acceptance of the corollary that in some cases it may *not* be chosen. In other words, even a belief in the superiority of American "civilization" over Indian "savagery" must leave a space for the maintenance of savagery, lest the "choice" of civilization seem coerced. And it is *choice* rather than "civilization" or "Americanness" that Jackson's novel ultimately seeks to affirm. As a result, being Indian in the novel signifies much more than being savage or oppressed; it also serves as a representation of the power to control the terms of one's national affiliation.

Moreover, much of the law's agonistic approach to the issue of Indian nationhood can be read in a similar way. There were certainly self-serving reasons to consider Indian tribes as nations in the early period of the republic; all-out war with the tribes would have been difficult for the United States to sustain at the time, and entering into treaties with Indians as if they were indeed foreign nations was thus the most expedient approach to U.S.-Indian relations. But by the 1850s the tribes no longer posed a serious threat to American expansion. The treaty policy was eventually abrogated by the federal government, yet the concept of Indian national sovereignty could not be easily buried, as cases such as *Crow Dog* make clear. The reason for this persistence may lie in the symbolic value that Indians had come to assume in American culture and American law. The very "inveterate habits" that so vexed individuals like Justice Johnson also represented an affirmation of choice in the construction of nationality — a visible manifestation of the principle that nationhood was a matter not for coercion, but consent. And consent, of course, lay at the core of the United States' sense of its own national identity.

Indian Resistance and Popular Sovereignty

The figure of the unassimilable Indian has a long history of representation in both American letters and American law. As Robert F. Berkhofer Jr. notes, such representations in nineteenth-century literature frequently sought to strike a precarious balance between worship and condemnation; Indians proved useful in literary efforts to repudiate European "overcivilization," but authors also emphasized that "White life ought not to degenerate into savage ways" (91). Of course, portraying Indians as a noble but nonetheless doomed race allowed for a celebration of "Indianness" without endorsing Indian culture per se. But while romanticized versions of the Indian unquestionably sprang in part from what Renato Rosaldo has called "imperialist nostalgia," such an explanation does not quite account for the stubborn survival of the concept of Indian national sovereignty within a legal discourse otherwise geared toward asserting the federal government's "plenary power" to regulate Indian affairs (Rosaldo 87). The romanticization of Indians within American culture may also be attributed to the very forms of Indian nationhood that both the government and reformers sought to destroy. For in refusing to relinquish their tribal identities, Indians came to symbolize the contractual ideology that lay behind the United States' own conception of itself as a sovereign nation.

Sovereignty has always been a troublesome concept in the United States. Having given birth to itself in the act of repudiating the power of the British sovereign, the nation maintained a distrust of centralized authority that led it to divide power among the three branches of government, each of which exercises a legal function. Since no one of these branches can claim sovereignty, it is their object — the law itself — which does; as Thomas Paine put it, "In America, the law is king." Yet Paine's metaphor is also misleading; because the law is an abstraction, it lacks the requisite agency that the concept of sovereignty requires. The form of positivism that came to dominate late nineteenth-century legal thought insisted that law must emanate from a concrete and definable agent. The most influential legal theorist of the time was the Englishman John Austin, whose principle work, *The Province of Jurisprudence Determined*, rejected natural law principles by maintaining (following Hobbes) that law was simply the command of a sovereign. Austin's thought had a large impact in the United States, but it also begged the question of who exactly qualified as "the sovereign." The answer, of course, was "the people." Although no less abstract than "the law," at least "the people" — as an accumulation of living individuals—were theoretically capable of exercising agency. Thus, while "the people" were subject to the law in their individual capacities, in their corporate capacity they could be imagined as the authors of the law, and the law was thus an expression of their collective free will. This theory of sovereignty sought to reconcile the tension between the personal constraint implied in submission to the rule of law and the popular consent posited by social contract theory as the foundation of the state. The law constrains persons, but it expresses the freedom of "the people." [15]

Moreover, the idea of free will that underlies the sovereignty of "the people" requires that this aggregate entity exist before its will is exercised. That is, "the people" cannot be *created* in the act of consenting to state authority, for that would make the acts of consent individual rather than corporate in nature and would elevate the state over the collective group that endows it with authority. "The people" must exist *prior to* the state that they call into being — the nation must precede the nation-state. The very concept of nationhood as it developed and became institutionalized during the Enlightenment presupposes a state of nature (either a literal one before the advent of the state or a figurative one within the self) in which communal identity exists wholly outside of political society. This is Benedict Anderson's "imagined community" without his requirement of sovereignty, for the existence of "the people" does not depend on the notion of state sovereignty — instead, it legitimates that sovereignty. "The people" makes sense as a political entity only if it is first conceived of as a natural one.

And it is for this reason that versions of nationhood continued to exert a power over legal and cultural representations of Indian identity throughout the nineteenth century. Since it made national affiliation seem more like a choice than an obligation, Indian refusal to consent to the terms of Americanization could be read by Americans as a validation of their own national identity. Indians' stubborn adherence to their tribal identities may have been proof of their "savagery," but their *lack of consent* to full assimilation ironically legitimated the *consent* that Americans saw as the foundation of their own state; behind that lack of consent was the same sort of corporate agent — a "people" — that lay behind the nation-state of the United States. Furthermore, white Americans saw Indians as a "people" who seemed to exist in something like a state of nature, since most could not understand the forms of governance that operated within Indian tribes.[16] Consequently, Indian nationhood served an important symbolic function within white American culture; it operated to legitimate the agency of an American "people" and thus to bolster the United States' sense of itself as a nation governed not by coercion or individual power, but by freedom and the rule of law.

The semiotic value attached to "Indianness" in American culture helps to account for the law's ambivalence toward Indian nationhood — its insistence on the "domestic" and "dependent" nature of the tribes, but its unwillingness to deprive them completely of the status of "nations." Justice Marshall's famous formulation was, in part, a response to Indian resistance to Americanization — a resistance the Supreme Court felt obliged to both disparage and acknowledge. But it also reflected the Court's sense of its own authority, for Marshall's very position was dependent upon the existence of a "people" that had called him, as Chief Justice, into being. His recognition of some measure of Indian national sovereignty affirmed the sovereignty of the communal entity that made his words authoritative. Only by imagining Indians as withholding their consent to assimilation — in other words, as a nation (or nations) composed of non-Americans — could Marshall speak with the legitimacy that springs from communal consent to the rule of law.

And the same symbolic significance also accounts for the ambivalent representation of "Indianness" in a reformist work like *Ramona*. By emphasizing the law's disregard for Indian welfare, Jackson argues that Indians need to be drawn into the legal fold — a project that requires both governmental action to recognize their rights and, at the same time, the willingness of Indians to assimilate into mainstream American culture. Yet Jackson ends up celebrating Indian identity by romanticizing its retention — Ramona's insistence on marrying Alessandro reflects a noble commitment to love as well as to the act of promising, and is also a decision that affirms her possession of an Indian self. Telling Alessandro that "your people are my people," and uttering it "as if registering a vow," Ramona marries both an individual and a "people" (185). The identity she assumes is one that Jackson cannot help imagining in national terms; after her heroine challenges the Señora's authority to forbid her marriage, Jackson tells us that "Ramona had passed now into a country where the Señora did not rule" (128). The "country" Ramona enters is the one she shares with Alessandro — a nation she chooses to become a part of and that therefore embodies the possibility of choosing "the people" to which one will belong. Jackson may have wanted Indians to choose American cultural ideals rather than Indian ones, but her novel reveals that she needed Indians to serve a symbolic function as well — a function best served by glorifying their resistance to Americanization.

That glorification involves equating "Indianness" with such virtues as naturalness, simplicity, honesty, and innate virtue. Jackson's use of a noble savage mythology in depicting Ramona and Alessandro is expressly designed to argue for the assimilability of Indians — they already possess the moral virtues admired by Western culture — but Jackson cannot represent those virtues without connecting them to an "Indianness" that is self-contained, integral, and *un*assimilable. Thus, when the two lovers flee the Moreno ranch, they take refuge in a remote canyon that Jackson presents as an edenic retreat into both nature and the deep recesses of Indian selfhood. The place becomes, to Ramona, "so like a friendly home, that she dreaded to leave its shelter," and the author connects that home to a shedding of the "miserable pretences of superiority, makeshifts of adornment, and chains of custom" (208). This is where Ramona begins her tutelage in being Indian, and its isolation from the outside world indicates the extent to which Jackson's version of "Indianness" is *not* reconcilable with the demands of white civilization. That point becomes clearer as Ramona and Alessandro are forced to flee from one Indian village to another, and into areas that are more and more remote, before finally ending up high in the hills near a village of the Cahuilla tribe. The Cahuillas are "veritable mountaineers in nature, fierce and independent" (318), and the homestead that Ramona and Alessandro establish in the hills partakes of the same qualities. As Ramona gazes down from her mountaintop home, she feels "that infinite, unspeakable sense of nearness to Heaven, remoteness from earth that comes only on mountain heights," and thinks to herself, "This is freedom! This is joy!" (309). And Aunt Ri, the Tennessee woman who befriends Ramona, notes after the couple have gone to live on the mountain, " 'Pears like she'd gone klar out 'er this yer world inter anuther" (303). The mountaintop retreat mirrors the secluded valley of the couple's initial flight — both sites embody a romantic core of the self that resists the demands of "civilization" and that, for Jackson, can only be represented through a discourse that affirms the sovereign integrity of Indian identity.

Of course, the lovers cannot completely escape the influence and aggression of white civilization. But while Alessandro's death at the hands of an angry American settler may reflect the impracticality of Indian attempts to remove themselves from all contact with whites, it does not undermine Jackson's celebration of "Indianness." In fact, Alessandro's death brings Ramona into close contact with the Cahuillas — the most purely "Indian" of all the tribes Jackson represents — and they serve, at least briefly, as her new "people." Her residence with the Cahuillas also coincides with her period of madness — a condition that mirrors the madness suffered by Alessandro's father after his ejectment from Temecula and that endured by Alessandro himself during his final days on the mountaintop. Madness in the novel springs from dispossession, but it also serves to sever the intersubjectivity that might otherwise exist between whites and Indians; that is, it acts as a psychic marker of a self-contained Indian identity, even if that identity has been twisted under the pressure of white injustice. Just as Ramona had entered "a country where the Señora did not rule" when she dedicated herself to Alessandro, both she and Alessandro enter another subjective country as the result of an "Indianness" that can exist only in complete isolation — either physical or psychological — from whites.

Moreover, that isolation does not end for Ramona even after she is rescued by Felipe. Although she is drawn back from her madness and agrees to marry Felipe, she clearly does so with only a portion of her will. The core of her self had been invested in Alessandro and in their shared Indian identity, and the Ramona that emerges from the ordeal of widowhood is clearly not the Ramona that had served as Alessandro's wife. Felipe himself recognizes this; he concludes that "the mainsprings of Ramona's life were no longer of this earth" and that he cannot enter "the world where Ramona really lived" (356, 359). Felipe, of course, is considering Ramona's love for Alessandro, but Jackson has already linked the lovers' romance with the romance of Indian nationhood. And Ramona's self-division — her unwillingness or inability to expose her "Indian" self to Felipe — reveals the extent to which that self survives her trials. Although Jackson's representation of Alessandro seems to relegate Indian national identity to the category of a noble but doomed form of savagery,

Ramona's retention of that identity even while married to the Mexican aristocrat, Felipe, indicates the author's sense that tribal affiliations lay deeper than most assimilationists were willing to concede. Acknowledging the depth of those affiliations allows Jackson to construct Indians as the very embodiments of collective free will — a quality that allows for the existence of both a "people" and a system of law that expresses "the people's" sovereignty.

In fact, while Jackson critiques the law's impotence in the face of Alessandro's murder, the terms of her critique simply confirm the idealistic principles that she invests in the notion of the rule of law. The failure to convict (or even to try) the murderer, Farrar, stems not from the law's ideals, but from its application — an application based on a false definition of the popular will. Judge Wells, assigned to conduct the preliminary hearing into the case, recognizes the criminal nature of Farrar's act and is personally outraged by it. But he also recognizes the gap between the demands of justice and the popular sentiment of the region's white Americans with respect to Indians:

> That Farrar was a brutal ruffian, the whole country knew. This last outrage was only one of a long series; the judge would have been glad to have committed him for trial, and have seen him get his deserts. But San Jacinto Valley, wild, sparsely settled as it was, had yet as fixed standards and criterions of popularity as the most civilized of communities could show; and to betray sympathy with Indians was more than any man's political head was worth. The word "justice" had lost its meaning, if indeed it ever had any, so far as they were concerned. (321)

Jackson's characterization of the area as "wild" explains the difference between its "criterions of popularity" and those expressed by more "civilized" communities. The judge's views reflect a perspective divorced from the narrow self-interest of the white residents of San Jacinto Valley — in subsuming individual desire in favor of the collective interest in executing justice, the judge's outlook is truly national in scope. Those white residents who would deny Indians access to justice may look like "the people," but their single-minded attention to their own personal gain actually separates them from the body of the nation, making them "wild," cut off from the standards of civilization, and thus representative of a local will that does not speak for the nation as a whole. Moreover, since Indians serve as Jackson's symbolic incarnations of this national will, it is fitting that Ramona's temporary madness after Alessandro's death prevents her from testifying at the preliminary hearing. Her testimony would have done no good anyway — "there would never have been found a San Diego County jury that would convict a white man of murder for killing an Indian, if there were no witnesses to the occurrence except the Indian's wife"— and her incapacity thus functions as an analogue to the judge's scruples about "justice" (321). Just as Alessandro's madness had indicated an unassimilable Indianness under assault from a bigoted local populace, Ramona's incapacity reflects the gap between the law's execution and its true foundations, between a popular will that is narrow and merely regional and one that can help forge an expansive and truly national collective entity. She cannot testify because that testimony would not make sense to a jury who think of themselves only as San Jacinto Valley residents, rather than as Americans.[17]

Jackson's concern with the usurpation of the national interest by merely local concerns also helps explain her use of a Tennessee woman, Aunt Ri Hyar, as a vehicle for depicting white acceptance of Indian identity. Writing less than twenty years after the end of the Civil War and in a post-Reconstruction era dominated by talk of national reconciliation, Jackson brings a Southern family out West and demonstrates its matriarch's embrace of national unity in her willingness to embrace a respect for Indians. Moreover, the Hyars are presented as Indian-like themselves: they live in a "primitive fashion," obtain much of their food by hunting, and are forced to be continually "on the move" (287). Aunt Ri eventually loses her prejudice toward Indians and learns to identify with Ramona's and Alessandro's Indian existence, finally exclaiming "'Pears like I'm gittin' heaps er new ideas inter my head, these days. I'll turn Injun, mebbe, afore I git through!" (349). A Southerner turning "Injun" might sound threatening to many Northerners — Indian resistance to white authority could function as a potential model for the reemergence of the Confederacy — but Aunt Ri turns out to be a Unionist through and through. And it is precisely her association with Ramona and Alessandro that makes her aware of the federal government's duties to American Indians. She argues for a full extension of the law to Indians and chastises the government agent for failing to prosecute Alessandro's murderer, while at the same time taking issue with the agent's tendency to refer to Indians in possessory terms. Aunt Ri does not believe Indians "belong" to the United States — they possess a self-sovereignty that defines them in her mind as rights-holders under the rule of law — but of course her conflicted position about Indian rights to self-determination and the government's duty to "protect" them mirrors the fragmented sense of Indian "dependency" and Indian "nationhood" so prevalent in American law and culture. But for Jackson there is also a logic to Aunt Ri's position; just as Southern resistance to the Union's authority ultimately served to strengthen the sense of American nationhood (through the fiction that Southerners eventually "consented" to reunification), Indian resistance to Americanization could serve a similar function. Aunt Ri can admire the fierce independence evidenced by Ramona's and Alessandro's life on the mountaintop precisely because it reflects the very cornerstones of an American *national* culture. By isolating themselves in an ideal "Indianness" that resists the coercive influence of American settlers, Ramona and Alessandro exhibit the form of freedom that lay deep within the United States' conception of "We, the people."

Notwithstanding her admiration for southern California's indigenous population, however, Aunt Ri never does "turn Injun." White and Indian characters flirt with true hybridity in the novel, yet ultimately remain separate. Felipe's marriage to Ramona is not that of a white man to an Indian woman, for Ramona keeps her "Indian" self hidden from Felipe. Moreover, Ramona herself establishes boundaries between her white and Indian identities that suggest their utter incompatibility, even within the figure of the mestiza.[18] Her marriage at the end of the novel is not the kind of spousal connection that had allowed for an intersubjective merging of her consciousness with Alessandro's, but simply another version of her sibling relationship with Felipe. While the sibling model allows Jackson to highlight a form of respect for "Indianness" and a recognition of Indians' place within "the family of nations," it also implies an inevitable distance. In the final analysis, Jackson does not want Indians to assimilate because the only way Indians might truly become American is if Americans, at least in part, "turn Injun." Recognizing (and even promoting) the "inveterate habits" that seem to make "Indianness" a form of nationality, Jackson fears the implications of a new nationalism that might reconcile that "Indianness" with being American. The question of who constitutes "the people" of the United States would have to be reexamined to account for a group who would now consider themselves both members of tribes and members of the United States, and Americans themselves might lose the sense of a collective "We" that lay behind their most cherished institutions.[19] Jackson's representation of Indian identity, like the law's, teeters in the precarious space between two equally terrifying versions of nationhood: one that is so homogeneous that it looks coercive —

without the possibility of resistance and therefore without consent — and one whose heterogeneity doesn't look like nationhood at all. Poised in the balance, her novel tries to maintain an unstable doubleness that rejects both alternatives.

Jackson's romanticization of Indian identity was colonialist, to be sure; the author could perceive her Indian subjects only through the lens of a civilized/savage dichotomy that dismissed tribal cultures in the name of saving individual Indians. But the novel was also written "In the Name of the Law," and Jackson's dedication to the logic of legal discourse and argument makes her novel "postcolonialist" as well. That is, its dismissal of the colonized Other is tempered by a sense of loss — a desire to retain that which it is in the process of destroying — in part because the Other has become part of the Self. If Justice Marshall's sense of the law's authority — and his own authority as a jurist — was dependent on preserving a public recognition of Indian nationhood, then Jackson's sense of her own position as an author (and a quasi-public official) addressing a national issue might have required the same recognition. Both Jackson and Marshall invest "Indianness" with a symbolic value that is largely self-serving, but they are able to do so only as a result of *actual* Indian resistance to assimilation — a resistance neither could afford to ignore. Between the pages of their respective texts, therefore, lies an Indian presence that resists all attempts to harness it for their own purposes. In seeking to define the terms of Indian national sovereignty, and thus to contain it safely within the bounds of an ideology of America, Jackson and Marshall are each forced to concede the free will and continued vitality of a "people" they cannot fully incorporate into the national "We."

While those concessions may seem insignificant in light of the devastation wrought by well-meaning judges and Indian reform advocates alike in the nineteenth century, the twentieth century witnessed a return of the concept of Indian national sovereignty that belies the demise it ostensibly suffered in the 1870s and 1880s. While individual tribes are by no means accorded the status of fully independent nations by the United States government today, there is now an acknowledged body of legal precedent that endows Indian tribes with sovereign rights not possessed since the beginning of Andrew Jackson's presidency. In the 1920s and 1930s, federal officials finally conceded that the Dawes Act and other assimilationist policies had failed, and the Indian Reorganization Act of 1934 inaugurated a new era of (limited) respect for tribal self-determination.[20] In other words, the vitality behind Indian nationhood has survived the most vehement and sustained efforts to eradicate it, and its endurance indicates that the Indian "presence" in even the most assimilationist of texts has proven stronger than the colonialist erasure those texts otherwise sought to impose.

Jackson's legalistic novel turned out to have an impact on American conceptions of Indians, but not the one she had anticipated. Rather than becoming the new *Uncle Tom's Cabin* by awakening a moral outrage over the current state of law and national policy, it would operate more like a legal brief intent on asserting the law's authority and its claim to respect. But in locating the sources of that authority, Jackson exposed the division that lies at the heart of any conception of national unity or an integral American "people." Its approach, like that of the law's texts, reflected the image of the nation off an indigenous "people" whose very status as aliens made them fitting mirrors of America itself.

CHAPTER 3

Narrating Citizenship in *Pauline Hopkins's* Contending Forces

> *The colored man's inheritance and apportionment is still the sombre crux, the perplexing cul de sac of the nation. . . . Attorneys for the plaintiff and attorneys for the defendant, with bungling gaucherie have analyzed and dissected, theorized and synthesized with sublime ignorance or pathetic misapprehension of counsel from the black client. One important witness has not yet been heard from. The summing up of the evidence deposed, and the charge to the jury made — but no word from the Black Woman.*
>
> *It is because I believe the American people to be conscientiously committed to a fair trial and ungarbled evidence, and because I feel it essential to a perfect understanding and an equitable verdict that truth from each standpoint be presented at the bar, — that this little Voice has been added to the already full chorus.*
>
> Anna Julia Cooper, A Voice from the South *(1892)*

> *The Afro-American is not a bestial race. If this work can contribute in any way toward proving this, and at the same time arouse the conscience of the American people to a demand for justice to every citizen, and punishment by law for the lawless, I shall feel I have done my race a service.*
>
> Ida B. Wells, Southern Horrors: Lynch Law in All Its Phases *(1892)*

Responding to those who would dismiss the fiction written by African American women at the turn of the century for its adherence to the conventions of literary domesticity, Claudia Tate and Hazel Carby have argued that we need to learn to read the political codes hidden within such conventions. Tate, for instance, maintains that "Black women's post-Reconstruction domestic novels aspired to intervene in the racial and sexual schemes of the public world of the turn-of-the-century United States by plotting new stories about the personal lives of black women and men" (9). Carby makes a similar point when she asserts that "the novel was seen by black women authors as a form of cultural and political intervention in the struggle for black liberation from oppression" (61). Both critics cite Pauline Hopkins's *Contending Forces: A Romance Illustrative of Negro Life North and South* (1900) as a work that exemplifies this form of literary "intervention." But while Tate and Carby thoroughly detail the ways in which works such as *Contending Forces* used sentimental conventions rooted in an idealized domestic sphere to critique matters of political and legal concern, they stop short of identifying the narrative means by which such novels could do so without reinforcing their own marginality — their own removal from the institutional realms they seek to transform.[1]

While I agree that Hopkins's novel "aspires to intervene" in the public world, I believe it seeks to accomplish its goals not by invoking a form of "sentimental power" that originates in a private, feminized cultural space, but by disavowing the distinction between private and public on which the tenets of literary domesticity were based.[2] Like Jackson's *Ramona*, *Contending Forces* places its conventional emphasis on courtship and marriage within a markedly legal framework, and in so doing recasts stories of individual identity and family membership as stories of citizenship. But while Jackson employed family affiliations to construct her Indian characters as non-Americans — citizens of nations other than the United States — Hopkins associates her highly domesticated characters with principles that lie at the core of American political and cultural life. Written at the end of a decade that had seen a dramatic rise in the lynching of African Americans — incidents often justified as punishments for the crime of rape — the novel denies that there can be such a thing as "private" justice, and thus serves as an indictment of the parodic form of judgment to which the victims of lynching were subjected. Along with prominent anti-lynching crusader Ida B. Wells, Hopkins recognized that such racial violence was largely condoned (or at least not effectively prohibited) by the criminal justice system; that the willingness of local authorities to treat it as a "private" matter, and the virtual impossibility of convicting its perpetrators (in the rare instances when they were tried), gave lynching a public — if nonetheless tacit — stamp of approval. And this awareness underwrote Hopkins's literary project — a project that involved representing the private spaces of domestic life in ways that hinted at their unacknowledged public content.

Contending Forces is, in part, a narrative about narratives. By infusing its domestic literary conventions with political and legal undertones, it exposes the literary quality of public discourse and undermines the distinction between literature and politics. For Hopkins, the act of narrating — in whatever form it takes — has potential consequences in the public sphere, and her novel thus engages the pervasive yet concealed fictions that determined the legal status of African Americans at the turn of the century. The most destructive of such fictions — those that, in effect, "legalized" lynching — constructed the black self as an entity entirely unfit for the responsibilities of citizenship, a presence constituted solely by desire and thereby incapable of exercising the kind of restraint that a respect for law entails. Hegel's influential treatment of the connection between historical narratives and legal systems had declared that blacks had no real "history" because they had no legal tradition and lacked the ability to subordinate self-interest to the rule of law. Such a self is beyond legal cognition, existing within the law's systems of representation only as an other, an alien presence to be controlled but not validated by extending to it the procedural safeguards accorded to fully constituted citizens. Hopkins, however, applies Hegel's connection between narrative, history, and law in a way that undermines his conclusions — conclusions that were shared by much of white America. *Contending Forces* combines literary, legal, and historical modes of representation to combat the form of legal erasure to which African Americans were subject and that made practices such as lynching possible. Its genteel characters are thoroughly representable within the conventions of the sentimental novel, and it is through this very conventionality that they emerge as legal entities. Strictly adhering to the literary codes governing domestic heroes and heroines, Hopkins endows them with a public (because generically familiar) weight and substance that identify them as responsible citizens as well as morally upright individuals. Moreover, by relating an antebellum past to a postbellum present and by telling a story gleaned from "records" she uncovers in a North Carolina courthouse, Hopkins identifies her work as one of history as well as of fiction.[3] The two fields are ultimately tied together through the legal implications of narrative.

But if narrating, for Hopkins, is an act with potential legal consequences, the law's ideals can also serve to inform the structure of narrative. The most important of those ideals in *Contending Forces* is the constitutional principle of due process — a concept that, for Hopkins, serves as a touchstone of literary representation as well as of judicial procedure. Her novel emphasizes the fairness and inclusiveness of its own narration and thereby legitimates both its authorial voice and the judgments it renders on the embattled African American legal subject. As the epigraphs to this chapter indicate, such prominent black women reformers as Wells and Anna Julia Cooper located their own reformist efforts within a conception of public debate that was essentially adjudicatory in nature; they saw themselves presenting "evidence," offering "proof," and thereby constructing their own authorship as a form of testimony in a process that would ultimately issue in judgment on the viability of African American citizenship. More than just a trope, their forensic imagery authorized their own public voices; by likening the public debate over race to a trial and asserting the testimonial nature of their authorship, black women declared a central role for themselves within a civil polity that defined itself by a respect for the rule of law. Like Cooper and Wells, Hopkins sought to enlist legal discourse in her project of (as Carby puts it) "reconstructing womanhood," but her concern over gender was ultimately one with her concern over race.[4] Both blackness and womanhood constituted disabilities in the eyes of the law — categories that negated the substance and import of their possessors' public selves. Yet for Hopkins that form of erasure could be — in fact had to be — combated from inside rather than outside the law, through an appeal to the law's own ideals. The disintegration of the law's institutional bounds that made lynching an "acceptable" means of limiting African American citizenship also made possible Hopkins's literary entrance into the legal arena, enabling her to summon the very legal authority seemingly renounced by the criminal justice system. If the official narratives of race in the United States were in the process of running amok and thus rendering the rule of law inapplicable to African Americans, that ideal could be revivified only through narratives that showed respect for the Constitution, for the discipline of history, and for established literary form.

Hopkins's dedication to these principles reveals the extent to which her method is informed by a professional ideology. Adhering to the formal constraints governing the newly professionalized fields of literature, history, and law, she uses those constraints to point to a content that has been suppressed. In so doing, she strives to bridge the gap between an institutionalized "inside" and a substantive "outside." Acknowledging that African Americans were essentially written out of the law, the dedication of *Contending Forces* states that the book was authored "by one of a proscribed race." Hopkins's novel seeks to counter that proscription with a form of literary inscription, imagining citizenship as a legal status mediated by narrative and available only to those who are representable within the parameters of established institutional discourses.

Historicizing the African American Legal Subject

Much of Hopkins's turn-of-the-century writing — both fiction and nonfiction — contributed either directly or indirectly to what August Meier has termed the "Negro history movement" (Meier 250). Although its participants varied in the goals and ideologies they brought to their work, one of the most common justifications these writers articulated for excavating an African and African American past was to present an argument for black citizenship rights. George Washington Williams, for instance, asserted that his *History of the Negro Race in America* (1883) was written to hasten the day "when there shall be no North, no South, no Black, no White — but all American citizens, with equal duties and equal rights" (Williams iii). While Hopkins's only work of explicit history — the *Primer of Facts Pertaining to the Early Greatness of the African Race* (1905) — would focus on a prediasporic past, a large amount of the nonfiction she published as a contributing editor of *Colored American Magazine* centered upon biographies of prominent African Americans, past and present. In her series entitled "Famous Men of the Negro Race" and "Famous Women of the Negro Race," she depicted the lives of these individuals in a way that emphasized their impact upon the public sphere (*Colored*, Nov. 1900–Oct. 1902). As C. K. Doreski notes, her idealized portraits presented history as a "great force that is 'literally present' in our actions" and emphasized "the precarious nature of African American citizenship in their insistence upon participation in history through public roles" (82). This promotion of equal citizenship through history was one of the broad goals of *Colored American Magazine* itself; the magazine's stated purpose was to perpetuate "a history of the negro race" and "to develop and intensify the bonds of that racial brotherhood, which alone can enable a people, to assert their racial rights as men, and demand their privileges as citizens" (*Colored*, May 1900, 2, 60).

The concern with African American citizenship that motivated much of the Negro history movement ties it to the assumptions behind Hegel's influential model of history. In his introduction to *The Philosophy of History*, Hegel asserted that "the term History . . . comprehends not less what has happened, than the narration of what has happened," and that such narration is possible only within "a community that is acquiring a stable existence" by promulgating "formal commands and laws" (60, 61). Maintaining that the "outward existence of a political constitution which is enshrined in its rational laws and customs, is an imperfect Present; and cannot be thoroughly understood without a knowledge of the past," he articulated a mutually dependent relation between historical narration and formally codified legal systems. More recently, Hayden White has invoked Hegel in reasserting this dependency:

> Hegel insists that the proper subject of [history] is the state, but the state is to him an abstraction. The reality which lends itself to narrative representation is the *conflict* between desire, on the one side, and the law, on the other. Where there is no rule of law, there can be neither a subject nor the kind of event which lends itself to narrative representation. . . . [W]e cannot but be struck by the frequency with which narrativity, whether of the fictional or the factual sort, presupposes the existence of a legal system against or on behalf of which the typical agents of a narrative account militate. And this raises the suspicion that narrative in general, from the folktale to the novel, from the annals to the fully realized "history," has to do with the topics of law, legality, legitimacy, or, more generally, *authority*. (12–13, emphases in original)

White's extension of Hegel's theory to incorporate fictional as well as nonfictional narratives points toward the rationale that united the efforts of black novelists and historians at the turn of the century. Both groups sought to depict an African American subject whose legitimacy was a function of participation in the legal history of the nation, a subject that was not simply created by legislative fiat in the wake of the Civil War but was entwined with the exercise and maintenance of authority in the United States. Moreover, these writers attempted to formulate such a subject in a way that made the value and efficacy of the rule of law dependent upon recognition of the equal citizenship of African Americans.

Encompassing both traditional "history" and novels infused with a strong sense of the past, Hopkins's writing reflected the connection between history, narrative, and law drawn by Hegel. But Hegel's historiography also constituted a force against which much of Hopkins's work — and that of other black historians and novelists — struggled. Celebrating the nineteenth-century European nation-state, Hegel's philosophy affirmed a political and cultural model of nationhood to which most African "nations" did not conform and in which African Americans were denied full participation. Thus, he maintained that Africa "is no historical part of the World" and that "What we properly understand by Africa, is the Unhistorical, Undeveloped Spirit, still involved in the conditions of mere nature" (99). He applied his view of Africa to blacks throughout the world, justifying his placement of the entire race outside of history by placing it outside of the law:

> In Negro life the characteristic point is the fact that consciousness has not yet attained to the realization of any substantial objective existence — as for example, God, or Law — in which the interest of man's volition is involved and in which he realizes his own being. . . . The standpoint of humanity at this grade is mere sensuous volition with energy of will; since universal spiritual laws (for example, that of the morality of the Family) cannot be recognized here. Universality exists only as arbitrary subjective choice. The political bond can therefore not possess such a character as that free laws should unite the community. There is absolutely no bond, no restraint upon that arbitrary volition. (93, 96)

Viewing the black self as motivated by pure desire, Hegel suggested that such a self cannot be represented by historical narrative for there is no system of legal authority in which it participates. Hegel's sense of authority is tied to "universality," but that universality can be realized only through the rule of law, which for him means a system by which rules are formally promulgated according to an established and consistent procedure. His sense of law's authority is similar to what Max Weber would later call "legal-rational" authority — an institutional form of legitimacy defined by its emphasis on the articulation of rules and procedures freely chosen, yet strictly administered.[5] This also emerges as the logic of the new professionalism in the late nineteenth century, and the efforts of black historians to methodically reconstruct the African American presence in the nation's past must be seen, in part, as an effort to employ the very professional discipline that blacks were accused of lacking. In true professional fashion, therefore, black writers at the turn of the century took on the task of affirming Hegel's connection between history and the law, yet using that model to undermine his racist conclusions. Those conclusions, of course, were white America's as well. The notion of unrestrained black desire served to justify a range of discriminatory practices in the South following the collapse of Reconstruction, from Jim Crow legislation, to disfranchisement, to lynching, and the North's unwillingness to intervene in these practices underscores the extent to which the theory of blackness that made them possible was not merely regional, but national.

A profile of Hopkins that appeared in *Colored American Magazine* (undoubtedly written by Hopkins herself) stated that her "ambition is to become a writer of fiction, in which the wrongs of her race shall be handled as to enlist the sympathy of all classes of citizens, in this way reaching those who never read history or biography" (Jan. 1901, 219). Her novel serves purposes normally reserved to nonfiction by narrativizing the African American self, locating it temporally within American history and thus debunking its construction as an ahistorical entity of pure desire. Consequently, the preface to *Contending Forces* insists that we read the book as a work of history as well as of fiction: "Fiction . . . is a record of growth and development from generation to generation. *No one will do this for us; we must ourselves develop the men and women who will faithfully portray the inmost thoughts and feelings of the Negro with all the fire and romance which lie dormant in our history*, and, as yet, unrecognized by writers of the Anglo-Saxon race" (13–14, emphasis in original). The passage suggests no tension between portraying the "inmost thoughts and feelings" of African Americans and depicting them on the larger canvas of history; for Hopkins, the two projects are not at odds. Implying that history is present within the individual, she seeks to define an African American subject whose "inmost feelings" are consistent with the process of historical "development." Furthermore, her invocation of the "fire and romance" contained within that subject renders it intelligible within the conception of selfhood intrinsic to the historical romance (a genre that, by the turn of the century, had largely abandoned its Hawthornian complexity in favor of melodramatic depictions of noble heroes and heroines overcoming perils to both themselves and the nation).[6] The very limitations of the genre are what make it useful for Hopkins's purposes. Not only must the black self be seen as a historical entity, she implies, but also as a representable "character" within any narrative form that history might take. Her insistence that fiction is a kind of "record" reveals her professional goal: she wishes to assemble and present the documentary evidence that will bolster her argument for African American citizenship rights — an argument that is legal as much as it is literary.

The preface goes on explicitly to link her historical goals with her legal ones, suggesting that an awareness of the black presence in American history can have decidedly legal ramifications. Lynching, in Hopkins's eyes, is made possible by the perceived unrepresentability of African American subjects — since they don't "exist" as citizens, she implies, they are essentially invisible on the American scene. Yet she also points to history as one way to combat this state of affairs: "In these days of mob violence, when lynch-law is raising its head like a venomous monster, more particularly in the southern portion of the great American republic, the retrospective mind will dwell upon the history of the past, seeking there a solution of these monstrous outbreaks under a government founded upon the greatest and brightest of principles for the elevation of mankind" (14). The African American subject her novel seeks to construct can be represented in the forms of narrative accepted by both historians and readers of novels, and she expresses the hope that in her own narrativization — her own decision to "dwell upon the history of the past" — that subject will emerge as the "solution" to such practices as lynching. For Hopkins, history and law function as overlapping structures of signification through which individuals become inscribed as citizens. Simultaneously literary, historical, and legal, her novel ties these fields together through the concept of narration — a practice by which private selves are turned into public citizens and rendered visible members of a national community governed by the rule of law.

Lynch Law and Storytelling in Contending Forces

The convoluted plot of *Contending Forces* centers around the legacy of racial violence perpetrated both before and after the Civil War. The first act of violence is the murder in North Carolina of a white planter from Bermuda named Charles Montfort, who moves to the United States because he wishes to avoid the terms of manumission required by the British Emancipation Act. Montfort intends to free his slaves, but wishes to do so gradually and with less financial hardship to himself. Anson Pollock, a local aristocrat who hears of Montfort's plan and has designs upon his wife, Grace (rumored to be partly black), organizes members of his secret "committee on public safety" and kills Montfort. Grace is brutally whipped in a scene that, as Carby notes, is markedly sexual and conjures the specter of rape. The committee on public safety justifies Montfort's murder as necessary to put down an insurrection of his slaves, an excuse that operates to "legalize" the violence; Hopkins's narrator tells us that "In those old days, if accused of aiding slaves in a revolt, a white man stood no more chance than a Negro accused of the same crime. He forfeited life and property. This power of the law Anson Pollock had invoked" (70).

Grace commits suicide rather than serve as Pollock's concubine, and her two sons, Jesse and Charles, are separated; the former eventually escapes to the North and the latter is sold to an Englishman, who vows to "collect the proofs" concerning Charles's family and to set him free (73). The descendants of Jesse — Ma Smith (owner of a Boston boarding house) and her children, Dora and Will — constitute the novel's main characters, along with a mysterious but beautiful boarder named Sappho Clark and an unscrupulous African American attorney named John Langley.

The postbellum acts of violence parallel the antebellum murder described in the novel's opening chapters. At a meeting of the American Colored League convened in response to a recent lynching, a delegate named Luke Sawyer speaks to the meeting of his own experiences with racial violence. Sawyer details first that his family was killed because his father, who "didn't care to meddle with politics," owned a successful store that was taking business away from a white-owned establishment. The father was hung after firing upon a mob that was attempting to drive him out of town by burning his house. Sawyer's mother and sister were whipped "and otherwise abused" until they died (256, 257). Sawyer then relates the story of the Louisiana family with whom he went to live after escaping this ordeal. The head of the family, Monsieur Beaubean, was a prosperous African American whose white father had left him a portion of his estate equal to those of his white heirs. After his daughter, Mabelle, was abducted, raped (the story implies), and placed in a house of prostitution by his white half-brother, Beaubean located her and swore revenge on his brother in federal court. That night a mob burned him alive in his house. Sawyer states that Mabelle died in childbirth, but by the end of the novel we discover that this is not true and that she is in fact Sappho. The stories of the Montforts and the Beaubeans come together not only through the Smith boarding house, but also through the character of Langley, who turns out to be a descendant of Anson Pollock and who tries to force Sappho to become his mistress by threatening to reveal her secret past. The Smith/Montfort family and the Beaubean family are eventually united when Sappho marries Will Smith.

Sawyer's accounts of violence are drawn from two actual lynchings with which Hopkins would have been familiar. In 1892, three black men were lynched in Memphis after they had opened a successful grocery store called the People's Grocery that challenged a nearby white-owned establishment. When a group of men with guns burst into the People's Grocery, the owners fired upon them in self-defense, only to find out later that the intruders were sheriffs in plain clothes that had been hired by the white competitor. The black owners were jailed but a white mob eventually took them from their cells and shot them. This incident was especially significant because it launched Ida B. Wells's anti-lynching activities, and Wells describes it in detail in her first published pamphlet on lynching, *Southern Horrors: Lynch Law in All Its Phases* (1892). Describing the owners of the People's Grocery as men who "believed that the [race] problem was to be solved by eschewing politics and putting money in the purse," she implicitly criticized Booker T. Washington's program of racial "uplift," and Hopkins's choice to emphasize the Washingtonian beliefs of Sawyer's father echoes Wells's sentiments (*Southern* 35). But the two writers' accounts of the event also highlight the fact that lynching was often not about black "bestiality" at all but about politics and economics. Thus, Wells described the lynching as an assertion of power rather than as a punishment for crime:

> Excitement was at fever heat until the morning papers, two days later, announced that the wounded deputies were out of danger. This hindered rather than helped the plans of the whites. There was no law on the statute books which would execute an Afro-American for wounding a white man, but the "unwritten law" did. Three of these men . . . were secretly taken from jail and lynched in a shockingly brutal manner. "The Negroes are getting too independent," they say, "we must teach them a lesson." (*Southern* 35–36)

Hopkins's use of this incident incorporates Wells's view that an "unwritten law" exists in the South that maintains white privilege through a quasilegal process of mob action in which law enforcement, either directly or indirectly, participates.

But if any of her readers believe that federal law can counteract such mob action, Hopkins's description of the Beaubeans' ordeal is meant to refute that notion. Monsieur Beaubean's death resembles the highly publicized 1898 lynching of Frazier B. Baker — a black postmaster in Lake City, South Carolina — who also was burned alive in his home by a white mob, and Beaubean's vow before his death to "carry my case into the Federal courts and appeal for justice" implicates the prosecution of members of the mob that killed Baker. Eleven individuals were brought to trial in federal court, and none was convicted. The invocation of federal remedies also highlights the national government's failure to enact a federal anti-lynching statute, for which activists such as Wells tenaciously fought.

Since most victims of lynching were not federal employees, their murderers could be tried only in state court, and even in the infrequent instances when criminal charges were actually filed, the all-white juries that typically heard such cases invariably acquitted the defendants.

The fact that Sawyer tells his story in Boston at a meeting of the American Colored League convened to protest a recent lynching serves as Hopkins's reminder of the reaction to Baker's murder. As Mary Frances Berry notes, "although Baker's death had failed to arouse the government, it unified the national black community" (93). After attending a mass meeting in Chicago in the wake of the lynching, Wells met with President McKinley and argued for federal prosecution of Baker's killers and for passage of a federal anti-lynching law. In Boston, an African American organization calling itself the Colored National League organized meetings at Faneuil Hall and at the Charles Street Church, at which "the best speakers of the race . . . demanded that the government should use every means in its power to bring the criminals to justice" (*Colored*, May 1900, 10). The meeting of the American Colored League in *Contending Forces* is modeled on the gatherings that occurred in the wake of Baker's murder, but unlike the participants in those meetings, Hopkins writes her account with the knowledge that the trial of the lynchers had not resulted in a single conviction. Thus, Sawyer ends his accounts of violence perpetrated against African Americans not with a demand for legal prosecution, but with a call for revolution: "I ask you what you think the American Colonies would have done if they had suffered as we have suffered and are still suffering? . . . Under such conditions as I have described, contentment, amity — call it by what name you will — is impossible; justice alone remains to us" (262).

Although the meeting calls attention to the law's apparent impotence in the face of mob violence, Hopkins's narrative uses this deficiency to assert its own respect for and adherence to those legal ideals seemingly renounced by the criminal justice system. In fact, lynching constituted a practice that challenged the bounds of the law in a way that was both murderously destructive and potentially empowering for African American advocates of reform, and it was thus from the very prevalence of lynching that activists derived their own authority to address matters of crime and punishment. For if the formalistic and restrictive interpretations of the Civil War amendments articulated by the Supreme Court in the *Civil Rights Cases* and *Plessy v. Ferguson* seemed to define those amendments in ways that stripped them of their power to affect significantly the state of race relations in the United States, the more expansive conception of law that Southern racists were willing to employ in executing "justice" paradoxically opened the door for newly invigorated legal arguments on the racial front.

Wells's career illustrates this point. Her activism began when she was forcibly ejected from a white railroad car in Tennessee and brought suit against the railroad in state court. Although she was awarded damages, the decision was ultimately overturned by the state supreme court — a result that caused her to lose faith in the legal system. She recorded this feeling in a diary entry in which she wrote, "I have firmly believed all along that the law was on our side and would, when we appealed to it, give us justice. I feel shorn of that belief and utterly discouraged" (quoted in Bederman 55). Nonetheless, the lynching of the owners of the People's Grocery in Memphis was an incident that, as Wells later wrote, "changed the whole course of my life" (Wells, *Crusade* 47). Her public activism against lynching was infused with the sense that the legal system had been utterly corrupted, yet she spoke in a voice that used the power of the law's ideals to criticize its actual practices. In *Southern Horrors*, she invoked this tension by subverting the normal usage of the word "legal" with question marks, noting that "One by one the Southern States have legally (?) disfranchised the Afro-American" and that a Southern court had "legally (?) hung poor little thirteen year old Mildred Brown . . . on the circumstantial evidence that she poisoned a white infant" (29, 45–46). Her question marks signal a belief in the possibility of law's objectivity and inclusivity even as they decry its racial bias. The institution of the jury trial embodied everything that Wells viewed as both right and wrong with the law. Acknowledging that the white press performed an essentially forensic function in the South by presenting the "evidence" that justified lynchings, she encouraged the black press to present its own evidence on lynching, asserting that "Afro-American papers are the only ones which will print the truth, and they lack the means to employ agents and detectives to get at the facts. The race must rally a mighty host to the support of their journals, and thus enable them to do much in the way of investigation" (42–43). For Wells, the real venue of the criminal trial had shifted from the courtroom to the press room; much like Howells's "Police Report" and his representation of Bartley Hubbard's legalistic form of journalism, she exposed the merging of legal and popular narratives. But while Wells criticized the legal system's willingness to bow to public opinion and, in effect, to condone the use of extralegal violence against blacks, she employed the very breakdown of the law's authority to assert the institutional authenticity of her activism. *Southern Horrors* carefully detailed the circumstances surrounding several notorious lynchings and presented the results of Wells's own investigation, thereby rebutting "evidence" that had appeared in white periodicals and modeling the process that should have taken place institutionally.[7]

Wells's effort to rehabilitate the ideology of the jury trial was a response to the "philosophy" that underlay the practice of lynching. Lynching may, in fact, have been an instrument of political and economic terror, but its overt rationale stemmed largely from its practitioners' belief that the official operation of the criminal justice system subverted the law's ability to deter African American crime — particularly the crime of rape.[8] Sometimes this justification was grounded in a critique of the court system itself; W. Fitzhugh Brundage asserts that "the great mass of southerners during the late nineteenth century had lost faith in the courts," and Edward L. Ayers notes that "the frequent claims about the inefficiency and corruption of the courts in the South . . . stood as an integral part of the justification of lynching" (Brundage 87, Ayers 246). An essay published in the *American Law Review* in 1894 relied upon this justification, arguing that "The cause of lynching is not a spirit of lawlessness. As a rule the men who participate in it wish ardently to enforce justice. . . . Whenever society has lost confidence in the promptness and certainty of punishment by the courts, then whenever an offense sufficiently flagrant is committed society will protect itself by a lynching" (Walter Clark 51–52). Yet such claims about the criminal justice system were often disguised complaints about the application of the formal protections of due process to African Americans. As the English writer James Bryce asserted, "The swift apprehension and slaughter of the culprit not only strikes greater dread than the regular process of justice, but does not gratify the negro's enjoyment of the pomp and ceremony of a formal trial before a judge" (quoted in Ayers 247). His comment invokes the commonplace minstrel stereotype of the ignorant "darky" who delights in gaudy shows and is unworthy of the respect that due process confers upon defendants. In a 1907 speech before the U.S. Senate, South Carolina's Ben Tillman would apply a similar argument to black defendants accused of rape: "And shall such a creature [the black rapist] . . . appeal to the law? Shall men coldbloodedly stand up and demand for him the right to have a fair trial and be punished in the regular course of justice? So far as I am concerned he has put himself outside the pale of the law, human and divine" (quoted in Gunning 5).

The idea that blacks were not entitled to "the regular course of justice" led to the view that lynchers were themselves enforcing the law, that they were administering a system of justice that applied specifically to African American men. Discussing the history of vigilantism in the South, James W. Ely Jr. and David J. Bodenhamer note the symbiotic relationship between official and unofficial punishment, asserting that "southern legal institutions co-existed well with this resort to extra-legal action. Since vigilantes acted to protect community values, southerners could extend support to both the judicial system and the practice of extra-legal redress" (Ely and Bodenhamer 23). When race was involved, the line between the "legal" and the "extra-legal" became increasingly difficult to draw; many white Southerners who recognized lynching as a threat to the notion of the rule of law proposed judicial reforms that would incorporate the summary "procedures" employed by mobs into the court system, attempting to resuscitate a respect for due process at the expense of the very elements that made that concept meaningful. Yet such "reformers" were unwilling to propose changes that would adversely affect large numbers of white defendants as well as black ones. As one proponent of limited judicial reforms stated, "It is better that a people exasperated by an atrocious crime should occasionally deal with it by extra legal methods than that methods which in themselves attack the guarantees of personal liberty should find lodgment in our legal system" (King 169). Such a view implied that the purity of the criminal justice system could be maintained only by establishing an alternative system for African American men. Given the institutional justification for lynchings, it is no surprise that many of them were preceded by mock "trials," often conducted at or near the town courthouse, at which the "evidence" against the victim was presented and he was accorded the opportunity to confess his crime. Thomas Dixon's novel *The Leopard's Spots* details such a scene, describing a crowd of vigilantes "swarming into the court-house square under the big oak where an informal trial was to be held" (381). Mimicry, therefore, extended in both directions; the courts began to imitate the "procedures" of the mob, and the mob parroted the forms of the jury trial, without its procedural safeguards.[9]

Like many African Americans at the turn of the century, Hopkins was unsure about where "the law" ended and lawlessness began. Yet rather than despair over this uncertainty, she employed it to authorize her own public voice. Like Wells's polemical nonfiction, *Contending Forces* places a question mark after the concept of "law" and thereby asserts its own legitimacy as a repository of legal principles that the courts, it implies, are unwilling to protect. The lynching of Montfort and Hopkins's resolution of the conflicts within the Smiths' family history illustrate the nature of the novel's legal engagement. Montfort is killed at the behest of the quasi-legal "committee on public safety" acting to protect the legal institution of slavery. By emphasizing the entanglement of this act of mob violence with officially codified law, Hopkins implicitly invokes the "legality" of postbellum lynching and, at the same time, exposes such racial violence as an "illegal" means of reinstituting relations that had been outlawed by the Thirteenth Amendment. Thus, the novel records both the legal justifications for the murder (Montfort was planning to manumit his slaves, an act that could have destabilized the institution of slavery in the region) and the illegal motive of Anson Pollock's sexual desire for Grace.[10] Montfort's killing ties together the past and the present in a way that complicates the ostensibly clear boundaries of legality and illegality.

Yet for Hopkins, those boundaries do not cease to exist simply by virtue of the legal system's failure to enforce them. If due process has been neglected by the courts and by law enforcement officials, the novel suggests, it nonetheless remains a vital principle latent within the law's texts — a principle whose life must flourish outside the courtroom when the courtroom renounces it. Even though Hopkins's literary invocation of procedural integrity lies "outside" the strict limits of the law, it leads to what is essentially an "inside" narrative — one that operates in a legal fashion and draws upon a kind of legal-rational authority. Thus, Hopkins resolves the racial conflicts of the Smith family's past through legal means. When Charles Montfort-Withington, an Englishman interested in "the negro question," arrives in Boston, he meets the Smiths and reveals himself as the son of Charles Montfort Jr. (who had married the daughter of his English benefactor). Ma Smith describes her own heritage to him and he embraces them as his kin, but asks if she has any "proofs" by which their identities could be legally validated. She informs him that her father, Jesse, had destroyed all the letters from his brother Charles in a fit of despondency, but Withington states that the letters from Jesse to Charles have been "preserved as a sacred legacy, together with a sworn statement of the main facts as we know them, in this remarkable case" (376). Furthermore, he tells her that Charles's English benefactor had sued the United States government on Charles's behalf and that half of the judgment obtained has been held in trust for Jesse's heirs. The law finally acknowledges the Smiths' "true" identities and restores their patrilineal rights:

> The case of Smith vs. the United States did not come to a public trial; it was heard privately before a court composed of the judges of the Supreme Court of the United States. The English heirs had received their portion years before; the Government only awaited the production of the necessary proofs to establish the identity of Mrs. Smith beyond a peradventure. Detectives went over the ground carefully. The records of real estate transfers, chattels, etc., were all found intact among the files of the courthouse at Newberne, North Carolina. . . .
>
> As Mr. Withington had said, the letters in his possession from Jesse to Charles Montfort, yellow and time-stained, completed a perfect chain of evidence. The sum of one hundred and fifty thousand dollars was awarded to Mrs. Smith as the last representative of the heirs of Jesse Montfort. Justice was appeased. (383–84)

Luke Sawyer's call for "justice" had invoked the American Revolution, suggesting the need for political violence by African Americans. Yet within the structure of the narrative, justice is "appeased" through the methodical and professional operation of law. The letters constitute the definitive "evidence" not only of the Smiths' relation to the Montforts, but also of the illegal circumstances of Charles Montfort's death. The legality of that death had been ambiguous under the regime of slavery, but in the postbellum legal world (the ideal one, at least) its unlawful quality becomes clear. Thus, the family is simultaneously written into history and the law; its place within history is given meaning through the legal definition of formerly equivocal events, and the present legal status of each of its members is determined through the excavation of an antebellum past. The Smiths emerge from Hopkins's narrative as fully constituted citizens, possessed of all their "rights" and officially acknowledged as integral parts of the nation's history. The "chain of evidence" that links the Smiths to the Montforts dislodges the last remnants of the "chains" of slavery, and also serves to discredit the faulty evidentiary "chains" relied upon as quasilegal justifications for the practice of lynching.

The legal resolution of the Smiths' genealogical claims is, of course, an ideal one, not intended by Hopkins to represent the present state of affairs. Consequently, its utopian quality is dampened by the fact that the Supreme Court hears the Smiths' case "privately" rather than publicly. There seems in fact to be no precedent for such a hearing, and Hopkins undoubtedly invented it to distinguish the sense of possibility she wished to convey from the reality of African American proscription. The just verdict is a consequence not of conditions external to Hopkins's narrative, but of an internal legal logic that informs the entire structure of the novel. Intensely critical of the criminal justice system's failure to adhere to the adjudicative ideals articulated by the Constitution's Fifth and Fourteenth Amendments, Hopkins constructs a story infused by a respect for due process. *Contending Forces* is a romance of the law; it eschews realistic representation in favor of an idealistic depiction of possibilities, yet its idealism is drawn from principles that are, in a sense, already present within the texts and ideology of the American legal system. In "publicizing" a decision that the Supreme Court hears "privately," she invokes a literary power that draws its authority from the law, even as it implicitly condemns the law's shortcomings.

It is no coincidence, therefore, that Hopkins's description of the detective work leading to the Smiths' legal victory echoes her reference to the research that underlay her novel; in the preface she states that "The incidents portrayed in the early chapters of the book actually occurred. Ample proof of this may be found in the archives of the courthouse at Newberne, N.C., and at the national seat of government, Washington, D.C." (14). The "proof," of course, has been transferred from the courthouse files to the pages of her own text, which now functions as evidence in the public trial of the African American legal subject. Moreover, Hopkins deemphasizes her own authorship to construct her text as a factual document relevant to the national debate over race. Maintaining that she has based much of the discussion at the meeting of the American Colored League on actual addresses from both white and black speakers, she states, "I feel my own deficiencies too strongly to attempt original composition on this subject at this crisis in the history of the Negro in the United States" (16). By denying "original composition," she presents herself not as ideologue or polemicist, but as professional attorney and historian, and this construction of her own authorship locates her novel as a site in which evidence, testimony, and respect for procedural integrity reign over the passion and prejudice of political interest.

Unlike the rumor, innuendo, and politically charged racial narratives that serve as the evidence justifying lynchings, Hopkins's evidence is presented in a restrained — even genteel — fashion. She thus specifically contrasts the biased account of a lynching printed by a Southern newspaper with the balanced response to it at the meeting of the American Colored League. The news story describes the victim, accused of rape, as a "black monster" and concludes that "the Negroes of this section have been taught a salutary lesson" (223–24). While the meeting called in response to this event contains expressions of outrage by individuals such as Luke Sawyer, its organizers also decide that "a conservative white man should be asked to address the meeting . . . and in this way each side could have a chance to represent the subject as seen from its point of view." In fact, the first three speakers at the meeting — the white Hon. Herbert Clapp, Dr. Arthur Lewis (a character modeled on Booker T. Washington), and the duplicitous black lawyer John Langley — all counsel the African American audience, as Langley puts it, not to "offend the class upon whom we depend for employment and assistance" (241, 253). After Sawyer suggests the need for violence, Will Smith (modeled on W.E.B. DuBois) delivers a forceful speech that is nonetheless balanced in its message between patience and restraint on the one hand and political agitation on the other. Thus, the meeting reflects a process in which each side obtains a fair hearing, with the result that the most compelling argument (for Hopkins it is clearly Will's) emerges triumphant.

This is also true of a dinner given by a white private club after the meeting. Doctor Lewis and Will Smith are invited to the event, and they engage in a debate with a white Southerner who defends lynching by asserting that "race is stronger than law." When Lewis replies that most rape accusations against black men are false, the Southerner — "white with passion"— exclaims "You cannot prove your assertions!" Lewis names the Georgia lynching of John Thomas and describes the hiring of a detective to investigate the charge of rape for which Thomas was killed. The detective had concluded that Thomas was innocent, and Lewis asserts that "If every case of Negro lynching could be investigated, we should discover fearful discrepancies between the story of the mob and the real truth" (297, 298–99). As in the meeting of the American Colored League, a free and open exchange of views leads to the emergence of "truth"; if allowed to come out, Hopkins implies, evidence will ultimately triumph over the "passion" of racial politics. Her novel serves as the forum for these exchanges and thereby assumes the functions of both the courtroom and the public arena of political debate. Yet it is the former site that she relies upon most, for the evidentiary and procedural questions she presents of criminal guilt, forensic integrity, and rightful inheritance are fundamentally legal ones. Due process functions as a principle of narration as well as adjudication in *Contending Forces*, and the debates that take place between the pages of the text all point conclusively to the legitimacy of African American claims to equal citizenship.

Domesticity and the Law

Hopkins's approach to legal reform on the racial front can be characterized as process oriented. She celebrates the procedural mechanisms that, theoretically, should operate to provide African Americans with a form of citizenship equal to that of whites. By doing so, she assumes that those mechanisms possess a content, that they are more than simply formal requirements that operate independent of any particular set of values or principles. In this sense, she exhibits her own reliance upon the logic of professionalism — a logic that affects the shape of her story as well as her representation of the law. For Hopkins, the truth will out, so long as the process used to uncover it is neutral, open, and honest. But the "truth" is also embedded in the very process itself — the truth about African American history and character is reflected in their demand that they be accorded due process of law. Form and substance here are indistinguishable.

Of course, we might well characterize Hopkins's faith in the neutrality of legal process as naive. The advent of legal realism in the 1920s began an intellectual challenge to the possibility of legal neutrality and openness that continues to this day. Members of the Critical Legal Studies movement have expanded upon the perspective of the legal realists by insisting that the law is *always* politically interested, that even its seemingly neutral procedural mechanisms bear an ideological stamp geared toward privileging some groups over others.[11] Though this perspective began to grow in force among intellectuals after World War I (not necessarily among rank-and-file lawyers), its roots can be traced back to the legal philosophy of Oliver Wendell Holmes Jr., who, as I have noted earlier, insisted that the law was informed as much by prejudice and self-interest as it was by principle. If this is so, then the liberal model of law as a neutral realm of mediation between different politically interested social groups begins to look not only suspect, but like a political argument itself — a form of rhetoric employed to achieve a particular set of self-interested goals, or even more insidiously, a form of ideology that allows for no critical position from which to combat it. Stanley Fish articulates this position when he asserts (in Holmesian fashion) that "the law is 'pre-eminently the discourse of power,' that is, a discourse whose categories, distinctions, and revered formulas are extensions of some political program that does not announce itself as such" (*Doing* 175).

But if we view Hopkins's procedural ideals in light of the advent of the new professionalism in the late nineteenth century, we might see those ideals neither as naive nor as evidence of Hopkins's capitulation to liberal ideology. In fact, her narrative functions both to vindicate traditional liberal principles and to call for their reconfiguration, and the concept of due process serves both ends. Her work implies that true procedural integrity in the legal sphere really *might* be possible if the procedures themselves were seen as more than just forms, but substantive elements of the law as well. In other words, if the law is charged primarily with establishing norms that regulate conduct outside the courtroom rather than determining individual questions of guilt, innocence, and liability, then due process might be seen as not just a means to an end, but an end in itself. "Neutrality" here would not be an absolute, but rather a concept constructed by the very forms that are supposed to reflect it — a concept laden with pluralistic and inclusive values. Of course, this perspective requires that we relinquish liberalism's insistence on the law's function as an arbiter of absolute truth and accept its role in defining principles — contingent and changeable ones — that can serve to bind a community together. If our legal epistemology requires a direct and unmediated relation between evidence and truth, we will invariably stray from our procedural safeguards in the name of that truth. But if due process's call for formal integrity embodies, first and foremost, a substantive principle of national inclusion, then that principle can determine the shape of the law's relation to reality. Such a relation, of course, must now be seen as mediated by rules and procedures, but those rules and procedures are, in this view, what the law really exists for anyway. For Hopkins (and for Ida B. Wells also), adherence to form is simultaneously a dedication to principle. And of course, the "truths" that emerge from this mediated epistemology are, in the end, more reliable (because less political) than those that result from an unconstrained (and unprofessional) pursuit of truth. The integrity of legal procedures is to Hopkins the very embodiment of the liberal goal of legal neutrality. That version of neutrality, however, no longer stands as a kind of universal truth; instead, it is related to the pluralistic ideals that have been built into the fabric of American institutions (though often suppressed) and into the very notion of American citizenship.[12]

It is in this light that Hopkins's use of well-worn nineteenth-century literary conventions takes on significance as a form of political intervention — an intervention that uses the constraints of literary genre as an analogue to the law's procedural constraints.[13] Her novel borrows from the genres of the historical romance, the domestic novel of marriage, and the melodramatic theater, doing so in pursuit of its goal of narrativizing the African American legal subject. These conventional elements constitute Hopkins's own forms — the mechanisms through which she articulates an authoritative version of the national community. If they do not convey the "truth" about African American experience at the turn of the century, they are not meant to. Instead, they make African Americans representable within a structure of signification defined by legal and literary professionalism, and thus serve as part of an argument that is ultimately institutional in nature.

The exaggerated gentility of her characters is a case in point. As Claudia Tate points out about the works of Hopkins and other African American women of the same era, "the idealized civility of black women and men in the private realm as wives and husbands becomes a gendered paradigm for responsible citizens in the public realm" (96). Will Smith, for instance, disavows Luke Sawyer's call to arms by stating in his own speech that "brute force will not accomplish anything," and his patience and restraint are finally rewarded through the orderly processes of the law (272). Furthermore, his willingness to overlook Sappho's unchaste past evinces a fairness that the novel associates with legal ideals, and he thereby proves himself worthy of full respect in the eyes of the law and the rest of the nation. Unlike Langley's desire for Sappho, Smith's is mediated by the concept of marriage, and this dedication to the institution of the family rather than to mere sexual gratification not only serves to combat the stereotype of the black male beast, but also evidences a personal ethic that transcends self-interest.[14] For Hopkins, the domestic subject was simultaneously a legal subject, and gentility could therefore serve as a signifier of both moral uprightness and responsible citizenship. But gentility here is also restraint — it is adherence to form and to correct procedure, in both a social sense (as in her characters' behavior) and a literary one (as in her own faithfulness to generic standards of representation).

While Tate notes a connection between gentility and citizenship, she also claims that Hopkins's version of citizenship is gendered female. Arguing that the novel rejects "male-centered expressions of racial protest" in favor of "female-centered expectations of domestic idealism," she maintains that this differentiation has legal implications:

> Although *Contending Forces* sustains both racial and domestic (or sexual) discourses, the former becomes increasingly reticent throughout the story, while the latter, which inscribes the "mother's law," becomes dominant. The mother's law centers a black matricentric morality; it metes out reward and punishment in direct proportion to the moral character of one's deeds, privileges a female-centered ethical context, and serves as a broader basis for redefining a virtuous woman other than on grounds of sexual chastity. Last, the characters turn to the mother's law for instruction, finding that the father's law is increasingly inappropriate for guiding their moral and ethical decisions. (174)

Without question, Hopkins's novel contains a critique of patriarchal values. Yet Tate's argument fails to account for the novel's explicitly legal resolution or to note the evidentiary premises through which it unfolds. Susan Gillman also neglects these factors in her discussion of the genre she terms "race melodrama," a literary category in which she places Hopkins's novel. Asserting that this genre draws "on a language of love and romance" and "bases its different conceptions of race on different conceptions of gender," she maintains that a work like Twain's *Pudd'nhead Wilson* does not ultimately fit the model: "[Twain's] institutionally based conception of race relations — in *Pudd'nhead Wilson*, race as a product of social institutions such as the law and science, race as a fiction of law and custom — differs fundamentally from the familial, kinship-based model of race that we get in the race melodrama. . . . For Twain the racial body is not a body at all, it is not at all gender-related or gender-specific" (227, 231). Like Tate, Gillman assumes an incompatibility between works that relate politics to gender and family relations, on the one hand, and those "institutionally based" works whose discourse is drawn from established systems of authority, on the other. Hopkins's novel, however, belies this distinction. Her narrative looks not to an alternative sphere of female-centered law defined by domesticity, but to the antiracist and antipatriarchal (one might say domestic) potential contained within the American legal system as it currently exists.

Citizenship is gendered in the novel only to the extent that Hopkins reconceives of the public sphere as a realm that authorizes female as well as male voices. Like Anna Julia Cooper's assertion that an "equitable verdict" on black citizenship was impossible without the testimony of African American women, Hopkins's perspective on gender places womanhood inside rather than outside the law, using the exclusion of black women's voices from the public sphere to expose the law's failure to adhere to its own standards rather than to assert the existence of an alternative realm of female-centered values (Cooper ii). Cooper's trial metaphor suggests that concepts such as due process were still potent sources of appeal for African American women at the turn of the century, despite the sense of proscription they experienced. Thus, the male-centered antilynching meeting of the American Colored League is balanced in Hopkins's text by the female-centered chapter entitled "The Sewing-Circle," which models the free and open debate of the political meeting while focusing on issues related to the construction of African American womanhood. Neither gathering takes precedence over the other within the structure of Hopkins's novel. Instead they complement one another by serving as paradigms for a political forum in which all perspectives are sought and each is evaluated on its own independent merits.[15] "The Sewing-Circle" introduces a character named Mrs. Willis, who has become a leading advocate on the "Woman Question" and who strikes Sappho as "insincere" (155). Yet Mrs. Willis articulates the principle that Will Smith will later use to judge Sappho, asserting that African American women "shall not be held responsible for wrongs which we have unconsciously committed, or which we have committed under compulsion. We are virtuous or non-virtuous only when we have a choice under temptation." The statement itself evinces the need to look beneath "appearances," a process that the sewing circle makes possible by enabling the existence of a genuine dialogue in which all feel free to speak their minds. As a result, Sappho begins to change her mind about Mrs. Willis, concluding that "there was evidently more in this woman than appeared upon the surface" (149, 157). Since Mrs. Willis's theory of responsibility points out the flaws of holding black women to account for the history of interracial sexual relations, Hopkins's chapter not only models the kind of public forum in which black women's voices are sought and respected; it also suggests that prevalent public narratives of an inherently lustful African American womanhood are themselves the product of a closed arena that silences the very individuals who have the most compelling evidence to offer.

That evidence, of course, would expose the role of white men in the sexual victimization of black women. In her preface to *Contending Forces*,

Hopkins states that she has "presented both sides of the dark picture — lynching and concubinage — truthfully and without vituperation" (15). Tastefully using "concubinage" instead of "rape," the assertion subtly alters the claim that lynching was the result of rapes perpetrated by black men against white women. Even those white leaders who condemned the practice of lynching often assumed the truth of this underlying rationale, thereby defending the motives of the mob while ostensibly repudiating its acts. For Hopkins, however, the "other side" of lynching is the rape not of white women by black men but of black women by white men. Symbolically veiled rapes of black (or reputedly black) women accompany the killings of Montfort and Sawyer's father, and more explicit sexual abuse results from the murder of Monsieur Beaubean. By connecting the lynching of black men and the rape of black women, Hopkins exposes the systematic nature of the violence that perpetuated white privilege in the South and places the ostensibly "personal" crime of rape in the wider legal context in which lynching occurred. If the image of the black male beast was an invention that concealed the political and economic grounds of lynching, the image of the sexually promiscuous black woman served the similar function of obscuring the historic sexual abuse of female slaves by white masters. Such abuse continued after the Civil War, as rape was one of the instruments of terror employed by the Ku Klux Klan during Reconstruction.[16] Hopkins reveals the perpetuation of this crime and suggests that, just as African American men accused of rape could not look to the law for protection or expect vindication after their deaths, African American women had no adequate legal redress when raped by white men.

But if politically charged racial narratives have served to corrupt otherwise egalitarian legal principles, Hopkins suggests, alternative stories can operate to reinvigorate them, so long as there is a forum in which they can be told. The literary genre of domestic fiction provides just such a forum. Although Hopkins's narrative makes use of both melodrama and domestic fiction, she distinguishes between these modes based upon the implicit methodologies by which each suggests the "truth" can be attained. Melodrama operates as a form of judgment that, in positing the existence of universal and unalterable essences directly available to human perception, eschews positivistic investigation and the consideration of mitigating facts. It is, the novel implies, the very genre that lies beneath the public narratives of African American dissipation and sensuality. Such narratives are able to exercise authority only by also exercising a kind of willful blindness, by discrediting — even silencing — specific evidence in favor of higher "truths" about race in general. Sappho's decision to keep the past a secret suggests that her background could be read only in light of dominant conceptions of black womanhood, and she thus assumes that her sexual victimization would be lost beneath the attention her "fallen" status would receive. Hopkins's story, however, rejects the melodramatic logic that would categorize her as a "fallen" woman, employing instead a domestic model of understanding and forgiveness — a model that allows the truth not only to emerge, but to be heard as well.[17] If melodramatic conventions require Sappho to keep quiet about her past, domestic ones enable her to speak, and even more important, provide her an institutionalized (because generically established) arena for doing so. The novel's domestic sensibility, therefore, serves not as a critique of institutional legal processes, but as a vindication of them; it exposes the inadequacies of the racial melodramas published as fact by the popular press and relied upon by vigilantes intent on executing "justice" without regard for the evidence. Although for Hopkins the very existence of these narratives has operated to suppress information that would tend to undermine their premises, the law's own positivistic ideology also implicitly keeps open the possibility that new evidence and testimony might eventually prove those narratives wrong, that its procedural mechanisms for determining the truth might function to undermine its most deep-seated assumptions.

The courtship plot of *Contending Forces* allows such subversive evidence to emerge, thereby supplementing the successful yet incomplete story of the Smiths' legal triumph. The overtly historical and legal concerns of the novel's Smith/Montfort story and the domestic elements of the courtship plot form a whole in which "both sides" of the violence against blacks — lynching and rape — are addressed. The description of the verdict in the Smiths' favor does not account for Grace Montfort's rape (just as the novel's depiction of it is carefully encoded as a "whipping"), but Hopkins fills that silence in her resolution of the relationship between Sappho and Will Smith. In love with Will but believing he would renounce their engagement if he knew of her checkered past, Sappho reveals the truth to him in a letter and runs away. Will, however, eventually locates her in New Orleans and declares his continuing love for her, stating that he does not hold her "responsible for the monstrous wrong" committed against her (396). His reaffirmation of their engagement serves as an analogue to the Supreme Court's adjudication of the Smiths' legal claims; both condemn the injustice of past racist acts and reinstate identities those acts had taken away. The verdict in Smith v. United States officially declares the illegality of Montfort's murder and acknowledges the Smiths' connection to the Montforts, and Will Smith's declaration of love decries the abuse suffered by Sappho and confirms her identity as a virtuous woman suitable for a genteel marriage. Thus, the courtship plot and the more overtly "legal" plot converge — both, it turns out, are ultimately about the process by which a legitimate judgment can be rendered on the African American legal subject.

Domesticity and the law are not finally at odds in *Contending Forces*; the former simply operates as a means of promoting a version of citizenship grounded in inclusion. The very practice of lynching, of course, excluded black men from the precincts of the law, and the refusal of whites to consult the experience of black women helped to make lynchings "legal." Hopkins's domestic story serves as a mirror image of her legal one and, as a result, her novel allows for no meaningful distinction between public and private, legal and domestic. By placing her characters within this legal/literary structure and revealing that structure's power to sort out identities and enact justice, she affirms both the representability of the African American self and the legal authority of her own narrative, even as she indicts the law for its failure to recognize the principles of equality and inclusion that undergird its very existence.

The first of Hopkins's four published novels, *Contending Forces* was also the one in which her legal and literary concerns converged in the most seamless manner. While conflicts surrounding justice, evidence, and punishment would continue to appear in her subsequent works, the narrative tensions within those works increasingly eluded legal resolution.[18] This is particularly evident in Hopkins's second novel, *Hagar's Daughter* (1901). Like *Contending Forces*, the story connects an antebellum act of violence to a postbellum one, and sorts through its characters' relations to these acts by means of a trial. Hopkins explicitly represents the details of this trial and employs it as the dramatic centerpiece of the narrative, but it nonetheless fails to mesh harmoniously with the courtship plot of the novel. In fact, the revelations that emerge in the trial set in motion a chain of events that eventually exposes the central female character, whom everyone had believed to be white, to be black — a disclosure that results in her white husband's hesitancy to affirm their marriage. He finally comes to his senses, but too late — his wife dies while traveling abroad. Like Charles Chesnutt in *The House Behind the Cedars*,

Hopkins relies on the tragic mulatta plot to conclude her novel, but unlike Chesnutt she employs it to suggest the law's inability to dismantle the social origins of racial caste. What seems like a triumph of justice (the innocent husband is acquitted of murder in the trial and the true killer is revealed) turns out to contain the seeds of injustice as well.[19] It is significant that the novel's postbellum setting is Washington D.C.; as time passed, the federal government's refusal to intervene in the ongoing violence in the South began to seem more and more permanent to advocates of federal action, and their suspicions were confirmed in 1902 (the year in which *Hagar's Daughter* ended its serialization in *Colored American Magazine*) when an anti-lynching bill grounded in the Fourteenth Amendment's equal protection clause was killed in the Senate Judiciary Committee as unconstitutional.[20]

Hopkins's last two novels would move even further from the legal structure that anchors *Contending Forces*. In *Winona* (1902), she would celebrate John Brown's Kansas activities in the 1850s, praising the "determined courage which faced his enemies in later years before the Virginia tribunal where, threatened with an ignominious death, he made the unmoved reply — I am about God's work; He will take care of me" (374). The novel seems to reject the legalistic gentility of the central characters in *Contending Forces* to adopt a position similar to Luke Sawyer's call to arms. Her final novel, *Of One Blood* (1903), looks to Ethiopianism and an incipient Pan-Africanism for the ideals that could lead to African American redemption, constructing its characters less as citizens of the United States and more as members of a global black nation. These works anticipate the aesthetic that would emerge much more explicitly in the literature of the Harlem Renaissance; the political transformations they envision spring not from existing institutional processes or discourses but from the direct agency of a transnational and transhistorical black self. Yet Hopkins's career reveals that this aesthetic rose from the ashes of an earlier one in which writing the African American self was equivalent to writing the legal and political history of the United States. If Hopkins's literary intervention in the legal sphere of turn-of-the-century America did not ultimately seem an answer to the state of proscription she decried, it nonetheless hinted at the potentially powerful strategy of using the law's own ideals to identify the shortcomings of its actual practices — a strategy that would soon underwrite the founding of the NAACP and that a later generation of civil rights activists in the 1950s and 1960s would employ to considerable advantage.

II

The Authority of Property

CHAPTER 4

Charles Chesnutt's Fictions of Ownership

*If he be a white man and assigned to a colored coach, he may have his action for
damages against the company for being deprived of his so called property. Upon
the other hand, if he be a colored man and be so assigned, he has been deprived
of no property, since he is not lawfully entitled to the reputation of being a
white man.*

    Justice Henry Billings Brown, Plessy v. Ferguson

In the legal brief he filed with the U.S. Supreme Court on behalf of
Homer Plessy in *Plessy v. Ferguson*, Albion Tourgée — the former
North Carolina judge and author of numerous novels of Reconstruction — asserted that Plessy's reputation as a white man constituted a form of property, and that this property had been forcibly taken
from him when he was ejected from a white railroad car. Although suc-
cinct and dismissive, the Court's response to Tourgée's argument nonetheless spoke volumes. Ostensibly refusing to rule on whether a white
appearance was a form of property, Justice Henry Billings Brown unwittingly articulated the terms by which whiteness might be "owned." For
Brown, a property interest in whiteness would be constituted by combining reputation with "lawful entitlement." His opinion deferred to state
law on the issue of who would be "lawfully entitled to the reputation of
being a white man," but since states typically defined race in terms of frac-
tional amounts of white and black blood, his formula implicitly incorporated this conception. Brown's opinion for the Court constructed white
blood as a form of title, the possession of which would transform a mere
reputation for whiteness into a legally cognizable form of ownership.[1]

Tourgée's failed argument in *Plessy*, and the Court's telling response
to it, expose the historical connection between race and property in the
United States. Recent legal scholarship — particularly that associated
with the movement known as Critical Race theory — has refocused attention on this relationship in an effort to explain the persistence of sys-

temic racial imbalances within a legal system that purports to ensure "equal rights" for all citizens. Cheryl Harris, for instance, asserts that "the origins of property rights in the United States are rooted in racial domination. Even in the early years of the country, it was not the concept of race alone that operated to oppress Blacks and Indians; rather it was the *interaction* between conceptions of race and property that played a critical role in establishing and maintaining racial and economic subordination" (1716). Notwithstanding the currency of this approach, Tourgée's argument in *Plessy* reveals that its roots lie in the late nineteenth century. Even before the Court officially sanctioned Jim Crow in 1896, it had been clear to many people — African Americans in particular — that whiteness was "worth" more than blackness and that American courts would not deny whites the use of their accumulated racial capital. Nevertheless, whether blackness itself could be conceived of as possessing tangible "value" of a kind that would be recognized by the marketplace and by American legal institutions remained an open question at the turn of the century. In the age of Booker T. Washington's philosophy of racial "uplift," it still seemed possible that the one-sided association of property with whiteness might be alterable.

Indeed, this hope lies behind Hopkins's representation of the African American legal subject in *Contending Forces*; the Smiths succeed to an inheritance in her novel that not only connects them to a history of wrongful enslavement, but endows them with a form of wealth that legitimates their claim to full citizenship and legal respect. Hopkins's faith in the law's power to bestow self-ownership is typical of much African American writing at the turn of the century, yet that faith was almost always tempered by an acute awareness of post-Reconstruction legal disappointments. Thus, Washington's sanguinity about black ownership inevitably generated questions: Weren't the rights granted African Americans by the Civil War amendments to the Constitution meant to endow them with a form of property — a free and unencumbered title to the self? If this legal effort had been unsuccessful, could the acquisition of land, homes, and businesses remedy the failure? And perhaps most important: Could blackness ever be "owned" on the same terms as whiteness?

Maintaining that "The Negro will be on a different footing in this country when it becomes common to associate the possession of wealth with black skin," Booker T. Washington answered the latter question in the affirmative, thereby constructing the "private" sphere of ownership as determinative of the "public" sphere of rights (176).[2] Despite his emergence as the most prominent black leader of the era, however, the questions and doubts persisted. One of the doubters was Charles Chesnutt. A friend and admirer of Washington, Chesnutt nonetheless disagreed with him on the issue of rights, and made his position clear in a June 1903 letter to Washington: "I appreciate all you say and have written about education and property; but they are not everything. There is no good reason why we should not acquire them and exercise our constitutional rights at the same time, and acquire them all the more readily because of our equality of rights. I have no confidence in that friendship of the whites which is to take the place of rights, and no expectation of justice at their hands unless it is founded on law" (quoted in Helen M. Chesnutt 183). For Chesnutt, ownership cannot logically precede rights because rights make ownership possible. Yet, implicitly acknowledging that rights cannot attach to an individual who is not already, in some sense, an "owner," his letter suggests that property and rights must be acquired "at the same time." Accordingly, much of his fiction not only registers his disagreement with Washington's panacea of property ownership, but also questions the efficacy of pursuing formally equal rights within a legal system that associates the black self only with absence and dispossession.

Chesnutt's novel *The House behind the Cedars* (1900) evidences his engagement with questions of ownership, rights, and the legal status of African Americans. The novel has seemed to many readers a somewhat anomalous work within Chesnutt's literary corpus; such readers have often praised his works for their astute renderings of political and cultural power struggles and their subtle approaches to the social construction of race, yet they have tended to read *The House behind the Cedars* as affirming a kind of racial essentialism in which fate and blood are inextricably linked. When we read the novel along with the short fiction that Chesnutt published at the turn of the century, however, its emphasis on blood and genealogy begins to look less like a capitulation to biological definitions of race and more like an exploration of the connection between race and property. Many of his tales operate as a kind of legal history; they expose the transformation of whiteness and blackness from antebellum status distinctions dictated by "nature" and officially codified by law into postbellum markers of ownership enforced through meanings concealed beneath the formal equality of the law's texts. These short works, along with his novel, seek both to critique this state of affairs and to intervene in it, to reveal the true meanings behind the concept of "blood" and to articulate the terms by which a property in blackness (a social rather than biological category) might be conceived.

Chesnutt was a lawyer, and his approach to the relation between the literary and the legal is both enabled and constricted by a professional ideology that requires strict adherence to institutional form. The formal elements of the law that he employs are the very concepts of property and rights that, by the late nineteenth century, had failed African Americans so miserably. For Chesnutt, however, these legal principles also contain a transformative potential — they accommodate versions of racial identity and community that the legal system has suppressed, but whose power nonetheless still resides within them. Countering the racial ideology of *Plessy* with the idealism inherent in the literary genres of the tragic mulatta tale and the domestic novel, Chesnutt — like Hopkins — attempts to tap this power. By reformulating legal concepts that had become racially charged, he seeks to revise such concepts as rights and self-ownership rather than abandon those foundational principles entirely. As Morton J. Horwitz has noted, the concept of property rights constituted an especially potent weapon for conservatism in the last decades of the nineteenth century, during which time "American courts came as close as they ever had to saying that one had a property right to an unchanging world" (151). Chesnutt's legal narratives accept the power of this discourse and acknowledge that, if whiteness has been endowed with the status of property, the only hope for African American equality lies in envisioning blackness in a similar way.

Deconstructing Reconstruction: "The Sway-Backed House"

A number of critics have questioned the literary merit of *The House behind the Cedars* by reading the novel as a conservative representation of the biological reality behind racial distinctions. Eric J. Sundquist, for instance, while applauding the insightfulness of *The Marrow of Tradition* and the stories contained in *The Conjure Woman*, criticizes *The House behind the Cedars* for its use of a "sins of the fathers" refrain in referring to its characters' mixed racial ancestry. By exposing the secret of Rena's genealogy, he maintains, Chesnutt abandons the epistemological complexity behind the construction of race and leaves the idea of sin "in an undisturbed category of governing genealogical facts" (399). SallyAnn H. Ferguson, reading the novel in light of Chesnutt's series of articles on "The Future American" published in the *Boston Evening Transcript* the same year as *The*

House behind the Cedars, asserts that "Chesnutt is primarily concerned with making a case for racial amalgamation" in the novel (82). Her position implies that, by offering a genealogical solution to racism, the author presents the problem as genealogical in origin.[3] And Donald B. Gibson argues that Chesnutt reveals his "class bias" in the novel by endorsing the notion that the "best people" are those with "good blood" (*Politics* 136).

But if *The House behind the Cedars* participates in the ideology of "blood," what then are we to make of a work like "The Sway-Backed House," also published in 1900?[4] The story takes place in North Carolina in the 1870s, and focuses upon a light-skinned black woman named Isabella who lives with her adoptive grandfather, Solomon. Solomon is a "very dark man" and likes to think he is the descendant of an African king. This sense of his own "royal" genealogy, however, leads him to show "a very distinct scorn for ordinary blacks" and to prefer those of a whiter complexion. He believes in "lightening up the breed" and, consequently, wants nothing to do with the offspring of his sister, who married "a good-fer-nothin' black nigger" ("Sway-Backed" 223, 226, 224). Solomon's perspective celebrates blood — a category, for him, of hierarchy and caste rather than familial connection. Solomon is also a property owner, but while the house to which he holds title is much larger than others in the neighborhood, it has a roof that sags in the middle, a roof that "could not, in his opinion, be remedied without an entire reconstruction of the house" (224). Chesnutt's presentation of Solomon relates his celebration of blood to his property ownership; both set him apart from others, yet both rest upon shaky principles in need of "reconstruction."

Isabella is of marrying age, and the narrator tells us that the "balance" hangs "trembling" between Professor Revels, a schoolteacher, and Tom Turner, a blacksmith. Professor Revels is light-skinned and manages to look even lighter through the use of "cosmetics," while Turner is darker — a fact increased by his trade (224, 225). The professor's character is distinctly Washingtonian, as he has "commended himself to the town authorities by abstention from politics and deference to the white people." Isabella ultimately decides on Professor Revels who, though already a property owner, admires the sway-backed house even more than he does Isabella's white complexion. Unlike Solomon, the professor feels that the roof "could easily be straightened" without tearing down the entire structure. When Solomon dies, it comes as a surprise to everyone that he has left his property not to Isabella alone, but to her and the ten children of his estranged sister, "share and share alike" (225, 230, 227). Naturally, Professor Revels feels disappointed and avoids meeting his fiancée for a while, during which time Isabella, facing eviction from the sway-backed house, finds the blacksmith to be more compassionate. Eventually, the professor decides to affirm their engagement, but when he asks Isabella where he may call for her on their wedding day, she informs him that she will be at her husband's, for she had married Tom Turner the night before.

Rather than essentializing race by accepting its biological foundation, "The Sway-Backed House" exposes the entanglement of blood and property; Solomon's restrictive and privileged sense of genealogy is manifested in his ownership of a house that distinguishes him from his neighbors, but Chesnutt's description of the house's unstable roof images the tenuous nature of such a perspective. The story ultimately discredits genealogy as a source of knowledge about the self and others, and implicitly rejects genealogical solutions to racism in favor of legal ones. Solomon's will is a legal document that enables him to control the terms by which he constructs his "family" of legatees. He redefines blood by granting equal shares of his estate to his nonbiological granddaughter and his biological nieces and nephews, thereby creating a "family" grounded not in social hierarchy or biology, but in the shared experience of being black. Drooping precariously under the strain inherent in the concept of black ownership, the sway-backed house embodies blood as a form of title, and Solomon's reluctance to tear it down reflects the failure of Reconstruction legal reforms to dismantle this notion and to replace it with a conception of self-ownership removed from racial distinctions. His will, however, makes amends; it reverses the biblical story, "splitting the baby" instead of leaving it intact, and in so doing accomplishes a version of the "reconstruction" that neither he nor the government had previously been willing to complete. Professor Revels (and by implication, Washington), on the other hand, would maintain an unstable status quo by promoting an exclusionary version of the self — a self that African Americans cannot own on equal terms with whites. Thus, while Solomon's will dispossesses Isabella of a property interest in her white blood, it bestows upon her the possibility of creating an identity that is not illusory — one that will be "forged" in her marriage to the blacksmith rather than "inherited" within a system of white privilege that, we know, will never allow her full participation. She loses a house but gains a home, and the form of selfhood she assumes will presumably disavow the hierarchical ideology embedded in the very foundation of the sway-backed house. The home that she finds with the blacksmith manifests the prospect of "owning" (and "sharing") blackness itself.

"The Sway-Backed House" is typical of much of the fiction that Chesnutt published at the turn of the century and casts considerable doubt upon interpretations of *The House behind the Cedars* that view it as endorsing the concept of blood. Chesnutt's advocacy of miscegenation in his "Future American" series acknowledges that the legal version of blood endows it with biological significance, but "The Sway-Backed House" suggests that he saw that version as a fictional construct. Thus, his suggestion that amalgamation would solve the problem of racism must be read in light of his belief that racial distinctions were creatures of law rather than nature. In fact, the argument he makes in the "Future American" pieces can be seen as a recognition of his own professional imperatives; rather than attacking the concept of blood from a privileged position outside the legal discourse that defines it, he employs that very discourse to undermine its exclusionary assumptions. This is also the method that lies beneath his fiction. By excavating the postbellum legal history of African Americans, he sought to identify the failures of Reconstruction and, at the same time, to locate and redefine the place of race in relation to the firmly entrenched discourse of property rights in the United States.

Race and Property: The House behind the Cedars

"How much would it be *worth* to a young man entering upon the practice of law, to be regarded as a *white* man rather than a colored one?" (quoted in Kurland and Casper 35). This question, posed by Tourgée's *Plessy* brief, was calculated to appeal both to the justices' own legal backgrounds and to an image of the African American community entering upon the pursuit of equality and civil rights.[5] Yet it would have also had a very personal resonance for Chesnutt, who knew Tourgée and may well have been familiar with the details of his brief.[6] After being admitted to the Ohio bar in 1897, Chesnutt had taken a position with a Cleveland law firm, but was eventually forced to focus his attention on stenography. Although his skin was light enough for him to pass — an option he had flirted with briefly when he was seventeen and that would have undoubtedly helped him achieve his professional goals — he ultimately chose to affirm his black heritage. His alter ego in *The House behind the Cedars*, however, takes the path the author eschewed. Having decided to become a lawyer, John Warwick (born John Walden) leaves his home town of Patesville, North Carolina, to achieve his goal by passing for white in neighboring South Carolina. He assumes the management of a large plantation (which includes slaves among its assets) and, marrying the daughter of the plantation's proprietor, eventually succeeds to ownership. Only then does he begin to practice law, implying that his success as a lawyer has been contingent upon his acquisition of property — more particularly, his establishment of a title to whiteness. Warwick's career affirms the merit of Tourgée's argument in *Plessy* and reflects the terms of racial acquisition articulated by Justice Brown's opinion — terms that Chesnutt had been unwilling to endorse through his own experience.[7]

The novel treats passing as a metaphor for the relationship between race and property; by manipulating reputation, it transforms the abstraction of white genealogy into a legally cognizable ownership interest. Chesnutt thereby highlights the legal narrative that lies concealed within the conventions of the novel of passing. His strategic use of the term "blood" throughout *The House behind the Cedars* furthers this goal, and it is no accident that he uses it most frequently in connection with the frame of mind of his lawyer, Warwick. Thus, his description of Warwick's decision to pass explicitly invokes it: "The blood of his white fathers, the heirs of the ages, cried out for its own, and after the manner of that blood set about getting the object of its desire" (109). "Blood" in this passage is both subject and object, possession and desire; conceived of as genealogical inheritance, it already exists within him, but as property it is as yet unrealized. The tournament that he attends in South Carolina with his sister, Rena, enacts the terms by which one becomes "lawfully entitled" to whiteness; it constitutes an elaborate social ritual meant to affirm blood as objective essence — a kind of Platonic ideal — even while it implicitly rests upon the shadow of reputation.[8] Rena's "title" to whiteness is confirmed when George Tryon crowns her "Queen of Love and Beauty," but the name by which she chooses to be known — "Rowena," from Walter Scott's *Ivanhoe* — reveals the fictional nature of blood. While Scott's "fair" Rowena is Saxon — her blood untainted by that of the corrupt Norman conquerors — Rena's appearance is more like Scott's dark-eyed Jewess, Rebecca. Warwick's name is taken from Bulwer-Lytton's *The Last of the Barons*, which, like Scott's novel, celebrates a precapitalistic past in which identity was rooted in genealogy. The use of these novels not only uncovers the social constructions that undergird legal definitions of race, but also reveals the extent to which such constructions formed a part of the cultural capital of whiteness — a narrative inheritance passed down by myth and encoded into the ostensibly objective and rational language of the law. Chesnutt wryly notes that the modern version of the tournament — modeled on the medieval one in Scott's novel — is "bloodless" (*House* 31). Its celebration of whiteness is simply a glorification of social dominance disguised as genealogy.[9]

Despite the fact that blood could never be more than a metaphor for something that did not in fact exist, the metaphor was needed to form an ideological property line around the concept of whiteness. As Cheryl Harris notes, "'blood' was no more objective than that which the law dismissed as subjective and unreliable." Among the assumptions it rested upon were that racial backgrounds had been accurately reported in the past and "that racial purity actually existed in the United States" (1714). Although courts charged with ferreting out racial backgrounds rarely questioned such assumptions, in practice their reliance on evidence grounded in appearance and reputation tacitly acknowledged that a scientific determination of race was impossible. Thus, the fiction of blood operated as an abstract ideal, a form of truth that could be known only through the mediation of physical and social signs. Yet the very concept had been developed precisely to anchor whiteness in something more objective and tangible. As Eva Saks notes about litigation over miscegenation laws, courts were "caught in an epistemological loop"; seeking "an authoritative legal representation of race," they were "led right back to social codes based on appearance, which was where the problem had begun" (58).

If the tournament in *The House behind the Cedars* highlights this "epistemological loop," Chesnutt's choice of South Carolina as the site of Warwick's and Rena's passing does so even more. Warwick's decision to move to South Carolina rather than staying in North Carolina or traveling to another Southern state is based on South Carolina's construction of whiteness and blackness — the state line embodies the color line, with all its attendant contradictions. Warwick's legal mentor, Judge Straight, informs him that the color line is more flexibly drawn in South Carolina than elsewhere in the South, and he reads from a South Carolina legal decision holding that race "is a question for the jury to decide by reputation, by reception into society, and by their exercise of the privileges of the white man, as well as by admixture of blood" (114). The case is actually a composite of two South Carolina cases; Chesnutt had quoted both in an 1889 article entitled "What is a White Man?" in which he surveyed various state laws defining the distinction between white and black with the clear purpose of exposing the arbitrary nature of racial categorization. His use of them in *The House behind the Cedars* reveals the tautology of blood; Warwick considers himself to be of white blood and therefore legally entitled to the privileges of whiteness, yet the only way he can gain the legal status of a white man is by exercising the privileges of whiteness first. Chesnutt's point is not simply that racial categories present a "chicken or the egg" problem (Which comes first, whiteness or the reputation for whiteness?), but that the very idea of race simultaneously incorporates both the idea of blood and the idea of reputation. The South Carolina decisions assert a belief in the existence of "African" and "European" blood, but at the same time implicitly acknowledge the constructed nature of whiteness. One of these decisions, in a portion not quoted by Chesnutt, states that "it may be well and proper, that a man of worth, honesty, industry and respectability, should have the rank of a white man, while a vagabond of the same degree of blood should be confined to the inferior caste" (*State v. Cantey* 616). Whiteness, in the court's formulation, is in part a kind of reward for good character and productivity, a legal acknowledgement of "worth, honesty, industry and respectability." The concept of whiteness thus transcended the biological boundaries of blood, tacitly incorporating reputation into its legal formulation. Its status as property, however, was still dependent upon its fictional construction as a creation of nature rather than law.

Indeed, it was precisely this identification with nature that endowed the concept of property with such far-reaching authority in nineteenth-century America — an authority that was remarkably resistant to professional efforts to reconfigure it. Although a new generation of legal thinkers, led by Oliver Wendell Holmes Jr., was beginning to imagine property as a mutable legal tool subject to redefinition according to public policy, orthodox legal thought on this subject still reigned supreme at the time Chesnutt was composing his fiction. That orthodoxy, defined by a liberal philosophical tradition traceable back to John Locke, also involved a particular reading of Lockean precepts — a reading that ossified the meaning of property in a way that confirmed the solidity of racial hierarchies. It is possible, of course, to see Chesnutt's treatment of whiteness as a capitulation to that interpretive tradition rather than as a critique of it. After all, if property is conceived of as a natural right, the protection of which is the chief end of government, then his presentation of whiteness as property might be read as validating its legal recognition, and thus its privileged position in the American system of caste. But Chesnutt employs Locke's defense of the institution of private property in a way that undermines the legal construction of race. Creating a property interest in whiteness, he suggests, transgresses the foundational principle of Locke's theory of property — namely, that individuals have a property right in their own persons. For Locke, this notion forms the basis of all owner-ship; he conceives of property as the creation of value through the appli-cation of labor to the state of nature, and ownership of the self is a pre-condition to the ownership of one's labor. This is the element of liberal thought that decisions such as *Plessy* craftily avoided, but which Chesnutt is quick to highlight. Although Warwick thinks of whiteness as his "in-alienable birthright," the fact that he marries into it suggests that it is not a category of selfhood, but of social status.

Moreover, Chesnutt's entire plot is constructed around his characters' attempts to recover value lost as a result of the Civil War. The postbellum creation of whiteness as property, he suggests, is grounded in a nostalgic effort to recapture the status relations that existed prior to the war. Just as the institution of slavery denied blacks the ability to own their persons or their labor, so the tacit recognition of a property interest in whiteness seeks to reinstitute that denial through the legal manipulation of private property.[10] The theme of lost value emerges initially when Warwick en-ters the house behind the cedars after his long absence and finds the fire-place screen decorated with Confederate banknotes. The detail sets the tone for the rest of the novel. The banknotes recall the extent to which the property of Southern whites had dissipated in the wake of the war, not only in the form of lost slaves but depressed land values and defaulted loan obligations as well.[11] As Chesnutt notes, "Few (whites) had anything left but land, and land without slaves to work it was a drug in the mar-ket." Tryon knows Warwick only because he has hired him to represent his interests in the settlement of his grandfather's estate, and his precar-ious financial situation is summed up by his friend, Dr. Green, who states that Tryon has "Lots of land, and plenty of money, if he is ever able to collect it" (91, 90). By pursuing a claim upon his grandfather's estate, Tryon seeks to realize value built during the antebellum era, when his family had been large slaveholders. Chesnutt structures his narrative in such a way that Tryon's attempts to collect on antebellum legal claims and his desire to marry Rena are mutually exclusive goals. Thus, Tryon also seeks to recover on an antebellum note given by Duncan McSwayne in his family's favor — a note that takes him to Patesville at the very time that Rena is there visiting her mother. Juxtaposing Tryon's attempt to profit on an antebellum financial transaction and his discovery of Rena's racial identity, Chesnutt reveals the extent to which Tryon's marriage to Rena is inconsistent with his attempts to restore his family's lost assets. This opposition suggests that the assets represented by the note are in fact tied to whiteness itself. Furthermore, immediately after finding out about Rena's secret, Tryon learns from Judge Straight that the legal claim on the note is sound and that the judge "had discovered property from which . . . the amount might be realized." And later, reconsidering his rejection of Rena, Tryon feels drawn toward Patesville by "an attraction stronger than the whole amount of Duncan McSwayne's note" (95, 138). Chesnutt suggests that he must choose one or the other. To marry Rena would be to undermine the property interest in whiteness that forms the basis for his family's postbellum economic recovery.

Such narrative strategies highlight the link between whiteness as legally sanctioned ownership and whiteness as legally sanctioned mastery. Far from defending its status as property, Chesnutt reveals that whiteness is grounded in constructions of race that look nostalgically back to the days of slavery, and that such constructions fly in the face of a conception of property based upon free labor. Furthermore, his depiction of the legal efforts that Tryon makes to restore his family's property specifically implicates the law in this process. Like the legislatures that instituted Black Codes in various Southern states after the Civil War, and like those that passed Jim Crow legislation later in the century, Tryon seeks to reinstitute white supremacy through legal means that are ostensibly nondiscriminatory. And just as Judge Straight, despite his good heart, is unable to successfully intervene in these efforts, federal courts eventually relinquished their own authority over the issue of race in the South.

The Right to Whiteness

Although both Rena and Warwick participate in the ritual celebration of whiteness that forms the basis of the South Carolina tournament, Warwick's renunciation of a black identity is a sacrifice that Rena is less willing to make. The distinction that Chesnutt draws between his two characters poses an unsettling question in an age dominated by Washington's philosophy of racial "uplift": To what extent is black ownership possible when the very terms of property acquisition incorporate an affirmation of whiteness? Warwick's success in the role of "owner" depends upon the extent to which his identity is defined by his white heritage. Rena, however, not only remains attached to their mother, by whom both siblings received their "black blood," but also continues to place faith in such African American folk beliefs as the predictive power of dreams. The fact that these two qualities lead directly to George Tryon's discovery of her identity, and thereby to the "loss" of her whiteness and all of its material benefits, suggests that Chesnutt saw the black self as an entity precluded from the kind of ownership available to the white self. As in "The Sway-Backed House," the attempt to acknowledge an identity grounded in blackness leads to dispossession (in the story the attempt is Solomon's; in *The House behind the Cedars* it is Rena's). Blackness, these works imply, constitutes a kind of legal disability, making African American title either to the self or to other forms of property unstable and insecure.

The house behind the cedars itself stands as a symbol of the conflicts inherent in the concept of black ownership. Located in an African American section of town, it maintains its own distinctness by being secluded from the street by its trees. Molly Walden, its owner and the mother of Warwick and Rena, sets herself above her black neighbors because of her own white heritage, although she is not white enough to pass. Whiteness for her is a kind of "paradise" from which she is shut out, though she likes "to see the glow of the celestial city" (107). Unable to claim whiteness by right, as Warwick claims to do, she maintains a sense of privilege through her exercise of the prerogatives of ownership. Thus, although she allows dark-skinned neighbors such as Frank Fowler into her house when they can be of use to her (Frank reads the letters she receives from Warwick and Rena), she excludes them from participating in such social events as the party she throws for Jeff Wain. Only mulattos are invited to the event, and Frank Fowler is left to view the proceedings from the piazza outside. One of the songs played at this party had also been played at the South Carolina tournament, thereby establishing a connection between Molly's title to her house and the title to whiteness that the tournament seeks to ratify. The former is but a lesser variant of the latter.

Molly thinks of her house as something that separates her from her darker neighbors. Nonetheless, Chesnutt's presentation of the manner in which she acquired title suggests that her ownership is more representative than she imagines. Her father had been a free black man of considerable success in the antebellum era. Possessing both property and, to some extent, rights, he reflected the possibility of black autonomy through ownership and equal citizenship. "In an evil hour," however, "he indorsed a note for a white man who, in a moment of financial hardship, clapped his colored neighbor on the back and called him brother" (105). After the father was called upon to pay the obligation, the family began a descent into poverty. Their hardships eventually led Molly to serve as mistress for a wealthy white man, who bestowed upon her his title to the house behind the cedars. The terms Chesnutt employs in describing her feelings of guilt reveal the true nature of the relationship; having come from a family of "old issue free negroes," she "did not have the slave's excuse" for engaging in sexual relations with a white man (104, 106). By invoking the specter of rape, the novel exposes the extent to which Molly's relationship, though voluntary in one sense, mirrored that of many white masters and female slaves. Molly receives something tangible for her sexual submission, but Chesnutt wonders whether the value received was worth the price. While white ownership seems to bestow autonomy upon the owner, the form of ownership that Molly's house embodies rests upon a loss of African American freedom and self-determination.

Although Molly puts herself into a kind of bondage, Chesnutt makes it clear that her decision is largely dictated by a system of economic relations centered not around ownership, but around white ownership. Consequently, her father's very success also contains the seeds of the family's misfortune, as his wealth requires participation in a market in which he is not an equal player. Molly eventually regains the family's lost status as holders of property, yet it is evident that she is more "owned" than "owner." White ownership is mastery, Chesnutt implies, but black ownership — at least on white terms — constitutes another form of slavery.

The House behind the Cedars suggests that racial hierarchies pervade the very concept of property in the United States. But while Chesnutt advocated the pursuit of civil rights as one way of addressing such imbalances, his advocacy was tempered by his knowledge of the history of Reconstruction legal reforms. By setting his novel "a few years after the Civil War" — or roughly the time of the Fourteenth Amendment's ratification in 1868 — Chesnutt invites us to consider it in light of this history (*House* 1). Accordingly, he presents Warwick's passing not only as a way of acquiring property, but of exercising rights as well: "Once persuaded that he had certain rights, or ought to have them, by virtue of the laws of nature, in defiance of the customs of mankind, he had promptly sought to enjoy them" (53–54). For Chesnutt, possessing rights is a way of possessing the self, but true self-ownership within the American legal system requires a form of title that rights alone cannot grant.[12] The rights Warwick imagines he has "by virtue of the laws of nature" are grounded in his white blood and therefore not possessed by blacks and whites equally. Chesnutt's use of a natural rights discourse that has its roots in the philosophy of John Locke and that formed a cornerstone of the Declaration of Independence is ironic; Warwick seeks not to assert that "all men are created equal," but that he is a member of a rightfully privileged — and propertied — race.

The blending of rights into caste privilege that Warwick's perspective embodies constituted a major obstacle to African American attempts to reimagine themselves in the wake of slavery. Joel Williamson has asserted that standards based in whiteness pervaded black culture during the Reconstruction era. Consequently, although "there was a positive pride in blackness," many freed slaves saw emancipation largely as "the freedom they needed to be more like whites" (49, 47). This feeling, of course, was grounded in the pervasive belief that "Anglo-Saxon" culture represented the zenith of civilized life, and that African Americans would now be free to "rise" to that level. Yet the ideology of Anglo-Saxonism also depended upon being able to identify and subjugate "inferior" races; Anglo-Saxons were natural masters. While ostensibly egalitarian, the "possessive individualism" that lay beneath the discourse of rights incorporated this racial hierarchy, with the result that many newly constituted black citizens viewed exercising the rights granted by the Civil War amendments not only as an assertion of equality, but also as a claim to the unequal privileges previously associated with whiteness.[13]

Chesnutt's presentation of passing reflects this paradox. When Judge Straight informs Warwick, upon hearing that he wants to practice law, that a lawyer is "everybody's servant," Warwick replies, "And everybody's master, sir" (110). His decision to pass is closely tied to his desire to practice law, and the exchange reveals his conflation of rights and privileges. Warwick's early career spent managing a slave plantation manifests his view that rights constitute the public sanction accorded to the exercise of mastery. But Chesnutt presents this perspective as part of a larger pattern as well; thus, Rena succumbs to similar feelings. After she assumes her new identity as Rowena and takes up residence in Warwick's house, the narrator informs us that "Here, for the first time in her life, she was mistress, and tasted the sweets of power" (43). Both characters mirror the tension present in Reconstruction legal reforms that ostensibly granted African Americans legal equality, but operated to legitimate the power relations that made the categories of "white" and "black" possible in the first place.[14] Chesnutt's point is not that the Civil War amendments inherently incorporated racial subordination, but that the interpretations given them were perverted from the start by racialized conceptions of ownership. As a result, their capacity for constituting equal citizens out of individuals previously enslaved turned out to be weaker than most African Americans had initially believed. The self-ownership granted by the Fourteenth Amendment's grant of citizenship was incomplete without whiteness, which consequently became the unstated ideal behind prevalent conceptions of rights in the aftermath of the Civil War.

Chesnutt's recognition of the problematic nature of black ownership and civil rights is particularly evident in the collection of short stories he published just prior to *The House behind the Cedars*. In *The Wife of His Youth and Other Stories of the Color Line*, he presents a series of characters, primarily of mixed racial ancestry, struggling to come to grips with the consequences of their heritage. Most of the stories included in the book were written during the 1890s, the period when Chesnutt was working on various versions of what would ultimately become *The House behind the Cedars*. As Robert P. Sedlack has shown, Chesnutt's first version of the novel was a short story entitled "Rena Walden," which he completed in 1891. He continued to work on the story throughout the decade, eventually expanding it and changing its focus considerably. The genesis of the novel, along with its color line theme, suggests a direct connection with the stories in *The Wife of His Youth*. Two pieces in particular from that collection — "Uncle Wellington's Wives" and "The Web of Circumstance" — address the manner in which whiteness complicates the black pursuit of both rights and property, thereby shedding light on Chesnutt's treatment of that issue in his longer work.

"Uncle Wellington's Wives" constitutes one of Chesnutt's most incisive treatments of the interaction among race, property, and rights. The narrative focuses on a mulatto man from Patesville who decides to go north to experience what he believes is "an ideal state of social equality." He imagines the North as "a land flowing with milk and honey, — a land peopled by noble men and beautiful women, among whom colored men and women moved with the ease and grace of acknowledged right" ("Uncle" 206, 207). Not doubting the assertions of a lecturer who states that racial intermarriage in the North is common, he decides to leave the woman he married during slavery to find a white wife. Uncle Wellington's rosy preconception about life in the North is formed by blending visions of wealth, whiteness, and rights into a harmonious whole. Chesnutt's narrator, however, has the benefit of hindsight and bitterly counters Uncle Wellington's naïveté by referring to the promise of equal rights as a "delusion" (204). Speaking from the jaded perspective of the 1890s, his more experienced voice casts doubt upon the entire Reconstruction effort at legal reform and links the "delusion" of legal equality to the celebration of whiteness in which African Americans such as Uncle Wellington participated. Although Uncle Wellington accomplishes his goal of marrying a white woman, the two are forced to move out of their predominantly white neighborhood and into a predominantly black one. He then loses his job as a coachman and, eventually, his white wife as well. His emphasis on the exercise of legal rights has by this time changed dramatically: "Liberty, equality, privileges, — all were but as dust in the balance when weighed against his longing for old scenes and faces" (252). He returns to Patesville in the hopes that his former wife, Milly, will take him back. Chesnutt does not reveal Milly's response to his reappearance, but suggests that she still loves him enough to forgive his transgressions.

As a story of Reconstruction legal reform, "Uncle Wellington's Wives" might be interpreted in at least two ways. In one reading, Chesnutt places blame on Uncle Wellington for misconstruing the nature of equal rights by imagining them as means of obtaining wealth, privilege, and "social equality" in the white world.[15] But while he presents his protagonist as a somewhat lazy man who lacks the solid good sense of his Southern wife, Chesnutt also makes it clear that Uncle Wellington has no access to any other view of rights. Having been a slave, exercising rights for him means assuming the place of master. Thus, in another reading, Uncle Wellington's interpretation of his rights is the only one available: if equal rights signify equal access to property, blacks can now aspire to become masters. But Uncle Wellington senses that the property he needs most is whiteness itself. Like Warwick, he attempts to marry into it, only to find its possession tenuous and unstable.

The story that concludes *The Wife of His Youth* suggests that Chesnutt's perspective was closer to that of the second reading than the first. In "The Web of Circumstance," a successful blacksmith named Ben Davis is arrested for stealing the riding whip of Colonel Thornton, a wealthy white man. Having commented on its elegance and looked at it "longingly," Davis is easily framed by his young mulatto employee, who has designs on his light-skinned wife. A successful black man who pays off the mortgage on his house just before being arrested, Davis celebrates the idea of African American property ownership. He tells a group of friends, "We colored folks never had no chance ter git nothin' befo' de wah, but ef eve'y nigger in dis town had a tuck keer er his money sence de wah, like I has, an' bought as much lan' as I has, de niggers might 'a' got half de lan' by dis time" ("Web" 293). He suggests that they stop wasting money on useless things that just "put money in w'ite folks pockets," and that they use it to build houses instead. His words, however, come back to haunt him at his trial, where the prosecutor calls him "a man whose views of property are prejudicial to the welfare of society, and who has been heard to assert that half the property which is owned in this country has been stolen, and that, if justice were done, the white people ought to divide up the land with the negroes" (298). After being convicted and serving five years in prison, he returns home to find that his wife has died, his son has gone to jail, and his house has been sold to pay debts. Holding Colonel Thornton responsible for his misfortunes, he goes to his house with the intention of killing him, but, seeing his young daughter and imagining her as "a little white angel," he changes his mind. Davis is himself killed when the colonel mistakenly thinks he is about to attack the girl.

Like "Uncle Wellington's Wives," "The Web of Circumstance" highlights the entanglement of property, whiteness, and rights. Davis's philosophy, like Booker T. Washington's, makes equality contingent upon property ownership, but Chesnutt shows that property ownership is not complete without the possession of whiteness as well. Thus, Davis's wealth relative to most blacks in the area does not save him. In fact, Chesnutt implies, it makes him a target by encouraging his employee to frame him and by making him a threat to whites. The prosecutor's characterization of him as a "communist" is, of course, a fiction (298). Davis threatens white dominance by employing the very instrumentality by which he had previously been enslaved — private property.[16] On the one hand, his ownership implicates a kind of black nationalism, as he expresses a desire to see black ownership increase in general. On the other hand, however, his success is partly gained by coveting the trappings of whiteness. Chesnutt's choice of a whip as the object of his undoing is no accident; as one of the primary symbols of white dominance during slavery, the whip embodies the kind of mastery that Davis hopes blacks can achieve through ownership.[17] Like Warwick, Rena, and Uncle Wellington, Davis can conceive of rights only by equating them with the privileges of whiteness; but without the requisite reputation as a white man, his plans are doomed from the start. Consequently, the "little white angel" serves as both savior and executioner; Davis's worship of whiteness in the form of the young girl spares him from the criminality that many whites at the end of the nineteenth century saw as an inherent trait among African Americans, but Chesnutt makes it clear that he worships a form of status from which he will be forever excluded.

Taken together, "Uncle Wellington's Wives" and "The Web of Circumstance" provide a perspective that says much about Chesnutt's use of passing in *The House behind the Cedars*. In addition to exposing whiteness as a form of property, the passing motif allows Chesnutt to underscore the extent to which property was a form of whiteness. Furthermore, it reveals that the rights that had been granted blacks by the Civil War amendments were significantly diluted by interpretations that left a property interest in whiteness intact. Although the amendments were meant to make African Americans owners of their own persons, there was still a kind of title that they could never hold. As "The Web of Circumstance" makes clear, other forms of property ownership could not replace that which blacks were excluded from, and the right to acquire property was therefore a right to aspire to — but never attain — the status of whiteness.

Thus, the limitations of legal discourse, and not "time and nature," account for what Donald B. Gibson calls the novel's "fatalism and pessimism." (*Politics* 136).[18] In *The Marrow of Tradition* and *The Colonel's Dream*, Chesnutt would explore these limitations further. The latter novel emphatically asserts that the entanglement of race and property is systemic and cannot be addressed on an individual basis. It depicts a reconstructed Southerner who returns south to infuse the social and economic system with his own "enlightened" capital. His property, however, simply enmeshes him in a web of relations that, much to his consternation, turn him into a new form of master. Yet the law for Chesnutt is not wholly a deterministic mechanism; as Sundquist notes, it is also "a discursive field charged with ideological ambiguity" — ambiguity that suggests its possibilities as well as its limitations (430). In *The Marrow of Tradition*, for instance, it is not the law itself that leads to the disfranchisement documented by the novel, but white disregard for the law.[19] Chesnutt's perception and use of the law's inherent ambiguity distinguishes his professional perspective from the rigidly defined legal absolutism exemplified by Justice Henry Billings Brown. Even at his most pessimistic, Chesnutt does not construct the mutually exclusive relation between blackness and property as natural or inevitable. He does, however, present it as a very real (if unacknowledged) aspect of contemporary racial formulations, as well as an authoritative way of inscribing those formulations into the language of the law.

Such deficiencies in contemporary modes of legal discourse help to explain Chesnutt's decision to end *The House behind the Cedars* with the tragic death of his heroine. Rena's acquisition of a temporary title to whiteness fixes her to a version of selfhood grounded in property rights, even after she resumes a "black" existence, and she is therefore doomed when defined by a form of blood that cannot be legally owned. Thus, when traveling with Jeff Wain to the town where she will take up the Washingtonian task of teaching grade school, she admires a "large white house" behind which lie "extensive fields of cotton and waving corn" (154). Having heard that Wain is a man of property, she assumes the house is his, but Chesnutt later tells us that it belongs to the Tryons. The house owned by Wain — her mulatto suitor who takes pride in being mistaken for white — not only lacks the splendor of the Tryons' house; it is also "mortgaged to the limit of its security value" (165). Rena's desire for the privileged form of ownership represented by the Tryon plantation reveals her inability to assume ownership of an African American self. Having valorized whiteness as a form of legal title, both she and Wain have "mortgaged" the value they might have found in their common black heritage. Yet the novel also wonders skeptically if ownership of an African American self is ever possible. Warwick, the only successful "black" owner in the novel, founds his identity on a complete renunciation of blackness. Taken together, the respective "success" and "failure" of Warwick and Rena expose the concealed realm within the legal discourse of property and rights where self-ownership and white privilege merge, and where "black ownership" becomes oxymoronic.

Houses and Homes: Owning Blackness

The female protagonists of *The House behind the Cedars* and "The Sway-Backed House" represent two sides of the same coin. The trial of racial identity that each undergoes may lead to either salvation or catastrophe, and Chesnutt's publication of the two narratives in the same year reveals his own uncertainty about which outcome was more likely. But while from a legal perspective these alternatives represent possibilities that, for the author, had not yet been decided, from a literary point of view the two endings are somewhat overdetermined. Both story and novel resolve themselves into genres already well established and easily recognizable by the turn of the century: the domestic novel of courtship and marriage and the tragic mulatta tale. Although these literary modes differed in the trajectories they mapped out for their heroines, they were both informed by a domestic ideology that sought to assert what Jane Tompkins has termed "sentimental power"— a form of authority grounded in the ethical and religious values associated with the home and distinct from the more worldly (and corrupt) authority of politics and law (Tompkins 122). Employing the domestic discourse of sentimentalism, Chesnutt offers a critique of the law from an alternative cultural space — a space that he invokes explicitly in the novel when he distinguishes Warwick's reliance upon rights from Rena's concern with "the domain of sentiment" (51). Nonetheless, the author never fully relinquishes his legal perspective; the home is for him as much a proprietary concept as it is a domestic ideal. Straddling the discourses of law and domesticity, his fiction struggles to articulate the terms by which legal transformation can take place, not to abandon the concept of ownership but to reconstitute its meaning through narrative.

Chesnutt's use of sentimental conventions drawn from the marriage plot of domestic fiction and the seduction plot of the tragic mulatta story reveals the extent to which he sought not only to identify a relationship between race and property, but to alter the nature of that relationship. His fiction, in fact, challenges definitions of literary realism that rest upon its rejection of sentimental conventions — a definition that Kenneth W. Warren has recently reasserted in his *Black and White Strangers: Race and American Literary Realism*. Warren argues that the constraints of realism prevented its practitioners from articulating in fiction the kind of progressive racial beliefs that they espoused outside of it, and that they inadvertently served the interests of racists by discrediting sentimentalism, a mode that Warren associates with "the political idealism of the New England tradition" (15). But it is significant that Warren's treatment excludes Chesnutt altogether, despite the fact that Howells promoted his work and considered him a literary ally (at least until the publication of *The Marrow of Tradition*). If we accept Warren's view that realists saw their fiction as "an instrument for altering social relations," then Chesnutt's property-oriented critique of race makes him a realist indeed. Like Howells, Chesnutt "locates the very vitality of art in its responsiveness to humanity's material needs," and it is for precisely this purpose that he engages the legal plane (Warren 72, 49). Rather than rejecting sentimentalism, however, his fiction attempts to translate it into terms cognizable within the distinctly material (and hence "realistic") world of the law. For Chesnutt, "the domain of sentiment" is no less legal than the domain of civil rights.[20]

This amalgamation of literary conventions suggests that we read Ches-

nutt's novel as a point of intersection between the fields of law and literature. While the social and material concerns of realism enable it to treat
legal issues in positivistic terms (or from within the law's own structure
and logic), the more idealistic bent of sentimentalism allows for a critique of law on ethical or religious grounds. The use of sentimental conventions in a novel such as *Uncle Tom's Cabin* implies that the province of
literature is necessarily removed from that of the law, and thereby provides the writer with an outsider's perspective. But Chesnutt's fiction alters such a configuration by suggesting that, just as realism and sentimentalism are not, in practice, wholly separable, neither are the spheres
of law and literature. If the sentimental tradition often highlights transcendent values that lie "outside" the law's internally constructed forms
and procedures, Chesnutt reveals the extent to which that "outside" can
also be seen as an essential component of the "inside" structure of legal
institutions. He articulates this connection in *The House behind the Cedars*
by emphasizing the fictive nature of passing — an act that creates simultaneously a narrative and a legally enforceable property interest. But although Warwick's and Rena's actions, like the novel itself, partake of both
the legal and the literary, their fictions nonetheless differ from Chesnutt's. The form of property that the two characters seek to author is, to
Chesnutt, a "house of cards" (*House* 45). Their passing accommodates —
and thereby confirms — the legal standards that create a property interest in whiteness, while Chesnutt's novel seeks to transform those standards by infusing them with a literary sensibility drawn from sentimental
fiction. At the same time, that sensibility is itself transformed through its
adaptation to the "realistic" demands of legal discourse.

Max Weber's discussion of "formally rational" and "substantively rational" legal systems sheds light on Chesnutt's form of literary interven-
tionism. For Weber, formally rational systems seek to subsume any given
fact situation under rules already articulated, and to reach a conclusion
based on the logical operation of those rules. Substantively rational systems, on the other hand, take into consideration such things as "ethical
imperatives" and "political maxims," and look not to maintain the integrity of rules but to "enact substantive justice in concrete cases for concrete individuals" (64, 355). Although Weber associated formal rationality with Western legal systems and substantive rationality with systems
such as the Islamic institution of the Khadi, he felt that no culture employed only one of these models in a "pure" state. Moreover, both institutional modes are often invoked by those who seek to challenge the le-

gal or political status quo, since formally rational systems present an egalitarian face to the world through their impersonality — their apparent disregard for class distinctions — while substantially rational ones allow for a form of justice that is intuitive, not bound by convention, precedent, or tradition. The concept of "title," of course, makes sense only within a formally rational system, but as Weber noted, property ownership is often challenged on substantively rational grounds:

> The propertyless classes in particular are not served, in the way in which the bourgeois are, by formal 'legal equality' and 'calculable' adjudication and administration. The propertyless demand that law and administration serve the equalization of economic and social opportunities vis-à-vis the propertied classes, and judges or administrators cannot perform this function unless they assume the substantively ethical and hence nonformalistic character of the Khadi. The rational course of justice and administration is interfered with not only by every form of 'popular justice,' which is little concerned with rational norms and reasons, but also by every type of intensive influencing of the course of administration by 'public opinion,' that is, in a mass democracy, that communal activity which is born of irrational 'feelings' and which is normally instigated or guided by party leaders or the press. (355–56)

Chesnutt's fiction reflects the quandary that Weber described. On the one hand, it reveals that the formal equality granted by the Fourteenth Amendment lacks substantive content because the legal establishment of a property interest in whiteness simply reestablishes the inequities that had existed prior to the war. The *Plessy* case provided him with a perfect example of this, as the Court rested its decision on the purely formal ground that the statute in question provided for "equal" accommodations, and refused to consider the substantive content of this particular form of "equality." On the other hand, however, Chesnutt was reluctant to relinquish the concepts of property and rights altogether, recognizing that they could also serve to undermine status distinctions grounded in blood. His use of sentimentalism constitutes an appeal to a kind of substantive rationality that he sees as immanent in the formal precepts of the Civil War amendments themselves. If Hopkins uses sentimentalism as a character template — a way to make her black figures cognizable as legal subjects — Chesnutt employs it as a mode of analysis intended to bridge the gap between the law's form and substance. The goal is the same in both cases: a revised version of the "official" African American. Moreover, Chesnutt's negotiation of form and substance, like Hopkins's invocation of genteel models of the self, is perfectly in keeping with the ideology of professionalism — an ideology that each author calls upon to challenge outmoded and oppressive forms of legal orthodoxy.

Chesnutt's manipulation of the sentimental marriage plot for reformist purposes is particularly apparent in "The Partners," a short story that appeared a year after *The House behind the Cedars*. The narrative focuses on two former slaves who try to pool their resources in the difficult times following emancipation. They draw up an agreement that reads,

> William Cain and Rufus Green is gone in partners this day to work at whatever their hands find to do. What they makes shall belong to one as much as the other, and they shall stand by each other in sickness and health, in good luck and in bad, till death shall us part, and the Lord have mercy on our souls. Amen. ("Partners" 254)

Part contract, part marriage vow, and part prayer, the agreement articulates a form of ownership grounded in shared identity rather than individual achievement. But when the two seek to purchase land from a tract that a Northern philanthropist has been selling to freedmen for nominal sums, their agreement gets in the way; "Learning that they lived in what they called partnership, he informed them that such a relation was incompatible with the development of self-reliance and strength of character, and that their best interests would be promoted by their learning each to fight his own battle" (254). The partners, therefore, buy separate but adjoining tracts of land, on which William flourishes while attempting to be of assistance to the struggling Rufus. The two grow apart and, when William accidentally floods a portion of his friend's land, the latter files suit against him. Rufus's pettiness comes back to haunt him, however, as a surveyor he hires in connection with the suit (whose slaveholding family had originally owned the land) finds out that his title is faulty and purchases it himself. The surveyor wins in court against Rufus but, on the day Rufus is to move, William comes to his assistance by telling him that his own lawyer can win an appeal. He reaffirms the domestic bond of their partnership agreement, stating "I've got money in de bank, an' w'at's mine is yo'n till yo' troubles is ended, an' f'm dis time fo'th we is podners 'till death shall us part" (260).

The story is particularly noteworthy for its reading of property rights in light of the history of Reconstruction efforts at land reform. As the Civil

War was winding down, many freed slaves were given tracts of land to farm from the plantations confiscated by the army, with the informal understanding, at least on their part, that it would be theirs to keep. In the Sea Islands of South Carolina, William Tecumseh Sherman's Field Order 15, issued in January of 1865, established a reservation for freed slaves, with each family receiving forty acres of land. Further efforts to distribute land to former slaves were initiated by members of Congress and other Union generals, including General Rufus Saxton, whom Eric Foner calls the "most dedicated of all to the idea of black landownership" (158). In June of 1865, Saxton announced his plan to use property under control of the Freedmen's Bureau to establish forty-acre homesteads. Chesnutt's decision to name his two protagonists William and Rufus identifies the story as a parable of the promise of black ownership through land reform.

Of course, such efforts at reform ultimately failed, as Andrew Johnson vetoed bills granting further land rights to freed slaves and, finally, ordered that land already placed in the hands of freedmen be restored to its original white owners. The story dramatizes this dispossession, revealing the extent to which black ownership was subject to arbitrary redefinition. Furthermore, Chesnutt shows that the terms of ownership themselves — the only terms by which any form of title to property can be obtained — are dictated by white interests. The communal ownership contemplated by the two partners is inconsistent with the individualized form of ownership required by whites, but conforming to the white model ultimately leads to black dispossession. Like *The House behind the Cedars*, the story implies that the very structure of the legal regime supporting private property in the United States is linked to the protection of whiteness and the negation of blackness as an equal form of racial capital.

Nonetheless, the partners' "marriage" significantly mitigates the destructive effects of property on racial identity and solidarity. Unlike his friend T. Thomas Fortune, Chesnutt did not adopt socialism as an answer to the United States' race problem.[21] Thus, rather than looking toward a coming revolution leading to the elimination of private property, the ending of "The Partners" foresees a legal restoration of Rufus's title — a restoration made possible by imbuing the formally rational notion of "title" with substantive content. The operation of the partnership agreement, the story suggests, will cause the law to recognize that which it had not before — not by directly affecting the terms of Rufus's landownership, but by constituting his ownership of blackness. The agreement endows the partners' shared heritage with the status of property by virtue of the tangible benefits it creates in the form of mutual support and shared profits, and this status will in turn make it cognizable in the eyes of the law. Unlike their title to land, however, their title to blackness is communal — the agreement establishes a kind of domestic union. The two partners will continue to be individual landowners after Rufus's title is restored (a prospect that William does not doubt), but the property line separating their respective tracts will not be mirrored in their personal relations. "The Partners" thereby posits a form of property that can be possessed only relationally and that, unlike whiteness, loses its value when located in the individual alone.[22] The same dynamic is at work in "The Sway-Backed House," in which Isabella loses her inheritance and breaks her engagement with Professor Revels, but gains both a marriage and a home with the blacksmith, and in "Uncle Wellington's Wives," in which Uncle Wellington first renounces and then reaffirms his marriage to Milly. In each of these stories, a "marriage" that had disintegrated is finally restored in a new form, and this restoration acts as a metaphor for the recovery of an African American selfhood that can be "owned" only by being "shared."

Chesnutt's critique of the law never leads him to abandon faith in its redemptive potential. Presenting the legal sphere as the receptacle of competing cultural narratives rather than as a monolithic entity with a single definable ideological function, his fiction seeks not so much to invoke norms that transcend that sphere as to reveal the latent possibilities within it. In this respect, he followed the lead of Frederick Douglass who, fifty years earlier, abandoned the moralistic disunionism of William Lloyd Garrison in favor of an approach to abolition that emphasized its consistency with constitutional principles (Chesnutt praised this aspect of Douglass's career in his 1899 biography of the black leader).[23] Sentimental literary conventions were a tool in Chesnutt's efforts; he enlisted them as a means of asserting legal principles now hidden beneath seemingly authoritative interpretations and to advise his readers that such "official" precepts — unlike the Mosaic Law — are not written in stone.

The internal struggle that Tryon experiences for much of the latter portion of *The House behind the Cedars* reflects this legalistic form of idealism.[24] At once the agony of the sentimental lover and the competition of conflicting legal standards, Tryon's dilemma is framed in terms that have ramifications within the rhetoric of the law as well as that of domestic fiction: "He was fighting a battle in which a susceptible heart and a reasonable mind had locked horns in a well-nigh hopeless conflict. Rea-

son, common-sense, the instinctive ready-made judgments of his training and environment,—the deep-seated prejudices of race and caste,—
commanded him to dismiss Rena from his thoughts. His stubborn heart
simply would not let go" (129). Linking reason and instinct with environment rather than nature, Chesnutt presents them as contingent phe-
nomena, socially constructed rather than fixed and absolute. Tryon eventually resolves his conflict by concluding that "Custom was tyranny. Love
was the only law" (194). The implication is that reason and instinct are
functions of custom, and that by abandoning custom Tryon enters a realm
where "the heart" holds sway — Rena's "domain of sentiment." Chesnutt's formulation of his dilemma, therefore, pits "reason," "instinct,"
and "custom" against "love" and "the heart."

Custom, of course, was the watchword of the conservative sociological jurisprudence of the late nineteenth century, a perspective embodied
in William Graham Sumner's assertion that "constitutional government
can never overcome the mores" (Sumner 87). Under this view, legal authority was solely dependent upon the extent to which the law enacted
principles that conformed with established custom — conceived of as an
essentially autonomous and natural realm removed from the influence of
law and politics. The Supreme Court's opinion in *Plessy* had made use of
this perspective, asserting that "If one race be inferior to the other socially, the Constitution of the United States cannot put them upon the
same plane." [25] Although the Louisiana legislature had already interfered
with the self-contained operation of the social sphere by passing its separate car legislation in the first place, the Court justified this intervention
on the grounds of its "reasonableness," a standard that incorporated "the
established usages, customs and traditions of the people" (*Plessy* 552,
550). Custom in *Plessy* functioned as an analogue to blood, securing title
to the white self by naturalizing racial distinctions (through an appeal to
"reason" and "instinct") and contributing to the establishment of Horwitz's "property right to an unchanging (that is, segregated) world."

Chesnutt's novel seeks to combat the stagnation inherent in the
Court's model of legal authority, to articulate a version of law that does
not simply recodify racial privileges as property rights. Yet Tryon's quixotic invocation of "love" as "the only law" is not the answer. Tryon imagines an escape from the stifling limitations of legal discourse; he hopes to
enter a "domain of sentiment" in which the terms of ownership dictated
by the domain of law no longer apply. His conception of marriage appeals to the transcendent authority that Tompkins associates with do-

mestic fiction, envisioning a world in which "the heart" can replace legal standards and emerge itself as "law." Chesnutt's form of idealism, on the other hand, refutes the distinction that his character draws between the domains of sentiment and law, and Tryon's failed attempt to abandon the latter in favor of the former reveals this map of the cultural terrain to be fatally flawed. Unlike Rena's and Tryon's version of sentiment, Chesnutt's has distinctly legal dimensions. As Rena notes — correctly — after Tryon abandons her, "The law would have let him marry me"; having established her reputation as a white woman, their marriage would not have constituted miscegenation under South Carolina law. Tryon's willingness to step outside the law — to overlook Rena's black heritage for the sake of "love" — offers a solution to the "race problem" grounded not in the "value" of blackness, but in its invisibility, and therefore constitutes no solution at all. The futility of his final declaration of the power of love stems from his inability to see the legal dimensions of sentiment, to find in it a potential source of legal transformation. Lying outside the legal domain, Tryon's starry-eyed rhetoric exemplifies the kind of answer to racism that, the novel suggests, will always be belated.

While Chesnutt would agree with Tryon's statement that "Custom is tyranny," he would disagree with the conclusion that such a realization makes it any less "law"; the law's mechanisms of oppression possess a "reality" for the author that no amount of idealism can fully counter. Nonetheless, by appealing to the domestic sensibility of his readership — by retelling the tragic mulatta story as a narrative of legal dispossession — he both exposes what is lost within a racist system of property relations and leaves open the possibility of legal transformation through a redefinition of what it means to be an "owner." Chesnutt's use of the tragic mulatta genre serves his purpose well; he genders blackness female to reveal post–Civil War legal history as a story of seduction and betrayal, in which yielding to the lures of whiteness (couched enticingly in terms of property and rights) leads inevitably to a loss of "home" in the form of racial identity.[26] The very tragedy of Rena's downward spiral invokes a meaning of "home" that is more expansive than a definition grounded in the right to exclude. Rena's death is tragic precisely because it should have been possible for her — like Isabella in "The Sway-Backed House" — to find a "home" in blackness, to forge an African American identity in which title to the self is also a title to race, and in which self-ownership does not preclude the possibility that all may "share and share alike." If the logic of possessive individualism ultimately operates to perpetuate white privilege, Chesnutt's property interest in blackness might be termed a kind of possessive communalism: a form of racial solidarity that balances the legal and economic "values" of whiteness and blackness and that implicitly claims equal citizenship for African Americans precisely because of — rather than in spite of — their race. Although neither Rena nor Tryon is able to reimagine marriage and home on such terms, those terms nonetheless permeate Chesnutt's novel as unrealized possibilities. Thus, the fatalism of the tragic mulatta plot of *The House behind the Cedars* turns out to be illusory. The novel acknowledges the bleak condition of the legal status of African Americans at the turn of the century, yet its appeal to domesticity keeps alive an alternative vision of "home," even as it recounts the law's failure to make that vision a reality.

Chesnutt's use of the domestic ideology of sentimental genres throughout his turn-of-the-century fiction underscores his literary commitment to engage and alter the self-contained and essentially conservative discourse of the law. In an 1880 journal entry, he wrote that "The Negro's part [in overcoming discrimination] is to prepare himself for recognition and equality, and it is the province of literature to open the way for him to get it — to accustom the public mind to the idea; to lead people out, step by step, to the desired state of feeling" (quoted in Helen Chesnutt 21). The "province of literature," here, sounds very much like the province of the law. That he perceived this literary project in quasilegal terms is even more clear in a 1903 letter to Booker T. Washington in which, disagreeing with Washington's program, he asserted, "We are directly concerned with the interests of some millions of American citizens of more or less mixed descent, whose rights are fixed by the Constitution of the United States, nor am I ready yet to accept the conclusion that those constitutional rights are mere waste paper. The Supreme Court may assent to their nullification, but we should not accept its findings as conclusive. . . . There is still the court of public opinion to which we may appeal" (quoted in Helen Chesnutt 195). Chesnutt bases his claim to civil rights on the Constitution, not on the higher law, and those rights, he suggests, have substance only in the minds — and hearts — of individuals. His fiction seeks to "lead people to the desired state of feeling," and to thereby supplement — without replacing — a discourse grounded in property and rights with one based in sentiment. Appealing to "the court of public opinion" — a concept charged with both formal and substantive rationality — Chesnutt hopes to build narratives more durable than Solomon's sway-backed house, narratives that move toward establishing the terms of a legal regime that valorizes the boundary lines of property and rights, but, in recognizing the "value" of blackness as well as of whiteness, effectively erases those of race.

Such "heartfelt" efforts notwithstanding, however, the conflicts inherent in imagining blackness as an "ownable" quantity ultimately remain unresolved in Chesnutt's fiction. The conclusion of "The Partners," for instance, suggests that the legal system will restore Rufus's title in his land and, at the same time, that the two partners will resume a "marriage" based upon communal rather than individual ownership. In other words, their reliance on a legal regime built around private property, including a property in whiteness, will not prevent them from feeling the emotional bonds that result from their common heritage of blackness. But while the agreement that William reaffirms at the story's conclusion reasserts the value of blackness in their own eyes, the story can look only to an unrepresented future for the restoration of Rufus's title that will fulfill the promise of a solid and secure form of black ownership. "The Sway-Backed House" and "Uncle Wellington's Wives" also seek to imagine forms of title that are free from insidious and divisive racial constructions, but neither Isabella's entrance into the blacksmith's house nor Milly's acceptance of Uncle Wellington are explicitly depicted. Although the tragedy of *The House behind the Cedars* is not replicated in the stories, the failure that Rena's death represents must be seen as a prospect that hovers ominously over the unrepresented futures of the shorter works. The sentimental transformation of the law's racial discourse exists as possibility only — unrealized, and perhaps even unlikely, yet nonetheless present as a subversive element in the very terms deployed to justify racial inequities.

The "unfinished" nature of these texts points to the dilemma in which African American professionals such as Chesnutt found themselves at the turn of the century. Unwilling to view racial distinctions in terms of class conflict by embracing socialism, but equally averse to affirming a system in which whiteness constituted a legitimate form of capital, they sought to find and promote the measurable "value" in blackness. Authorized by professional credos requiring the mediation of form and substance, "inside" and "outside," Chesnutt's fiction — like Isabella's choice of husbands — manifests the delicate "balance" his endeavor involved. If the legal underpinnings of American capitalism remained unchallenged in his work, it was largely because of his steadfast refusal to posit a world not based, in some form, on the idea of ownership. Chesnutt's endorsement of private property relations was hardly unequivocal — indeed, it was fraught with misgivings — yet the author nonetheless held out hope for a truly meaningful form of black ownership. Presenting the color line as a kind of property line — and in part accepting this formulation — Chesnutt's swaybacked texts sag precariously beneath the weight of the racialized forms of title they compellingly bring to light.

CHAPTER 5

Privacy and Subjectivity in
Edith Wharton's The House of Mirth

What is one's personality, detached from that of the friends with whom fate happens to have linked one?
    Edith Wharton, A Backward Glance

The pivotal moment of Edith Wharton's *The House of Mirth* (1905) occurs during Lily Bart's second visit to Lawrence Selden's flat. Having decided to use Bertha Dorset's love letters to Selden as ammunition to redeem her own social standing, Lily finds herself passing by Selden's building and is drawn to his "quiet room." The flat seems a kind of domestic retreat to Lily; during her earlier visit it had struck her as "part of the outer world," but "now the shaded lamps and the warm hearth, detaching it from the gathering darkness of the street, gave it a sweeter touch of intimacy." The sense of privacy it conveys evokes a desire to reveal her true self to Selden, to make him "see her wholly for once, before they parted" (*House* 304, 305, 307). Yet the lawyer never does "see her wholly," and neither do the novel's readers. Although Lily's consciousness forms the subject of intense scrutiny throughout much of the work, the subjective process that leads her to change her mind — to burn the instruments of her salvation — remains opaque, and even the act itself is filtered through the "tranced" perception of Selden, who "hardly noticed the gesture" (310). The scene condenses the novel's drama of subjectivity into a few brief pages; Lily's desire to reveal herself and Selden's inability to interpret her signs form the backbone of their tortured relationship and highlight the fact that their minds never fully meet. Moreover, the shifts in the work's narrative point of view — the periodic intrusion of Selden's limited perspective — lead to a similar dynamic between Lily and the reader; just when we think we are getting to know "the real Lily Bart," Wharton discards her authorial omniscience and withholds from us central elements of Lily's consciousness. "Intimacy" seems no more possible between Lily and the reader than it does between Lily and Selden.

But Wharton is not simply being coy, for her narrative strategy has much to do with the obstacles inherent in representing female subjectivity at the turn of the century. As Gillian Brown has persuasively argued, the home served as a model for the inner self in nineteenth-century America by figuring a private space in which a "masculine selfhood" grounded in possessive individualism could exist removed from the public pressures of the marketplace (Brown 2). What Brown's analysis does not tell us, however, is that the home was an appropriate model for the subject because of its unitary nature; although the home was composed of husband and wife, the wife's consignment to the domestic sphere made her thoroughly "knowable" as object, while the husband's ownership of the home signified his existence outside of its bounds, and hence his ability to know without, in turn, being known.[1] The home thereby authorized a (male) self that was private without being insular. By placing ownership at the center of the fully realized subject, domestic ideology manifested the logic by which the subjective could serve as an essential component of selfhood yet maintain a connection to an objective, material universe. Nonetheless, it could do so only by denying that women possessed inner lives comparable to those possessed by men.

The power of the home to harmonize oppositions made it useful in grounding legal as well as domestic versions of subjectivity, and it thus emerged as an especially important element in late nineteenth- and early twentieth-century debates over the existence of a right to privacy. The argument for such a right arose ostensibly out of increasing outrage at the intrusiveness of the press, but its more fundamental concern was with the viability of the law's possessive, rights-bearing subject. The language of rights derives its authority from the liberal conception of selfhood — a conception whose emphasis on self-ownership and autonomy comes dangerously close to affirming a kind of radical subjectivism, yet whose rationalist assumptions presuppose the universal nature of truth and knowledge. The home helped to resolve this tension, functioning as a metaphor for what might be termed the ideal legal subject; by imaging a form of ownership that allowed for both privacy (subjectivity, autonomy) and knowledge (reason, objectivity, universality), it brought the seemingly irreconcilable values of liberalism together under one roof, as it were. Relying heavily on a domestic vocabulary, the legal discourse of privacy sought at once to fortify the bounds of the self and to contain the threat to the law's authority that an insular and solipsistic version of subjectivity seemed to pose. Consequently, when Samuel Warren and Louis Brandeis articulated their famous 1890 argument in favor of a right to privacy, they used the idiom of property relations to link individual "personality" to the sanctity of the home, thus gendering "personality" as male. Yet legal actions testing their theory were often brought by women — a development that challenged not only the domestic model of privacy and subjectivity, but the validity of the ideal legal subject. Furthermore, arguments in favor of women's rights were frequently couched in terms that suggested the need to "divorce" the concept of privacy from its moorings in the home. Such arguments threatened to create an autonomous female subject whose very existence would transform the home — and the law itself — from a realm of unity and knowledge to one of duality and uncertainty.

The House of Mirth situates its heroine within this field of combat, recording the extent to which her consciousness both reflects and struggles against dominant discourses of privacy and subjectivity. Fluctuating between dreams of marriage and equally strong impulses to maintain her independence, her inner turmoil marks the threat that the notion of female privacy posed to the concept of "personality," while Selden's dogged insistence on uncovering "the real Lily Bart" associates him with the model of unity and knowledge upon which "personality" hinged. Wharton invokes the law's version of that model not only through Selden's occupation, but also through the legal language of her narration and, even more emphatically, through the letters in Lily's possession. The letters, after all, constitute the essential elements in George Dorset's plan to divorce Bertha (New York allowed divorce only for adultery), and their status as both evidence and property connects them to a positivistic epistemology grounded in a gendered legal subject. Lily's act of destruction, however, denies them their evidentiary weight and places her own motives beyond the pale of Selden's decidedly legal cognition. The novel highlights this illegible element at the core of Lily's self, exposing the fragile nature of the system that constructed the "private" female subject as a form of public property.

Wharton endows Lily with a complex inner life and, in the process, testifies to a form of female subjectivity that domestic and legal discourse would deny. Yet in exhibiting the respect for Lily's privacy that Selden does not, she also significantly complicates the terms of her own authorship. The shifts in the novel's narrative perspective reflect Wharton's desire to depict the richly subjective existence of her female protagonist and, at the same time, her awareness of the consequences of such depiction — namely, its potential to reaffirm the form of "knowledge" that she strives to denounce.[2] Her attempts to negotiate this dilemma in *The House of Mirth* raise questions not only about the gendered premises that lie beneath institutional forms of authority, but also about the role of literary representation in valorizing those premises. Ultimately refusing to expose her heroine to the unimpeded gaze of her readers, Wharton suggests that the "real Lily" may be unrepresentable, that she may defy the legal, domestic, and literary parameters of "personality" altogether. Viewed from this perspective, Lily's tragic death begins to look less like a case of victimization and more like Wharton's own act of evidentiary destruction, preserving her character's privacy by ensuring that the reader, like Selden, never does "see her wholly."

Ownership and the Right to Privacy

Like Charles Chesnutt, Wharton recognized the way in which conceptions of property rights in America tend to translate into conceptions of selfhood. In the antebellum era, the limitations applied to female property ownership (such as the doctrine of coverture that prohibited married women from controlling property they had possessed before marriage) had helped construct a public version of female identity that denied women any claim to personal autonomy. Although they began to achieve greater control over property after the Civil War thanks to such legal reforms as married women's property acts, by the early twentieth century women were still subject to a gendered discourse of property rights in which owning was imagined as a masculine prerogative that they could only mimic, and rather poorly at that. The female self lacked the requisite self-ownership that would make title to physical things an outward expression of individual power and depth. Again and again in her early works, Wharton highlights the extent to which her female characters are deprived of the ability to construct forms of identity that are truly possessory — that function as bounded spaces in which the self can define itself on its own terms, denying the "rights" others might assert to interfere.

Thus, property and privacy are intimately connected in Wharton's works. Her early novella, *The Touchstone* (1900), for instance, explores this connection by focusing on the publication of love letters written by a famous author, Margaret Aubyn. The man to whom they were written,

Glennard, had not returned her love and agrees to publish the letters after her death as a way of earning enough money to marry his intended wife. His justification for doing so is that Mrs. Aubyn's "name had so long been public property" that there could be no issue of personal privacy involved. As one reader asserts after reading the letters, however, "It's the woman's soul, absolutely torn up by the roots — her whole self laid bare" (*Touchstone* 5, 45). Tormented by his decision, as well as by his attempt to conceal his involvement from his wife, Glennard finally realizes that the ordeal has given him a new sense of respect for the depth of Mrs. Aubyn's private life, and he comes to love her in a way he could not while she was alive. Wharton's story places a woman's privacy — indeed her very "soul" — at the mercy of a man who sees her only as "public property," thereby exposing the tenuousness of female privacy and self-ownership. The public is only too happy to consume Mrs. Aubyn's "soul," and Wharton suggests that the "souls" of all women may be subject to the same fate.

The House of Mirth returns to similar ground, but with greater attention to the legal meanings attached to property and privacy. While the two concepts possess a moral weight in *The Touchstone* that makes them foundational and self-explanatory, Wharton's later work delves into the social construction of those terms in a way that casts doubt on their transcendent significance. The very genre of the novel of manners is ideally suited to this kind of critique, and Wharton's use of it undermines the notion that property is something we are born with (a Lockean principle) and that privacy exists within every home and every mind. Instead, property and privacy are constructed in the novel through an elaborate system of social codes, conventions, and narratives, rendering concepts such as ownership and even individual subjectivity amenable to redefinition depending on the current configuration of norms and power relations. Moreover, these standards operate with the force of law, and Wharton is quick to point out throughout the novel that Lily Bart is essentially on trial. The novel of manners, of course, is a perfect vehicle for presenting a Holmesian vision of the law as an ever-changing mixture of politics, morality, economics, and brute force; the "inside" norms of Wharton's New York seem actuated by nothing "outside" the thoroughly contingent and always temporary narratives that help define the social world of her characters. Yet it is just as true that embedded within the genre is an assumption that there *is* indeed an "outside" — a space from which the author writes in which those beliefs that look so foundational to the work's characters appear without their transcendent aura. Wharton's approach to the literary geography of the novel of manners, however, complicates her own position as authorial "outsider"; while she is more than willing to undermine the most cherished tenets of the New York social world her novel critiques, she also constructs her own narrative in a way that places herself within the circle. Rather than offering a narrative that is "truer" than those that destroy Lily Bart, she constructs one that emphasizes its own contingency. Her method, therefore, employs a professional logic requiring that "truth" be mediated by the established rules and conventions governing its production. At the same time, however, she employs those rules and conventions in a manner that points her readers to a form of "knowledge" that she cannot fully reveal. Property and privacy may be socially constructed concepts for Wharton, but what they serve as signifiers for — the self — possesses a reality she can invoke only by silence.

Wharton's concern with property and privacy in *The House of Mirth* need not, in itself, direct our attention to the law. Yet the novel's central conflicts — organized around terms that are both domestic ("home," "marriage") and legal ("rights," "ownership," "personality") — closely resemble those at the heart of legal debates over privacy at the turn of the century, and this likeness suggests that the law serves as one of the discourses structuring Wharton's narrative. It also points toward the seminal 1890 article written by Warren and Brandeis as a starting place for excavating the work's legal context. The argument advanced by the two lawyers in favor of a right to privacy affirmed a subtle connection between domesticity and legal authority, relying heavily upon the image of the home to bolster its persuasive power. Although it posited the existence of an "inviolable personality" that inhered in each individual, this space within the self was unimaginable without recourse to a similar space within American culture. Maintaining that the home itself was under attack from the forces of publicity, they decried the way in which "Instantaneous photographs and newspaper enterprise have invaded the sacred precincts of private and domestic life," and argued that the "idle gossip" of newspapers requires a ruthless "intrusion upon the domestic circle" (Warren and Brandeis 205, 195, 196). By defining "personality" in domestic terms, they inflected it with masculine qualities. Despite taking pains to emphasize that a legal right to privacy need not be grounded in ownership, they nonetheless likened the "inviolability" of the self to the "impregnability" of property rights, and thereby implicitly constructed the "domestic circle" as a realm within the exclusive control of men. Thus, they concluded their essay by asserting, "The common law has always recognized a man's house as his castle, impregnable often, even to its own officers engaged in the execution of its commands. Shall the courts thus close the front entrance to constituted authority, and open wide the back door to idle or prurient curiosity?" (220).[3]

The willingness of Warren and Brandeis to fall back on the language of property, while at the same time asserting a distinction between privacy rights and property rights, underscores the delicate balance they sought to strike. Employing the image of the home as the most powerful cultural symbol of seclusion and retreat, they also needed it to ground the "personality"— to embody a subject whose "inviolability" did not imply solipsism. As a realm of ownership as well as of privacy, the inner self could be envisioned within a framework in which subject was never without object, and owner never without property. In an essay on reputation and privacy that appeared in the same year as the article by Warren and Brandeis, E. L. Godkin employed a similar logic:

> [The] recognition by law and custom of a man's house as his *tutissimum refugium*, his place of repose, is but the outward and visible sign of the law's respect for his personality as an individual, for that kingdom of the mind, that inner world of personal thought and feeling in which every man passes a great deal of time. The right to decide how much . . . of his own private doings and affairs, and those of his family living under his roof, the public at large shall have, is as much one of his natural rights as his right to decide how he shall eat and drink, what he shall wear, and in what manner he shall pass his leisure hours. (65)

For Godkin, the house is an appropriate figure for the "kingdom of the mind" because it is ruled by a unified subject. The male owner has the right to decide not only how much to reveal about himself, but also how much will be revealed about his family as well. The right to privacy threatened to create a world of "inviolable personalities" endlessly colliding with one another, and Warren, Brandeis, and Godkin sought to counter that threat by anchoring privacy in the epistemological order of the patriarchal family.[4]

At the turn of the century, of course, that epistemology was being challenged rigorously by advocates of women's rights. In her famous address entitled "Solitude of Self," for instance, Elizabeth Cady Stanton asserted that "In discussing the rights of woman, we are to consider, first, what belongs to her as an individual, in a world of her own, the arbiter of her own destiny, an imaginary Robinson Crusoe with her woman Friday on a solitary island" (325). Stanton's metaphor imbued rights with epistemological significance; they served to constitute individuals as self-contained entities inhabiting subjectivities construed as "worlds" and "islands." Just as Helen Hunt Jackson grounds her argument for Indian rights and national sovereignty in the notion that Indians are in fact aliens, Stanton invoked principles that were both legal and extralegal — her version of female consciousness exempted women from legal control while simultaneously constructing them as rights-holders. Unlike Warren, Brandeis, and Godkin, however, she made no effort to ground subjectivity in material referents, arguing instead for legal recognition of the essentially unknowable nature of female as well as male consciousness. Charlotte Perkins Gilman, in her 1903 work entitled *The Home*, sought to achieve similar ends by deconstructing "the filmy fiction of the privacy of the home" (*Home* 45). Maintaining that no family members — male or female — have any privacy at home, she nonetheless emphasized the psychic loss to women of this state: "The mother — poor invaded soul — finds even the bathroom door no bar to hammering little hands. From parlour to kitchen, from cellar to garret, she is at the mercy of children, servants, tradesmen, and callers. So chased and trodden is she that the very idea of privacy is lost to her mind; she never had any, she doesn't know what it is, and she cannot understand why her husband should wish to have any 're-serves,' any place or time, any thought or feeling, with which she may not make free" (40). Gilman imagined "the mother" as a woman who lacks subjectivity entirely, whose environment is so "invaded" by others that she has no inner life she can truly call her own. She "cannot understand" her husband, whose dual existence within and without the domestic sphere endows him with a private sense of self that she lacks. Warren and Brandeis had defined their right to privacy as "the right to be let alone" (205), but no such right could possibly exist for women within the intrusively communal environment pictured by Gilman. Much of Gilman's writing attempted to redefine the home on new grounds, but these efforts also involved redefining the structure of female consciousness; she sought to fortify it against "invaders" and, in so doing, to make it as inaccessible as the form of consciousness possessed by men.[5]

The differences between the positions of Warren, Brandeis, and Godkin on the one hand, and Stanton and Gilman on the other, expose the stakes involved in formulating a right to privacy at the turn of the century. By seeking to endow women with a form of privacy grounded in self-ownership, female reformers threatened to disrupt the cognitive foundations of male subjectivity. Such a transformation would also challenge the law's claim to epistemological authority; American law in the late nineteenth century came to rely increasingly on a rights discourse that required its own subjectivism to be grounded by the concept of ownership; without such "objective" means of distinguishing between adverse interests, all rights would indeed be "equal" and the very notion of rights, in essence, rendered meaningless. In 1883, the attorney Charles Savage noted that there was an "irresistible movement" in the development of family law "in the direction of the most perfect legal equality of the married partners, consistent with family unity" (quoted in Keller 469).[6] His qualifier, of course, virtually destroys the assertion it qualifies. Applying the liberal model of rights to women raised the specter of a world composed of owning subjects without any objects to be owned. A space whose privacy was impregnable yet whose unity was grounded in the perfect harmony of subject and object, the home countered this threat, imaging the ideal legal subject in a way that made rights intelligible and imbued them with force.[7]

Given the gendered meanings of privacy during this era, it was only fitting that one of the central cases addressing the right to privacy should involve the unauthorized publication of a woman's image. In 1902, the New York Court of Appeals (the state's highest court) decided the case of *Roberson v. Rochester Folding Box Co.*, and its decision was widely noted in both law reviews and the popular press.[8] The plaintiff in the case was a young single woman (the action was filed on her behalf by a guardian ad litem) named Abigail Roberson, whose picture appeared, without her consent, on printed advertisements for flour milled by the Franklin Mills Company. Above the lithographic print of her image were the words "Flour of the Family." Conceding that the likeness was an accurate one, the plaintiff did not claim that her property interest in her reputation was damaged — a claim that would have fallen under libel law. Instead, she maintained that publication of the image violated her right to privacy, and that she had suffered "great distress" by virtue of the "scoffs and jeers" of those who saw it and recognized her face. In a close decision, the court denied her claim, rejecting the arguments raised in the article by Warren and Brandeis and refusing to recognize a common law right to privacy. Since "the subject-matter of the jurisdiction of a court of equity is civil property," Chief Justice Parker asserted in his opinion for the majority, the plaintiff's claim of injury stemming from invasion of an "inviolable personality" was not legally cognizable (*Roberson* 446).

What is especially noteworthy about the decision is the court's mystification over why Abigail Roberson had filed suit in the first place. Noting that "the likeness is said to be a very good one," Parker's opinion summarized the plaintiff's claims of mental distress by dismissing them: "Such publicity, which some find agreeable, is to plaintiff very distasteful, and thus, because of defendants' impertinence in using her picture . . . she has been caused to suffer mental distress where others would have appreciated the compliment to their beauty implied in the selection of the picture for such purposes" (442, 443). For Parker, there was no inconsistency in identifying a woman as a domestic ideal — the "flower of the family" — and yet publishing her image on an advertisement posted in "stores, warehouses, saloons, and other public places" (442). Between the lines of his opinion lies the assumption that the female self is public rather than private, and that defamation law governing injury to reputation is the only protection that women need, or in most cases, desire.

Although the exact nature of Abigail Roberson's "distress" remains a mystery, it is conceivable that her sense of domesticity generated something more personal than a public persona. Acknowledging this possibility, the dissenting opinion refused to assume "that the plaintiff's complaint is fanciful, or that her alleged injury is purely a sentimental one." Yet its claim that "if her face or her portraiture has a value, it is hers exclusively, until the use be granted away to the public," reveals its inability to frame her "distress" in a manner that did not associate it with an injury to property (449). Her concern, of course, may indeed have been motivated by a sense of diminished value. As a single woman, her beauty was an asset that could lead to an advantageous marriage, and its indiscriminate publication may well have affected its value in the eyes of potential suitors. It is equally plausible, however, that in publicly exposing her as the epitome of domesticity, the advertisement also destroyed the possibility that she might actually achieve the ideal her picture represented. The true "flower of the family," after all, shrinks from the public eye, or presents herself in public only in the most morally discriminating manner. In this interpretation of the plaintiff's "distress," what was lost in the translation of "flower" into "flour" was the very core of her sense of self, the privacy that (theoretically) accompanied domesticity and that served as the only available model of female subjectivity.

The *Roberson* decision reveals how tenuous that model was and helps to explain the need felt by reformers to ground female privacy and subjectivity in rights. It also exposes the cognitive assumptions that lay beneath the construction of privacy in the article by Warren and Brandeis and the essay by Godkin. Unable to take full possession of a self defined by domesticity, women inhabited a realm — ostensibly private but, for them, primarily public — in which reputation established the bounds of identity and made the female subject available to male consciousness. While the *Roberson* court sought to fortify this system by denying the existence of a right to privacy, its attempt revealed the fragile nature of the structure it hoped to protect. The court's inability to account for Abigail Roberson's "distress" exposed the law's version of the female subject as incomplete, and pointed toward the menacing possibility that lurking beneath the transparent clarity of women's domestic identities were "personalities" that were just as "inviolable" as those possessed by men.

Risking Reputation: Lily Bart

At first glance, Abigail Roberson and Lily Bart would seem to have little in common. Lily, of course, relishes her existence in the public eye and recoils from the prospect of being sheltered and concealed from view. Yet the terms of her self-exposure must be her own. The form of selfhood she seeks to achieve through carefully measured publicity is just as "private" as that which Abigail Roberson sought to protect by preventing publication of her image. Lily views herself as a kind of artist whose ability to manipulate conventions and appearances presupposes a certain distance from them; her sociability points toward a selfhood not defined by publicity, but in which subjectivity becomes possible through the control she exerts over her own public image. Like Abigail Roberson, Lily loses control over the terms of her self-exposure, and thereby faces the possibility of *being* her reputation rather than *owning* it.

Lily's lack of self-ownership is directly related to her unmarried status. For women in the novel, being married constitutes a form of capital, not only by facilitating access to their husbands' bank accounts but also by shielding them from the uncertainties of reputation. Possessing a seal of domestic virtue that mere suspicions cannot undo, their status renders them as impervious to "talk" as to the vicissitudes of chance (the married women always seem to win at cards). But such is not the case with Lily. At the mercy of the public gaze, Lily's being lacks the kind of safe haven that marriage provides, and Wharton employs a property discourse throughout the novel to communicate this state of uncertainty. Thus, during her first visit to Selden's flat, she notes, "How delicious to have a place like this all to one's self! What a miserable thing it is to be a woman" (7).

While it is clear that Lily is partly joking, it becomes equally clear during the course of the novel that Wharton is not; Lily's increasingly desperate straits stem largely from her inability to possess herself fully. The "assured possessorship" with which Lily had entered into society has disappeared by the time the novel opens, leaving her "struggling for a foothold on the broad space which had once seemed her own." Her mother had treated her beauty as "the last asset in their fortunes," keeping watch over it "as though it were her own property and Lily merely its custodian," and this lack of ownership leads Lily to feel like "a mere pensioner on the splendor that had once seemed to belong to her" (38, 34, 26). Her eventual disinheritance by Mrs. Peniston acts as a metaphor for the unpropertied condition in which she finds herself throughout the novel.

This concern with the terms of female self-ownership manifests itself in Wharton's insistent use of the language of finance. As Walter Benn Michaels has noted, Lily lives in an environment permeated by speculative activities, and she participates in these activities as much, or more, than the novel's male characters. For Michaels, her participation reveals the manner in which her selfhood is defined by market relations; she cannot imagine herself as "free" unless she can discard an oppressive sense of self-control by engaging a world of risk. Yet Wai Chee Dimock asserts that Lily's status within the market-oriented economic system of New York society is lower than that of other characters, that she ends up "paying" where others do not. These two positions place Wharton in opposite corners with respect to the economics of capitalism. For Michaels, Wharton affirms the logic of the market, while for Dimock, she seeks to articulate an escape from it — an escape that Dimock finds "aristocratic" (Dimock, "Debasing" 790).[9]

The difference between Michaels and Dimock, however, diminishes when we view the novel's financial language in legal as well as economic terms. If the form of self-ownership with which the law endowed women at the turn of the century was grounded in reputation, Lily's willingness to speculate actually represents an attempt at rebellion. The only form of capital she owns is her reputation itself — the very foundation of her legal identity — and by continually risking it she affirms it as something separate from, rather than coextensive with, the bounds of her self. Beneath the public identity on which she speculates lies a private one that, in willing such actions, is not itself put at risk. While the *Roberson* court refused to draw a distinction between *owning* reputation and *being* it, Lily's recklessness insists that there is indeed a difference. In fact, it is precisely at those moments when her reputation for domesticity is most at issue — when her marriageability is on the line — that she indulges an inner life removed from the public identity she has worked so hard to cultivate. For instance, having played the role of the quiet, demure, and pious woman that Percy Gryce seems to seek, she nonetheless finds that, on the morning she is to attend church with him, "the whole current of her mood" carries her toward spending the morning with Selden. Her feelings project outward in her subjective description of the morning: "the day was the accomplice of her mood: it was a day for impulse and truancy. The light air seemed full of powdered gold; below the dewy bloom of the lawns the woodlands blushed and smouldered, and the hills across the river swam in the molten blue. Every drop of blood in Lily's veins invited her to happiness" (58). Wharton's juxtaposition of Lily's "duty" to attend church and the effulgent inwardness of her feelings suggests the relationship between the two; the urgency she feels to project an appropriately domestic image gives rise to an inner life that asserts an equally urgent demand for privacy.

Identifying domesticity with reputation and thereby divorcing it from privacy and subjectivity, Wharton counters the flawed epistemology of the home. But she also underscores the extent to which that epistemology determines the official bounds of female selfhood, acting to define the "real" in a way that protects the integrity of both the domestic sphere and the ideal legal subject. While Wharton may or may not have been familiar with the *Roberson* case, she was unquestionably familiar with the paradigm upon which it rested; the willingness of New York society to accept the rumors about Lily's unchaste life as truth reproduces the cognitive assumptions behind Justice Parker's opinion, and the language Wharton uses to describe the decline of Lily's reputation situates her novel within a decidedly legal universe. After suffering the public humiliation of Bertha's accusations in Europe, Lily returns home to find that "all the actors and witnesses in the miserable drama . . . had preceded her with their version of the case; and, even had she seen the least chance of gaining a hearing for her own . . . she knew it was not by explanations and counter-charges that she could ever hope to recover her lost standing" (227). Lily's "case" has been decided without her own testimony and in accordance with a version of reality grounded in reputation. Merging the language of the stage and the language of the trial, Wharton highlights the artificial nature of the evidence against her heroine, but she also makes it clear that such evidence is nonetheless determinative. Replying to Gerty's question about what really happened in Europe, Lily states, "the truth about any girl is that once she's talked about she's done for; and the more she explains her case the worse it looks" (226). Lily's property interest in her reputation is illusory; rather than constituting her as an "owner," it leads to a loss of autonomy and subjects her to a form of knowledge that denies the evidentiary weight of her private experience.

Wharton's New York is founded upon judgment and dependent upon the ideology of domesticity to imbue its judgments with authority. It is an oppressively legal environment — so oppressive that even those, such as Selden, who attempt to distance themselves from it unwittingly reproduce its mechanisms of power. In fact, it is precisely Selden's claim to "take an objective interest in life" that connects his perception to that of the rest of New York; despite the idealism seemingly inherent in his "republic of the spirit," he is "rather fond of the law," and his judgments with respect to Lily reveal his own investment in the legal and domestic status quo (184, 68, 12). Convinced that Lily possesses an identity distinct from her public persona, he nonetheless refuses to acknowledge the possibility that such an identity may not be fully knowable, that it may, in fact, be as private as his own. In Europe, Selden hopes to "preserve his privacy" by not seeing Lily, for the "impenetrable surface" she presents challenges the epistemic assumptions upon which he relies (191). His commitment to these assumptions is particularly evident in the tableau vivant scene, in which he fails to see the "artistic" value in Lily's decision to portray Reynolds's Mrs. Lloyd and instead interprets her performance as an unveiling of "the real Lily Bart" (134, 135). While Wharton tells us that "she had selected a type so like her own that she could embody the person represented without ceasing to be herself," the irony of such a statement is evident. Reynolds's figure, besides being a married woman, is pictured in the act of inscribing "Lloyd" on the trunk of a tree — the very name proclaiming the unity of her being with that of her husband. But Lily's success is attributable precisely to her unwillingness to marry; because she does not define herself by domestic ideals, she is all the more capable of rendering them artistically. Imagining Lily's personality and that of Mrs. Lloyd merged in the tableau vivant, Selden believes he has caught a glimpse of the "reality" that lies beneath Lily's outer shell of artifice. Such "knowledge," however, requires a kind of willful blindness, a determination to look for the "reality" of female existence only through the prism of domesticity.

Judgment and Gender

Equating owning and knowing, *The House of Mirth* suggests that male subjectivity can exist only by exposing women to "the glare of publicity" (216). The home is the site that authorizes this system of relations, the place in which the unity of subject and object becomes gendered and makes possible a form of male privacy whose "inviolate" nature does not prevent its possessor from looking outward. As a result, Selden's "objectivity" signals not a detachment from the judgments of New York society, but an immersion in them. Again and again in the novel, he relies upon a combination of rumor and appearance to reach conclusions about "the real Lily Bart," and his assumption of omniscience with respect to Lily's "private" life, Wharton suggests, is connected to his own investment in a form of "knowledge" that reconciles the tensions within the ideal legal subject. Yet the novel also reveals the cracks in this structure, thereby suggesting the possibility of a "knowledge" not analogous to ownership.

In her short story "The Other Two"—published a year before *The House of Mirth*—Wharton explored this possibility explicitly. The story opens shortly after the protagonist, Waythorn, has returned home from a shortened honeymoon with his wife, Alice. Waythorn's life had been "a gray one," but his wife's "unperturbed gaiety" serves as "ballast to his somewhat unstable sensibilities" in such a way that he is willing to overlook the fact that she has been married twice before and has a daughter — Lily — by her first husband ("Other" 380, 381). The scandalous implications of her past do not bother Waythorn, since her "grievances were of such a nature to bear the inspection of the New York courts" and since he considers "a New York divorce" to be "a diploma of virtue." Waythorn's expectations for a life of domestic serenity, however, are upset when Lily becomes ill and Alice's first husband, Haskett, asserts his "right" to visit the child. To further complicate matters, Waythorn's business leads him into contact with Alice's second husband, Varick. Finding this situation "intolerable," Waythorn is disturbed by the "elasticity" with which his wife handles it, and he begins to wonder who she really is: "Alice Haskett—Alice Varick—Alice Waythorn—she had been each in turn, and had left hanging to each name a little of her privacy, a little of her personality, a little of the inmost self where the unknown god abides" (381, 393).

Wharton makes it clear that Waythorn's concern with the integrity of his wife's "privacy" and "personality" is equally a concern with his own, and even more important, with the inviolability of his property rights. Haskett's repeated visits make him seem to Waythorn "a lien upon the property," and, associating marriage with "the joy of possessorship," the property involved is simultaneously his home and his wife (392, 386). What seems at first to make his wife both ownable and knowable is her sharply defined legal status, but that status blurs as Waythorn questions the "diploma of virtue" he thought she possessed:

> It was she who had obtained the divorce, and the court had given her the child. But Waythorn knew how many ambiguities such a verdict might cover. The mere fact that Haskett retained a right over his daughter implied an unsuspected compromise. Waythorn was an idealist. He always refused to recognize unpleasant contingencies till he found himself confronted with them, and then he saw them followed by a spectral train of consequences. His next days were thus haunted, and he determined to try to lay the ghosts by conjuring them up in his wife's presence. (391)

Waythorn becomes Hawthorne in this passage, or to be more precise, he plays Young Goodman Brown to his wife's Faith. In Wharton's story, however, the certainty at issue is more legal than spiritual. The law's discourse of property and its moral claim to reward virtue and punish vice — even in divorce proceedings — function to ground Waythorn's perception, and the collapse of this structure leads to a profound inner crisis. But unlike Goodman Brown, Waythorn does not retreat into a grim and insular certainty. The story's conclusion places him in the same room with both previous husbands, an uncomfortable situation that Alice defuses by offering everyone tea, and Waythorn takes "the third cup with a laugh" (396).

The scene of communion with which Wharton ends her story suggests a transformation on Waythorn's part. Believing Alice to be officially certified as a paragon of domestic virtue, he thinks her at first the perfect object of both ownership and knowledge, and assumes that her domesticity will make possible his own form of self-possession. What he finds, however, is that she challenges the very bounds of identity that make knowledge possible. Alice's previous marriages figure a form of "privacy" grounded not in domesticity but rather in the distance between the self and the domestic role of wife.[10] Although Waythorn's crisis stems from the inaccessibility of this self, his anxiety eventually turns to irony; the "laugh" in which he indulges transforms him from Goodman Brown into Robin Molineux, relieving his "gray" disposition by sacrificing the domestic "idealism" that had prompted his marriage in the first place.

The story also highlights the relationship between identity and rights, but in drawing the connection, it simultaneously deconstructs it. Waythorn's property rights clash with Haskett's visitation rights, and neither provides the means to establish firm boundaries between individuals. Only Alice seems to draw a distinction between legal identity and personal identity, yet it is precisely this fact that renders her such a "ghostly" presence in Waythorn's life. If on one level, Waythorn is troubled by the thought that she has no "inmost self," on another his problem seems to be that she *does* in fact have one, and its name is not "Mrs. Waythorn." Wharton refuses to delineate the nature of her "real" personality, leaving both Waythorn and the reader pondering the possibility of a female subjectivity whose very existence removes it from the regime of knowledge embodied in legal and domestic discourse.

Resolving its conflicts by not resolving them, Wharton's short story seems to offer a literary alternative to such legal absolutes as truth, justice, and right. Legal discourse is a discourse of certainty, and even the subjectivism inherent in the concept of rights must situate itself within a framework that valorizes the law's claim to objectivity. This has been the case in the United States at least since Justice John Marshall articulated the principle of judicial review in *Marbury v. Madison* in 1803, but it was never more true than it was in the late nineteenth and early twentieth centuries. Responding to the growing militancy of challenges to the inequities of industrial capitalism — particularly by the burgeoning labor movement — and to the legislative reforms that accompanied those challenges, the United States Supreme Court began to read the Constitution in an increasingly conservative manner, using the concept of rights to undergird the autonomous and property-oriented nature of the Lockean liberal self. Rights became "substantive" in a way that suggested their utter impregnability, and with the Court's decision striking down a maximum hours law on the basis of "liberty of contract" in *Lochner v. New York* (1905), the era of "substantive due process" reached its peak.[11]

But if the skepticism of Wharton's short story suggests the possibility of an escape from the absolute nature of rights discourse, *The House of Mirth* — published in the same year as the decision in *Lochner* — expresses considerably less optimism. Lily's ownership of Bertha's letters figures her possession of "knowledge" and provides a means of asserting her own rights. Her decision to renounce the legal philosophy they stand for, however, leads not to communion with others in a shared sense of irony, but to self-destruction. Suspecting that Lily is in possession of the "positive proof" that he needs to divorce Bertha, George Dorset pleads with Lily, as "the only person who knows," to reveal her secrets, stating, "all I need is to be able to say definitely: 'I know this — and this — and this' — and the fight would drop." Lily responds by maintaining "I know nothing — absolutely nothing," repeating the phrase "as if it were a charm" (244, 248). While Selden insists upon deriving truth from the flimsiest of evidence, Lily does the exact opposite; she refuses to rely upon the epistemic value of her "positive proof," and thereby disowns the very knowledge that her ownership of the letters makes possible.

By denying her possession of "knowledge," Lily also renounces her "rights." When she acquires the letters from Mrs. Hafner, she thinks she has "no right to keep them" (107). She begins to change her mind, however, as she comes to understand that the "social order" of New York is also a kind of legal order:

> What debt did she owe to a social order which had condemned and banished her without trial? She had never been heard in her own defence; she was innocent of the charge on which she had been found guilty; and the irregularity of her conviction might seem to justify the use of methods as irregular in recovering her lost rights. . . . After all, half the opprobrium of such an act lies in the name attached to it. Call it blackmail and it becomes unthinkable; but explain that it injures no one, and that the rights regained by it were unjustly forfeited, and he must be a formalist indeed who can find no plea in its defence. (300)

On one level, this passage constitutes an appeal to the law's claims to justice and objectivity; Lily's "conviction" had been "irregular," and therefore not really "legal" at all. On another level, however, Wharton's metaphor implies that legal processes are always "irregular," always founded upon false claims of cognitive privilege, and that those cultural practices that assert similar claims to the "truth" partake of the same form of bad faith. Lily's ownership of the letters figures the form of self-ownership that make rights imaginable and situates her in an environment in which she "knows" rather than merely being "known." In disavowing this system she disavows her title to the self, drifting into a private oblivion in which not knowing equals not being.

This dissociation of privacy from rights undercuts one of the central tenets of turn-of-the-century feminism. Privacy and subjectivity in *The House of Mirth* do not emanate from the Crusoe-like self-possession envisioned by Stanton, but from a sense of dispossession. Lily's descent on the social scale takes her further and further away from the public world of New York society, yet the growing inwardness that accompanies this fall does not result in a corresponding level of self-definition or self-knowledge; in fact, it has just the opposite effect. Her decision to write a check to Trenor is based on not knowing whether she will have the courage to do it later, and springs from her feeling of being "something rootless and ephemeral, mere spindrift of the whirling surface of existence, without anything to which the poor little tentacles of self could cling" (319). The "real Lily" for which she searches turns out to be plural rather than singular. At the critical moment when she burns the letters she imagines herself possessing two selves, a fact that complicates her "passionate desire to be understood" and her desire that Selden "see her wholly" (306, 307). Lily's decision to use the "proof" she holds had made possible a self constituted by its tie to a legal and domestic epistemology grounded in truth, certainty, and unity, but when she renounces her legal option she relegates her existence to one of duality, and hence uncertainty. Holding Nettie Struther's baby following her last encounter with Selden, she imagines it "penetrating her . . . as though the child entered into her and became a part of herself" (316). This process of merging creates not so much a state of unity as one of boundlessness; a selfhood that is indefinable, without distinct outlines or individual traits; a personality that is violable and, as a result, ceases to be a personality at all.[12]

While Waythorn learns to live with and laugh about his uncertainty in "The Other Two," Wharton denies this option to Lily. Both novel and short story depict social environments grounded in judgment but in which the conditions that give judgment meaning are conspicuously absent. Yet *The House of Mirth* also delves into the mechanisms that prevent alternative constructions of subjectivity from being recognized and articulated.[13] Lily's refusal to "explain her case" reflects the extent to which her situation constitutes a legal problem without a legal solution. Her "personality" — like Abigail Roberson's — is what people say it is, and Wharton's novel indicates that the very systems of authority defining the bounds of the self rely upon a steadfast refusal to account for the subjective "distress" that suggests a fracture in this equation.

Disowning "Personality"

On one level, Lily's death serves to denounce a legal and social order that denies women the "inviolable personalities" possessed by men. On another, however, the novel's conclusion might be seen to offer a resolution as well as a critique of this problem — a problem that, for Wharton, is as much literary as it is legal or domestic. Lily's death is tragic, to be sure, but it also completes a process by which the narrative voice has alternately revealed and concealed the nature of "the real Lily Bart" to the reader, and these modulations indicate a relationship between the novel and the discourses it employs that is more complex than mere commentary or critique.[14] In fact, by identifying Lily's reputation as a function of "stories," the author not only casts doubt upon legal constructions of the female subject, but suggests literature's potential complicity in perpetuating them. As Rosedale tells Lily regarding the "stories" circulating about her, "they're there, and my not believing them ain't going to alter the situation" (255). "Stories," for Wharton, possess a "reality" wholly independent of their truth value, and it is in this domain of "the real" — this common epistemological ground — that literature itself becomes "legal," that it enacts versions of the truth that delimit the possibilities of selfhood. This is a Howellsian version of the public sphere — one dominated by storytellers such as Bartley Hubbard and Bertha Dorset, but possibly amenable to a more responsible form of narrative intervention. Just as Lily ponders her ability to survive outside the carefully codified world of New York high society, Wharton wonders if literary representation can ever free itself from the kinds of "facts" given reality through the force of legal and domestic discourse. Is it possible to tell a story, the novel asks, that does not affirm a form of truth grounded in gendered conceptions of subjectivity?

Despite the fact that Lily "knew herself by heart . . . and was sick of the old story," she is unable to respond when Gerty asks her for her "story" in the wake of her humiliation in Europe: "My story?" she replies, "I don't believe I know it myself" (100, 226). But Wharton knows it no better, or if she does she's not telling. Exposing the ideal legal subject as a fiction, she refuses to offer a transcendent authorial subject in its place. Thus, while she provides her reader with glimpses of what might be "the real Lily Bart," she ultimately withholds significant details of her character's consciousness and thereby posits the existence of literary truth while disavowing her own access to it. It is through this unwillingness to speak that Wharton seeks to intervene in the legal constructions of "privacy" and "personality," to disrupt the form of "knowledge" that is gendered male and that rests upon the utter transparency of female consciousness. This practice casts doubt upon Ruth Bernard Yeazell's assertion that Wharton "offers us an interior view, the privileged access to another's consciousness" and that "Consciousness in [the novel] primarily defines itself by negating the world of appearances" (731). "Appearances" are all that Selden has, and Wharton's decision to filter crucial moments of her narrative through his perception complicates the opposition Yeazell articulates. In fact, much of Lily's interiority is also a kind of exteriority: she frequently sees herself through Selden's eyes, and the result is a version of double-consciousness in which the essence of her identity is no more apparent to herself than it is to her observers — a category that includes the novel's readers.

Consequently, Lily's renunciation is Wharton's as well. The act of burning the letters preserves the concept of privacy at the expense of the concept of rights, and Wharton valorizes Lily's choice by protecting her privacy, by keeping her intentions opaque and indecipherable. Lily becomes "unknowable" in both a legal and a literary sense at exactly the same moment, a moment when there is no longer a recognizable regime of knowledge to which she subscribes and through which she can be represented or observed. Renouncing her authorial "right" to omniscience, Wharton discredits literary knowledge as much as legal knowledge, steadfastly refusing to reveal the "reality" behind the stories that constitute her characters' legal identities. Whether Lily intends to kill herself is left unresolved — the very notion of intention complicated by her fragmented identity — and the author thereby relegates "the real Lily Bart" to a realm somewhere outside the bounds of her novel.

Wharton's New York is a place that Oliver Wendell Holmes Jr. would have recognized. For Holmes, concepts such as property and rights were fluid, subject to an ongoing process of definition and redefinition by the community at large.[15] Yet he also recognized that it was in the nature of legal discourse to retain a sense of its own transcendence, to employ a "moral language" in spite of its worldly engagement with politics, expediency, and power. Rosedale is the most self-conscious legal positivist in the novel, able to see through the fictional constructs of others while still recognizing the force that such stories contain. His proposal that Lily use

Bertha's letters to redeem her social standing makes this option seem to Lily like "a transfer of property or a revision of boundary lines" and suggests a view of the world in which the "play of party politics" can replace the problems associated with "fluctuating ethical estimates" (259). By not taking Rosedale's advice, however, Lily acts in a very un-Holmesian manner. While Wharton and Holmes shared a skepticism about the law's claims to transcendent authority, Holmes accepted as inevitable that any legal regime would assert that authority to justify itself. Wharton, on the other hand, sought to expose the costs involved in treating "stories" as "truth." If Holmes imagined a legal universe in which "boundary lines" were being constantly revised, Wharton attempts to imagine a state in which the arbitrary nature of such lines leads not to their perpetual readjustment, but to their disappearance altogether. Thus, Lily renounces the fiction of "right" for a state of "no right," and in so doing commits a kind of legal suicide. Rebelling against the establishment of boundaries that are not "real," she abandons the boundaries that delineate her very existence.

Yet in abandoning those boundaries, she also discards the insularity inherent in the liberal model of the self. Just before taking the fatal dose of chloral, Lily imagines that all she has left is "the emptiness of renunciation" (320). As she drifts off to sleep, however, she pictures Nettie Struther's baby in her arms, and Wharton thereby constructs her death as an establishing of connection rather than a severing of it. The "emptiness" that accompanies dispossession is more a matter of perception and representation than reality; the space vacated by "personality" seems "empty" when viewed through the lens of a rights-based model of the self, but appears peopled by others when this model is discarded. Rather than defining the limits of Lily's resistance, therefore, her death marks the limits of Wharton's literary medium — the bounds of her novel are precisely the bounds of "personality" itself. Lily becomes unrepresentable when she achieves a form of privacy that cannot be defined as "the right to be let alone," and Wharton enforces that privacy by removing her heroine's consciousness from the sight of even the most omniscient narrator. The lifeless body that confronts Gerty and Selden testifies to the limits of both legal and literary epistemology, imaging a subject that, in its very boundlessness, can never be reduced to an object of knowledge.

Responding to Lily's question about whether the falsity of the "stories" about her does not matter, Rosedale asserts that "the truth" matters "in novels," but not "in real life" (256). Yet for Wharton, literary truth matters only to the extent that novels affirm their own phenomenal existence — their removal from a noumenal world they are able to posit without representing. *The House of Mirth* seeks to be such a novel. Selden's hesitant "explanation" of Lily's life and death at the novel's conclusion models the only form of "knowledge" that Wharton will sanction: "Did the cheque to Trenor explain the mystery or deepen it? At first his mind refused to act — he felt only the taint of such a transaction between a man like Trenor and a girl like Lily Bart. Then, gradually, his troubled vision cleared, old hints and rumours came back to him, and out of the very insinuations he had feared to probe, he constructed an explanation of the mystery" (328–29). The truth that Selden perceives is a "constructed" one, gleaned from "hints," "rumours," and "insinuations," able only to approximate a reality whose "mystery" cannot be fully obliterated. After reimagining Lily based upon her unwillingness to live with the debt to Trenor, Selden concludes that "That was all he knew — all he could hope to unravel of the story" (329). Modifying his legal orientation, he finally accepts his cognitive limitations, and it is only then that Wharton allows "the word that made all clear" to pass "between" the would-be lovers. "The word," of course, is unspeakable; passing "between" a living person and a dead one, it affirms its independence from the dictates of "personality" and from the forms of knowledge communicated by the narratives of both law and literature.[16]

Lily's predicament, and the tragic nature in which Wharton resolves it, suggests comparison to another novel of female subjectivity from the same era — Kate Chopin's *The Awakening*. Wai Chee Dimock has offered an interpretation of Chopin's work that reads it as "a tribute to the primacy of jurisprudence in American life: a tribute to its adversarial language, its tendency to saturate other domains of discourse, not the least of which being the discourse of subjectivity" (*Residues* 209). For Dimock, Edna Pontellier is "a not so remote descendent of the Lockean moral subject," and her determination to assert the primacy of her own consciousness against the claims of others affirms an absolute concept of rights, a form of subjectivism that makes her "unintelligible to others." Her death, however, also seems to critique such a concept, and Dimock concludes that the "voice of subjectivism" in the novel "is allowed to speak both on behalf of its heroine and in testimony against her" (*Residues* 202, 204). Yet while Dimock's reading perceptively identifies Chopin's concern with liberalism and rights, her conclusion seems flawed; the "testimony against" Edna pales in comparison to the testimony in her favor. Edna's death is essentially a taking possession, a perfection of the form of ownership she had asserted earlier in the novel by moving out of her husband's house into one purchased with "her own resources" (Chopin 91). The "sensuous" physicality of her final act completes the process; having already rebelled spiritually, she retakes her body itself from her husband and children, who "need not have thought that they could possess her, body and soul" (124). Chopin's refusal to depict her actual demise reveals the act as one not of loss, but of gain, as Edna's subjectivity is released from all referential bounds and achieves the inviolability her marriage had taken from her. Thus, rather than critiquing the absolutization of right, the novel affirms it, leveling its criticism at a society that fails to accord a right of self-ownership to women as complete as that it grants to men.

The Awakening and *The House of Mirth* are often read together, their perspectives seemingly joined by the deaths of their heroines and by their intense scrutiny of female subjectivity. But while both novels engage a discourse of rights and highlight the challenge presented by that discourse to domestic ideology, Wharton and Chopin reach very different conclusions about female self-possession. For if Edna's subjectivism ultimately results in an assertion of ownership so complete that it leads to her death, Lily's leads to a form of selfhood that cannot be owned. Asserting "no right" to the letters that embody her salvation, she has "no right" to life itself, and her death reflects none of the triumph of Edna's. Yet Wharton does not condemn Lily for renouncing her rights; the letters may be legal evidence, but Lily has come to realize that such a status makes them no more "real" than the evidence that forms the basis for her reputation. Unlike Chopin, therefore, Wharton dissociates rights from reality, and suggests that self-ownership depends upon accepting the epistemology of a legal regime that disguises stories as facts.

The discourses of law and literature, it turns out, have much in common for Wharton. Highlighting the fictions that lie beneath concepts such as property and rights, she discredits the liberal model of legal authority grounded in the transcendent subject. At the same time, by disavowing authorial omniscience and locating reality outside the pages of her text, she places literature in roughly the same position as the law. The two fields operate on the same cognitive plane, each divided from reality by a mask of "mystery." Maintaining a self-conscious sense of its own phenomenology, however, literature provides a potential corrective to the law's desire for unity — a desire whose fulfillment can come only through fictions that divide individuals into subjects and objects, owners and property.

Thus, Wharton's fiction seeks not to replace the ideal legal subject with a more "knowledgeable" authorial one, but to speak to the law in the skeptical voice that it will not acknowledge as its own. Limiting her own narration by the evidentiary principles and definitions of selfhood employed by the law, Wharton presents her work as a form of legal analysis — a narrative brief that speaks the law's language in a way that also exposes that language's inadequacies. By doing so, she implicitly concedes the power of legal discourse to construct the terms of identity for women, but at the same time presents that discourse as divided, ambivalent, and therefore subject to reinterpretation. *The House of Mirth* is addressed, in part, to such individuals as Justice Parker of the New York Court of Appeals, whose mystification over Abigail Roberson's "distress" resulted in a refusal to recognize a form of privacy that seemed to threaten the authority of both the home and the law. And it is also addressed to turn-of-the-century suffragists, whose reliance upon a discourse of rights, the novel implies, ultimately affirmed the very tenets such reformers wished to challenge. Insisting upon the interchangeability of domestic and legal versions of the subject, Wharton suggests that the kind of "Solitude of Self" for which Stanton argued would implicitly replace the confining walls of the home with the equally confining contours of the possessive, rights-bearing self.

There is, of course, considerable irony in Wharton's conception of authorship, for the self-conscious skepticism it promotes is most powerful at the point when the author stops writing. If one of her goals in *The House of Mirth* is to rewrite the gendered language of privacy, her success is tempered by the limitations of a vocabulary that makes rebellion and renunciation indistinguishable. As a result, the most compelling image of authorship in the novel is not the writing of letters, but the burning of them. Lily's death enacts a Bartleby-like logic in which refusing to participate constitutes the only way to identify the weaknesses of a system that is all-pervasive and that delimits the nature of reality itself. Preferring not to endorse this system, Wharton sacrifices her own desire for knowledge by sacrificing Lily, turning death into a state that communicates truth through the very finality of its silence.[17]

Rights and Renunciation in The Age of Innocence

Wharton's literary project in *The House of Mirth* is without question a feminist one. Yet her reluctance to affirm a form of female selfhood grounded in rights places her fiction in opposition to the brand of feminism that predominated at the turn of the century. Refusing to underwrite the ideal legal subject, Wharton suggests that the kind of "Solitude of Self" for which Stanton argued constituted an implicit acceptance of a world in which human relations were dictated by boundaries grounded in power. Wharton's ambivalence about the women's movement would emerge again in *The Age of Innocence* (1920), and it is only fitting that the novel should appear in the same year that Stanton's dream of female suffrage was finally realized in the ratification of the Nineteenth Amendment. Once again celebrating renunciation, the novel picks up where *The House of Mirth* had left off, but it seeks to articulate the way in which such renunciation can lead to life rather than death, and thereby become representable within a literary framework.

If Selden's legal consciousness limits Wharton's otherwise omniscient depiction of Lily's subjectivity in *The House of Mirth*, this limitation becomes even more pronounced in *The Age of Innocence*. Wharton filters her entire story through the mind of Newland Archer, his legal field of vision determining what we see and don't see of May Welland and Ellen Olenska. Like Selden, Archer believes he wants a life free of the conventions of domesticity, but also like Selden, his view of reality is grounded in the utter intelligibility of female selfhood. Thus, the lens through which he views the two women is both legal and domestic. His feelings for May are connected with "a thrill of possessorship in which pride in his own masculine initiation was mingled with a tender reverence for her abysmal purity" (*Age* 7). Her "purity," of course, renders her consciousness an open book, giving her a "transparency" that confirms Archer in his knowledge of her; seeing her in Saint Augustine after experiencing doubts about their marriage, he thinks, "Here was the truth, here was reality, here was the life that belonged to him" (189, 140). But while Archer's attraction to Madame Olenska appears to spring from something different — from a sense of mystery — his only tools for breaking through this mystery are the domestic conventions with which Old New York provides him. As a result, his legal advice to her regarding the possibility of obtaining a divorce is colored by rumors that she has had an affair with her husband's secretary — rumors arising from a letter written by Count Olenski himself — and when she asserts her desire for "freedom," it flashes across Archer's mind that "the charge in the letter was true." Since "she would not or could not say the one word that would have cleared the air," Archer decides "to cover over the ugly reality which her silence seemed to have laid bare" (111). "The word" that Ellen refuses to utter is the very one that renders both her and May intelligible to Archer — innocence. May's being is defined *by* it and Ellen's *against* it, but in both cases it acts as a cognitive link binding the discourses of the law and the home and serving as Archer's primary means of access to the "reality" of female subjectivity.

Wharton, of course, significantly complicates the "reality" that Archer perceives. His "tendency to weigh his evidence" is a part of the larger process involved in Old New York's acceptance of Madame Olenska — a process that makes her visit to the opera seem to Archer like appearing before an "august tribunal before which . . . her case was being tried" (17). Yet neither Archer nor New York society ever breaks through the rumors to the "reality" underneath, and Wharton's determination to reveal only Archer's thoughts and perceptions keeps Ellen a mystery to the reader as well. Furthermore, despite Archer's insistence on May's "transparency," the denouement of their unspoken conflict reveals that she has been more aware than he had guessed. Archer, in fact, commits the same mistake that the willfully blind older generation of New Yorkers commits with respect to women, and May herself intimates as much when she tells him, "You mustn't think that a girl knows as little as her parents imagine. One hears and one notices — one has one's feelings and ideas" (148). Not until the novel's conclusion, however, does the meaning of this hint finally become clear to Archer. Thoroughly convinced that "never, in all the years to come, would she surprise him by an unexpected mood, by a new idea, a weakness, a cruelty or an emotion," he finds himself surprised to learn that she had understood about his love for Ellen all along, that she had — like him — a private life of her own and was therefore more than "the embodied image of the Family." During their marriage, he had "given up trying to disengage her real self from the shape into which tradition and training had moulded her," but he discovers, after her death, that she had accomplished this disengagement herself (295, 332, 326–27). May's "real self" turns out to be as mysterious and inaccessible as Ellen's.

Wharton's emphasis upon the impenetrability of female subjectivity, however, does not give rise to a corresponding representation of female self-ownership and rights. Archer feels that each woman has a "right to her liberty," but his view of Ellen's rights is clouded by his suspicion that she is guilty of a moral transgression. While rights for Archer inhere in the individual, they are also connected to "reality" in a way that ties them to the domestic code of New York. For both May and Ellen, on the other hand, rights have no meaning. Noting that "There was no use in trying to emancipate a wife who had not the dimmest notion that she is not free," Archer refuses to consider the possibility that May's conception of freedom may not be tied to the possession of rights (195). And after advising Ellen not to pursue a divorce — advice grounded in a suspicion of her own adultery — he is dismayed to learn that she has interpreted him to mean something very different:

> "May is ready to give me up."
> "What! Three days after you've entreated her on your knees to hasten your marriage?"
> "She's refused; that gives me the right —"
> "Ah, you've taught me what an ugly word that is," she said. (173)

Archer, of course, intended to teach her no such thing. Yet the "ugliness" of rights for Ellen springs not simply from the harm they may do to others, but also from the insular model of the self they articulate. Thus, in renouncing rights, she gains a form of privacy that is also a form of connection, and she tells Archer, "I shan't be lonely now. I *was* lonely; I *was* afraid. But the emptiness and the darkness are gone; when I turn back into myself now I'm like a child going at night into a room where there's always a light" (172–73). As in *The House of Mirth*, "emptiness" dissipates with the achievement of privacy, with the act of disowning the self. Her renunciation makes no sense to Archer who, finding her "enveloped . . . in a soft inaccessibility," groans out, "I don't understand you!" (173). Understanding, for him, can occur only within a universe of ownership, rights, and knowledge, and the subjective "room" to which Ellen directs him seems to negate the meaning of such terms.

By the end of the novel, however, Archer does "understand." His decision not to ascend to Ellen's room in Paris is a form of renunciation paralleling Ellen's determination to disavow her right to a divorce. "It's more real to me here than if I went up," he tells himself while remaining "rooted" to a bench outside (362). The version of "reality" implied in his statement is relative rather than absolute, contingent instead of transcendent, and its fluidity allows his imagination to link him to Ellen in a way that sensory contact could not. Although "there was nothing now to keep her and Archer apart," he constructs a barrier whose arbitrariness and artificiality make possible a subjectivity that is connective, that avoids the solipsistic implications of the "real" self conceived of as absolute possession bounded not by imagination but by nature (357).[18] Furthermore, Wharton finds a way to depict this barrier without invoking death, thereby suggesting the possibility that literary representation might transcend the limitations with which she had struggled fifteen years earlier. The separation between Archer and Ellen celebrates not so much the divisions *between* individual subjects as the divisions *within* individual subjects, making duality an "understandable" alternative to the unity of the home, the law, and the "personality."

"What is one's personality, detached from that of the friends with whom fate happens to have linked one?" (*A Backward Glance* 169). Wharton's question, posed in her autobiography at the beginning of the chapter dealing with Henry James, reveals the extent to which the contours of selfhood occupied her throughout her career. As *The Age of Innocence* indicates, her "argument with America" (as Elizabeth Ammons has called it) was not simply over the terms of female selfhood, but over the limited and constraining construction of subjectivity, both male and female, inherent in the liberal model of "personality." The "victim" of society in *The Age of Innocence* is a man rather than a woman, and his name — a composite of James's Christopher Newman and Isabel Archer — seems to endow him with both feminine and masculine qualities. For Wharton, the costs of an epistemology grounded in domestic unity and legal truth are exacted against knower as well as known, and Archer's experience of both roles suggests that the genders with which the author was most concerned in 1920 were located within each consciousness and were embedded in the very notions of subject and object.

But while we might also read *The House of Mirth* in this way, the tragic death of Lily makes Selden's victimization seem pale by comparison. Unable to anchor itself in either "right" or "no right," Lily's uncertain form of selfhood arises from the official lack of privacy that made Abigail Roberson's subjectivity invisible, and therefore nonexistent, to the New York Court of Appeals. The cost of renunciation seemed greater to Wharton in 1905 than it did in 1920, and the troubling aspect of the conclusion to *The Age of Innocence* is that its relatively sanguine presentation of rights renounced and subjectivities enhanced becomes possible only after the movement for women's rights had reached a climactic moment and many of its benefits had been realized. If the novel had been written fifteen years earlier, would anything have remained after Ellen Olenska's renunciation? Would we not be left, as in *The House of Mirth*, with a form of female privacy representable only by death?

CHAPTER 6

Theodore Dreiser's Progressive Nostalgia

The spirit of America at that time was so remarkable. It was just entering on that vast, splendid, most lawless and most savage period in which the great financiers, now nearly all dead, were plotting and conniving the enslavement of the people and belaboring each other for power. These crude and parvenu dynasties which now sit enthroned in our democracy, threatening its very life with their pretensions and assumptions, were just in the beginning.

Theodore Dreiser, A Hoosier Holiday

Writing in 1916 of the prevalent mood in the United States in the mid-1890s, Theodore Dreiser summed up this "lawless" era in terms that suggested both its passing and its continued presence. Although his description defines a "period" that had died with its "great financiers," Dreiser nonetheless characterizes the time as the "beginning" of something that is still extant, still "threatening." One can read it as a kind of mini-narrative, in which a natural past gives way to a more civilized present, but in which the "lawless and savage" fountain from which the new regime springs continues to haunt it, even while testifying to that regime's order and legitimacy.[1]

The simultaneously synchronic and diachronic nature of Dreiser's description might be termed one of the hallmarks of nostalgia — a narrative mode that, in effect, "kills" the past in order to preserve its legacy. Its appearance in Dreiser's text is not surprising, because nostalgia was everywhere in the first two decades of the twentieth century. Whether it was nostalgia about the "passing" of Indian nations, the Old South, the American frontier, or the small town, the feeling was widespread that the old models had rapidly transformed into new ones and that the past could be preserved only through acts of narration that identified its demise. Although it was not limited to any particular group or ideology, nostalgia structured much of the discourse regarding business reform employed by individuals who thought of themselves as "progressive" — so much so, in fact, that it is difficult to discuss progressivism without discussing progressive nostalgia. Richard Hofstadter has asserted that the "general theme" of progressivism was "the effort to restore a type of economic individualism and political democracy that was widely believed to have existed earlier in America and to have been destroyed by the great corporation and the corrupt political machine" (5). While his description aptly captures the kind of nostalgia that fueled progressive business reforms, his emphasis on "restoration" overlooks the fact that such nostalgia was aimed largely at extinguishing the idyllic state of affairs whose memory it so warmly invoked. Progressives needed to invoke the spirit of the past to legitimate their reforms, but they first had to render the past obsolete. Renato Rosaldo's definition of "imperialist nostalgia" as "the curious phenomenon of people's longing for what they themselves have destroyed" encompasses much of the backward-looking romanticism of the Progressive Era (particularly with respect to American Indians), but like Hofstadter's characterization, does not account for nostalgia's *agency* (87). More than serving as justification after the fact, nostalgia can take an active part in the destruction by defining beginnings and ends, by consigning periods, concepts, and ideologies to extinction, and in the process releasing their narrative power.

In this sense, the progressive movement can be characterized not only by its politics and economics, but by its literary qualities as well. "Progressivism" has been a notoriously difficult term to define — a problem that I do not propose to remedy here — but two elements stand out prominently among the many diverse features that united people who employed that label: a desire to adjust the relation between the state and the market that classical formulations of liberal economic theory seemed to dictate, and a willingness to posit a now defunct past grounded in the bedrocks of "nature" and "property" in pursuit of that adjustment. The latter element indicates the extent to which progressive business reform went hand in hand with the practice of storytelling. While the battle over reform was fought primarily on the terrain of antitrust and corporation law, the issues extended far beyond the courtroom and the legislative halls; they involved the very foundations of liberal ideology, and the narratives that imbued that ideology with authority.

As Carol M. Rose has noted, many of the founding texts of liberal political economy — such as Hobbes's *Leviathan*, Locke's *Second Treatise of Government*, and Blackstone's *Commentaries on the Laws of England* — rely upon stories beginning in a state of nature to ground their respective philosophies of law, government, and property. Rose maintains that such stories are necessary to explain the conflict between the self-interested individualism that justifies private property and the existence of a legal system that protects that property — a system that can be maintained only through cooperation. She asserts that "the existence of a property regime is not in the least predictable from a starting point of rational self-interest; and consequently, from that perspective, property needs a tale, a story, a post hoc explanation" (38). Her exploration of the relationship between property and narration reveals as much about narratives in the early twentieth century as it does about those in the seventeenth and eighteenth. Locke's theory of natural rights was an especially important point of reference for lawyers, judges, and laypersons during the Progressive Era, predominating over Hobbes's and Blackstone's more positivistic approaches to legal theory. And no wonder, for Locke's story of the origins of property and governments is itself quite nostalgic. The Lockean state of nature is a kind of paradise in which land is plentiful and reason is universal; individuals are self-interested, but no one appropriates more than he (the gender is Locke's) can use. Yet Locke also acknowledges that there is a disruption in the smooth translation of natural rights into the positive rights protected by the social contract, a disruption occasioned by the invention of money. Money, for Locke, is distinct from property; the very physicality of property makes it a source of order, since there is no reason to acquire more than can be used, but money is bound by no such physical limitations. Its appearance implies a fall from nature and suggests the obsolescence of property itself. Since the protection of property forms the foundation of the Lockean social contract, money serves as a disturbing and potentially subversive force with which Locke's narrative of the movement from nature to society ultimately fails to come to grips.

The omnipresence of Lockean narratives in the Progressive Era highlights the fact that not only were the *meanings* of "nature" and "property" at issue, but their very *existence* as well. And the anxiety generated by this uncertainty accounts for reformers' frequent resort to nostalgic narratives. Through such narratives, progressive advocates of antitrust enforcement were able to celebrate the virtues of ownership while at the same time rejecting the laissez-faire theories that legitimated the concentration of wealth in corporate hands. Like Locke and his Scottish heir, Adam Smith, these proponents of trust-busting relied upon a conception of property grounded in a distinctly materialist conception of nature: property could be seen, touched, experienced in a physical way. Moreover, because it was limited by its own physicality, it was inherently self-regulating. The trust, on the other hand, was the very embodiment of money — intangible, manipulable, a means of accumulating more than one has rightfully earned — and consequently, an anti-egalitarian source of disorder. This Lockean insistence on the difference between money and property was especially important to such prominent progressives as Woodrow Wilson, Thorstein Veblen, and Walter Lippmann, each of whom identified the disappearance of traditional forms of private property and their transformation into immaterial kinds of wealth accessible only to those who knew how to "manipulate" it. But while progressive discourse raised the banners of nature and property in justifying the need for business regulation, it did so in a way that relegated those liberal essences to the scrap heap of history; only by turning them into objects of nostalgia could progressives invoke their authority to legitimate a legal incursion into the formerly private relations of the marketplace.

Dreiser's novels of business, *The Financier* (1912) and *The Titan* (1914), exhibit a similar form of nostalgia, thus pointing toward the progressive impulses that underlie their conflicted treatment — at once critical and celebratory — of the business world. Although their hero, Frank A. Cowperwood (modeled on streetcar tycoon Charles T. Yerkes), is first and foremost a "natural" man — a "savage" — he deals in money as well as property, and this tension suggests Dreiser's own engagement with (and anxiety about) the archetypal liberal plot.[2] The strong influence of Darwin and Spencer notwithstanding, Dreiser's novels are informed equally by the legal and political stories told by Locke and by Locke's self-appointed descendants in the Progressive Era.[3] Consequently, Dreiser presents Cowperwood as the embodiment of nature and, at the same time, of individual ownership. Property in his two works is natural, physical, a means of liberating stagnant and plutocratic accumulations of capital in the name of individuality and competition. Even more significant, however, is property's tendency to undermine *combinations* of capital, and Dreiser's emphasis on this tendency associates his novels with the version of liberal ideology contained within the logic of antitrust. Cowperwood's ability to "manipulate" appearances and intangible values, of course, also associates him with money and corporatism, but as the novels progress it becomes clear that he is defined less by his deceptiveness than by his refusal to deceive — a refusal that underscores the nostalgia beneath Dreiser's downward plots. *The Financier* and *The Titan* are stories of defeats, not victories, and Cowperwood's losses result from his adherence to a logic of property rather than money. Retelling Yerkes's successes as Cowperwood's failures, Dreiser turns his protagonist into a kind of progressive hero — a staunch individualist and an owner of tangible things rather than intangible interests, whose business demise authorizes the very forms of regulation advocated by progressive proponents of business reform. Dreiser sympathized little with "reformers," disdaining the pious and moralistic rhetoric he felt they used, but his novels express the kind of nostalgia that made legal intervention (such as it was) possible in the economic sphere during the Progressive Era.

Perhaps more strongly than any other author in this study, Dreiser fulfills Howells's vision of the author's simultaneously legal and literary role in American public life. By suggesting that a self-regulating economy grounded in individual ownership no longer exists, *The Financier* and *The Titan* incorporate a professional ethic that justifies the emergence of the "official" regulator and the financial expert — those progressive figures charged with creating the rules and codes that would do the work "nature" could no longer do. And these novels also open a space for the progressive author in this now denaturalized economic arena. At a time in which vast differences in the concentration of wealth seemed to be "threatening" the "life" of democracy itself, Dreiser's narratives indicate how difficult it was to write a novel of business without writing a novel of business regulation.

"In the Beginning . . ."

If "nature" and "property" were especially vexing concepts for legal and economic theorists in the Progressive Era, it may be because their meanings within classical liberal thought had always been conflicted. Although the preservation of natural law and property rights justifies the existence of the state in liberal theory, "nature" and "property" also function as narrative markers of the past — signs of Derridean "presence" whose values depend largely upon their absence from our own time and place. This conflict is especially evident in Locke's *Second Treatise*, a work that qualifies not only as one of the ur-texts of liberal political philosophy, but as one of the most influential examples of the paradigmatic liberal narrative as well. In Locke's state of nature (prior to the invention of money), individual self-interest leads to appropriation but never to gross inequalities, for the tangible quality of property places reasonable limits on what can be effectively used. Yet Locke's rather reluctant admission that money and property are distinct leads to a kind of narrative within a narrative.

If Locke's primary story was of the translation of nature into society — and of the survival of nature in the natural rights that serve as society's foundation — he also told a more subversive story of the demise of nature altogether:

> In the beginning all the World was *America*, and more so than that is now; for no such thing as *Money* was any where known. Find out something that hath the *Use and Value of Money* amongst his Neighbours, you shall see the same Man will begin presently to *enlarge* his *Possessions*. . . . This partage of things, in an inequality of private possessions, men have made practicable out of the bounds of Societie, and without compact, only by putting a value on gold and silver and tacitly agreeing in the use of Money. For in Governments the Laws regulate the right of property, and the possession of land is determined by positive constitutions. (343–44, emphasis in original)

Locke strongly suggested that the invention of money precedes the social contract. In the abstract, his theory of natural right assumed that there is no such intermediate step: that governments are formed to preserve rights acquired through individual labor, and that those rights are thus translated directly from nature into the language of "positive constitutions." But when he attempted to describe this process temporally, he was forced to admit that nature (and the form of property that it authorizes) has already died by the time of the social contract, that it has been killed by the introduction of money. If Locke's conception of property was essentialist (derived from nature), his conception of money was decidedly conventionalist, and his philosophy comes dangerously close to acknowledging that there is no such thing as property for civil society to protect, that all ownership is really just money and exists in a world of "tacit" negotiations that take place "out of the bounds of Societie." It turns out that the very cornerstone of his political theory — property — exists only nostalgically and that, like the state of nature itself, its authority in the present is dependent upon its placement in a bygone past.

Adam Smith's celebration of free competition presided over by the market's "invisible hand" was grounded in the same assumptions about the materiality and rationality of nature that Locke had articulated. For both theorists, property is immune from state interference because it is governed by nature's physical laws (which, for Smith, are also economic laws). Smith's "invisible hand" is ultimately rooted in a world of visible things.[4] Thus, when advocates of antitrust enforcement in the late nineteenth and early twentieth centuries referred to the "natural laws of competition," they were employing a discourse grounded in a materialist conception of property — a conception that served to repress the subversive presence of intangible wealth. Yet they were also forced to concede that government might occasionally have to step into the economic sphere to maintain competition, that left to its own, nature might become artificial and competition turn anticompetitive. The logic of antitrust required belief in both the continued presence and vitality of nature and, at the same time, its constant tendency to become too socialized, to renounce its own order by turning property into money.

These were the assumptions latent within Justice Harlan's 1903 opinion in *Northern Securities Co. v. United States* — one of the most celebrated antitrust cases of the period and, more than any other, the one that earned Teddy Roosevelt the much-undeserved title of "trust-buster." Roosevelt instituted the case against a holding company that had been created by James J. Hill and J. P. Morgan to combine their respective interests in the Great Northern and Northern Pacific railroads. The holding company was a relatively new invention at the time and New Jersey (where the Northern Securities Company was incorporated) had been the first state to allow the incorporation of businesses whose only assets were the stock of other corporations.[5] The Supreme Court held the combination to be in violation of the Sherman Anti-Trust Act of 1890, and Harlan's opinion for the Court (joined by only three other justices — no single opinion garnered a majority of five) was grounded thoroughly in the authority of nature. He referred to the two railroads as "natural competitors"; described as "plainly deducible" the proposition that "the natural effect of competition is to increase commerce"; and concluded that "the public convenience and the general welfare will be best served when the natural laws of competition are left undisturbed" (*Northern* 328, 331, 337–38). In describing the transaction itself, however, Harlan suggested that his concern was not only with preserving "nature" but with the continued viability of the liberal conception of property as well. Upon transferring the shares of the railroads to the holding company, he asserted, "The stockholders of these two competing companies disappeared, as such, for the moment, but reappeared as stockholders of the holding company" (326). His characterization suggests a kind of alchemical transformation; individuals who had been owners of the railroads had magically (unnaturally) "disappeared," to be replaced by entities who seemed to own nothing but pieces of paper. By ordering the dismantling of the Northern Securities

Company, Harlan sought to undo this financial wizardry, to restore a version of property that was natural, material, and hence, self-regulating. The irony, of course, was that the only way to accomplish this goal was through the regulatory apparatus of the Sherman Act.

Although the philosophical origins of Harlan's assumptions about nature went unacknowledged in his plurality opinion, Justice Oliver Wendell Holmes Jr. made them explicit in his dissent. Pointing out that Harlan's logic would seemingly allow either Hill or Morgan, acting individually, to combine ownership of the two railroads by purchasing a majority interest in each, Holmes made it clear that the real dispute was not over "competition," but over the meaning and significance of property. Like Harlan, he resorted to a narrative of the origins of property, but unlike Harlan, he did so self-consciously and with the intent of exposing the assumptions Harlan would have left unstated. At the end of his dissent, Holmes wrote, "I am happy to know that only a minority of my brethren adopt an interpretation of the law which, in my opinion, would make eternal the *bellum omnia contra omnes* and disintegrate society so far as it could into individual atoms. If that were its intent, I should regard calling such a law a regulation of commerce as a mere pretence. It would be an attempt to reconstruct society" (*Northern* 411). Holmes's language was carefully chosen. Recognizing the Lockean narrative embedded in Harlan's opinion, he recurred to Locke's predecessor and nemesis — Hobbes — in articulating his own version of property's origins. Like Locke, Hobbes invoked nature in tracing the genesis of civil authority, but his version of nature was anything but nostalgic. For him, the state of nature is a state of war, and governments and laws are established not to preserve any aspect of such a state, but to escape from it. As a result, Hobbes imagined property as a purely conventional rather than natural institution, asserting that "justice and propriety begin with the constitution of commonwealth" and that "where there is no coercive power erected, that is, where there is no commonwealth, there is no propriety" (*Leviathan* 113). Holmes's legal positivism owed much more to Hobbes than to Locke, and he would make his own Hobbesian views on ownership clear in a later opinion in which he referred to property as a "creation of law" (*International News* 246). In *Northern Securities*, his dissent sought to expose the extent to which Harlan's conception of property was grounded in an arguable view of nature and to assert that the "community of interest" that had led to the railroad combination could also be seen as a civilizing gesture — an attempt to escape from the savagery of nature through the kind of cooperation that makes "society" possible in the first place (*Northern* 406–7).

Embodying more than just different interpretations of the Sherman Act, the opinions of Harlan and Holmes can be seen as microcosms of property narratives that diverge in their respective constructions of "nature." But while Roosevelt was furious with Holmes for his dissent, it is not easy to say which narrative, in the end, was more "progressive."[6] Roosevelt's progressivism was grounded in a kind of rugged individualism that Holmes seemed to critique, but by the time Woodrow Wilson came to office in 1913 the face of progressivism had changed considerably. It was no longer the era of the robber baron or of the Horatio Alger hero, but of the "organization man"— the business specialist defined not by individualism but by (as Martha Banta has termed it) a "culture of management" grounded in efficiency and self-sacrifice (Banta 5). Wilson continued to use the progressive language of nature, competition, and individualism, but at the same time he accepted as inevitable the rise of the corporate economy. As Locke's nostalgia makes clear, however, Wilson's views on ownership and business were not necessarily inconsistent. Wilson's appeal to the individual — the "man on the make"— was akin to Locke's appeal to nature before the invention of money; in both cases the power of the ideals invoked stemmed from a latent sense of their extinction.

Like Dreiser in his comment on the era of the "great financiers," Wilson looked back on the late nineteenth century as a period in which nature rather than artifice held sway. In his book *The New Freedom* (1913), published shortly after he took office as president, he asserted that "big business is no doubt to a large extent necessary and natural. . . . But that is a very different matter from the development of trusts, because the trusts have not grown. They have been artificially created" (*New* 164–65). He then went on to place his views on nature and artifice in a temporal setting: "The trusts do not belong to the period of infant industries. They are not the products of that old laborious time, when the great continent we live on was undeveloped, the young nation struggling to find itself and get its feet amidst older and more experienced competitors. They belong to a very recent and very sophisticated age, when men knew what they wanted and knew how to get it by the favor of the government" (165). Wilson told the story of the nation's economic development as a fall from grace, proceeding from a "struggling" and "laborious" youth lived within nature to a descent into knowledge and sophistication. But if his narrative suggested that the "old laborious time" was long gone, another narrative he related in the same chapter (entitled "Monopoly, or Opportunity?") implied that its passing was more recent. Wilson told the tale of Andrew Carnegie in decidedly Algeresque terms, celebrating his natural business instincts while, at the same time, recounting their obsolescence:

> Mr. Carnegie could build better mills and make better steel rails and make them cheaper than anybody else connected with what afterward became the United States Steel Corporation. . . . He had so much more brains in finding out the best processes; he had so much more shrewdness in surrounding himself with the most successful assistants; he knew so well when a young man who came into his employ was fit for promotion and was ripe to put at the head of some branch of his business and was sure to make good, that he could undersell every mother's son of them. And they bought him out . . . because they couldn't beat him in competition. (*New* 180)

Carnegie was just the sort of natural competitor that Wilson associated with the "young nation." Yet the steel magnate could serve as exemplar only because he had already been "bought out" by the monopolists.[7] Nature and property, it seems, had been alive and well until the end of the nineteenth century, when they suddenly began to "disappear" amid a haze of corporate combination and financial manipulation. Although Wilson sought to distinguish between the naturalness of "big business" and the artificiality of the trusts, the only reason for doing so was to preserve through nostalgia a conception of ownership that had passed away. In fact, one might say that part of Wilson's intent was actively to consign this conception to extinction, since his own political agenda was rooted in a form of legal regulation to which property (in the liberal tradition) would have been immune. Wilson legitimated state intervention in the marketplace by infusing regulation with the status once held by individual proprietorship, thus bringing the lessons of a rational and natural past to bear on an artificial and conventional present.[8]

Looking Backward: Frank Cowperwood

To say that Dreiser's novels of business reflect a form of progressive nostalgia is not to deny his status as one of the preeminent practitioners of American literary naturalism. It is rather to argue that the naturalists' insistence on writing about "nature," even when they emphasized its continued presence and power, arose in part from an uncomfortable suspicion of its possible demise, and that this anxiety stemmed largely from the tenuousness of the legal and political authority that "nature" stands for in the liberal tradition. Walter Benn Michaels has asserted that the "logic of naturalism" is at one with the logic of capitalism, and that Dreiser "thinks of nature in all her manifestations as capitalistic" (83). But Dreiser's decision in *The Financier* and *The Titan* to present Cowperwood's "naturalness" as the product of a previous era suggests a distinction between nature and capitalism, or to be more precise, between nature and the form of industrial capitalism based upon large-scale corporate enterprise. This mode of economic activity, Dreiser implies, aligns itself not with nature, but with art, and while Cowperwood participates in its rise, his career ultimately affirms the anachronistic virtues of ownership over the ascendant uncertainties of corporatism and money. In the end, of course, progressivism was more successful at keeping socialism at bay than it was at "democratizing" the market, and in that sense Dreiser's own progressive impulses might be characterized as innately capitalistic.[9] Yet the specific shapes that capitalism takes are not without their significance, and the "logic" of Dreiser's novels authorizes forms of legal regulation that, twenty years earlier, had been widely viewed as anticapitalistic.

Dreiser frames his account of Cowperwood's life with two visions of nature: the struggle between the lobster and the squid that Cowperwood observes as a boy, and the "equation" by which power alternates between "the individual" and "the mass" invoked by Dreiser at the end of *The Titan* (551). The battle between the lobster and the squid illustrates the Darwinian essence of nature — the rule that individual organisms are necessarily in competitive relationships for limited resources, or as the young Cowperwood puts it, the principle that "Things lived on each other" (*Financier* 8). The struggle between the individual and the mass (a model Dreiser draws from Spencer) would seem at first glance to be equally competitive. But in what way can "the mass" act self-interestedly? This model of nature is, in fact, quite different from the Darwinian one, for it allows that people might come together into a "community of interest" that eliminates the need for competition among self-interested individuals. And this is precisely what happens at the end of *The Titan* — Cowperwood's attempt to extend his streetcar franchises is defeated by a popular revolt against his unscrupulous exercise of power, and the governor of Illinois refuses to take a bribe that clearly would have been in his own self-interest. But while Dreiser implies that the "equation" will eventually turn the other way, Donald Pizer's observation that "the bulk of [*The Fi-*

nancier] is devoted ... to [Cowperwood's] difficulties and defeats" applies equally to *The Titan* and suggests that Cowperwood's legacy is one of failure (*Novels* 171).[10] The two works thus reflect what Philip Fisher calls "the Naturalist plot of decline"— the rise and inevitable fall that characters such as Hurstwood in *Sister Carrie* and Clyde Griffiths in *An American Tragedy* experience (169). Furthermore, Dreiser's decision to end *The Titan* with Cowperwood's defeat was by no means dictated by Yerkes's biography; although Yerkes lost his battle for the franchises, he sold his Chicago streetcar interests for some 20 million dollars and used the amount to become the principal financier of the London Underground.[11] Dreiser's insistence that Yerkes's story was, at bottom, one of failure arises not from the author's dedication to fact or philosophy, but from his sense that the version of nature and individuality that the "great financiers" stood for had, in an age of corporate growth and regulatory reform, become archaic.

For Dreiser as for Locke, self-interest is "just there," instinctive and axiomatic. Yet it also serves as a beginning that makes sense only as something that no longer exists in its original form. Cowperwood's dedication to the self— to an autonomous, natural version of selfhood rather than to a socialized one — is precisely what renders his ultimate success in business elusive. What he wants most of all is to be a monopolist, but as the opinions by Harlan and Holmes in *Northern Securities* make clear, the monopolist was thought of as someone willing to sacrifice an individuality grounded in nature to establish an artificial "community of interest." For Harlan, the monopolist represented a threat to a society founded upon individual rights, but for Holmes, the monopolist was society itself in microcosm — a visible manifestation of the way in which we have all renounced nature to enter a web of social relationships. Dreiser likewise highlights the fact that monopolists are anything but autonomous. Yerkes himself chose to pursue his dreams of monopoly by investing in streetcars, but the streetcar business depended upon being granted public franchises by municipalities. Similarly, his rise to financial success in Philadelphia was a result of obtaining the sole right to sell and redeem city loan certificates, an endeavor that required his participation in a market in which values are a function solely of public perception. Dreiser's decision to use Yerkes as his model emphasizes the irony inherent in monopoly; in the abstract, monopolists appear to be answerable to no one but themselves, but in practice their monopolies are always dependent upon others, always the result of a "community of interest."[12] Monopolists only seem like the ultimate individualists; in reality, they are tied to others in ways that make the realization of individuality and autonomy impossible.

Cowperwood's motto, "I satisfy myself," reflects the fears about monopoly that prompted the antitrust movement, fears grounded in the assumption that large corporate consolidations would result in a control of the market for a given product that would be completely self-contained, a form of dominance in which the "natural" laws of supply and demand — Smith's "invisible hand" — would no longer apply (*Financier* 121). But this fear operated largely in the abstract, because antitrust reformers also recognized that in practice monopolistic enterprises were almost always established through cooperation — sometimes between sets of businessmen and other times between businessmen and government. The fear that motivated such reformers was that corporate ownership would assume the attributes that liberal theory ascribed to individual ownership, that it would be free from all external reference, absolute, immune from interference. Cowperwood's motto, therefore, reflects a dream of monopoly that was really a dream of individual proprietorship; he does not actually want to become a monopolist, but an owner whose property rights would be dependent on nothing outside of himself. The real monopolists in *The Financier* and *The Titan* are the powerful interests who work together to run their respective cities for their own benefit — Butler, Mollenhauer, and Simpson in Philadelphia and Schryhart, Merrill, Hand, and Arneel in Chicago. Cowperwood serves as their nemesis; his natural self-interest continually foils their collusive schemes and thus prevents them from achieving the kind of oligarchical control they desire. In *The Financier*, Cowperwood dreams of "a city-wide street-railway system controlled by a few men, or preferably himself alone" (103). In *The Titan*, he comes close to realizing his dream. What keeps him from it is precisely his unwillingness to combine, his insistence upon reaching his goals "alone," and he thus relegates himself to the role of perpetual outsider by his refusal to "satisfy" the powerful men who run both Philadelphia and Chicago.

Even at the beginning of his career, when Cowperwood seems most amenable to using social "connections" to achieve financial success, his own self-indulgence functions to undermine that success. His affair with Aileen Butler, for instance, ends up destroying the goodwill he had established with her powerful father — a member of the city's ruling "triumvirate" — and leads directly to Cowperwood's bankruptcy and criminal prosecution. Dreiser depicts Aileen as the very embodiment of nature and physicality, describing her as a "spirited animal" for whom artifice is impossible, and his devotion to her thus manifests his devotion to his own nature — particularly his sexuality (*Financier* 113). His sexual indulgences work against his financial interests throughout both novels; he has a self-destructive tendency to engage in affairs with the wives or daughters of men whose financial or journalistic support he could most use. But while Dreiser sought to make a point about sexual prudery in American life (the affairs seem to be drawn more from his own experiences and fantasies than from Yerkes's life), he also used Cowperwood's insatiable sexual drives to illustrate the conflicts inherent in corporatism and monopoly; the more one seeks to "satisfy" the physical demands of nature, the less one is able to achieve the more communal satisfaction of the monopolist.

Cowperwood's refusal to conform to a newly emergent corporatism makes him a relic — an anachronistic embodiment of a "savage" time that no longer exists. His individualistic perspective is more effective at defeating monopolistic tendencies than in promoting them, and it is this element of his character that identifies him as both a progressive hero and a throwback to the past. In *The Titan*, he thwarts the attempts by Chicago's "quadrumvirate" of ruling interests to reap the benefits of their investments in American Match, which had been "trustified" and, as a result, promised to yield rich profits to those who controlled it (436, 401). The four oligarchs hope to manipulate the stock price in their own favor, but find themselves at Cowperwood's mercy when he gains control of a large block of the stock. Acting in his own self-interest, Cowperwood throws the stock on the market, thereby depressing its price and forcing the company into bankruptcy. Dreiser takes delight in describing the meeting at which Cowperwood faces down the large banking interests of Chicago, who seek to punish him financially for his self-interested actions. One of the quadrumvirate, Anson Merrill, expresses a grudging admiration for Cowperwood, calling him "a man with the heart of a Numidian lion," and Dreiser editorializes by telling us that "It was true" (437). Cowperwood may aspire to be the ultimate monopolist — one whose ownership is so complete that he needs no "community of interest" to support it — but this very goal paradoxically turns him into a trust-buster.

Cowperwood's triumph in the American Match episode, however, is fleeting. His unwillingness to work in concert with other powerful interests, along with his inadvisable sexual liaisons, is ultimately his undoing; the newspapers, controlled by men whom he has alienated, work diligently to oppose the extension of his franchises, and even Cowperwood's bribes are unable to counteract their power. Yet the defeat is predetermined from the start, not by Dreiser's knowledge of Yerkes's life (which did not, in itself, dictate Dreiser's interpretation), but by the naturalness with which the author imbues his hero. Associating Cowperwood with the beginning of an era, the author preordains his downfall by virtue of the very temporal terms of his structure. Dreiser calls Cowperwood "one of those early, daring manipulators who later were to seize upon other and ever larger phases of American natural development for their own aggrandizement" and tells us that his carefully controlled manipulation of the city loan certificates "was no different from what subsequently was done with Erie, Standard Oil, Copper, Sugar, Wheat, and what not. Cowperwood was one of the first and one of the youngest to see how it could be done" (*Financier* 141, 94). By comparing his protagonist to those who would put together famously powerful and monopolistic enterprises, Dreiser depicts him as a transitional figure in the development from nature to society, someone who ushers in a paradigm that renders his own existence obsolete. As the title of Edward Bellamy's popular 1888 utopian novel had inadvertently suggested, the act of "looking backward" was really a way of looking ahead, since the past could be "seen" only by severing it from the present and the future. "The mass" triumphs over "the individual" in both *The Financier* and *The Titan*, and Dreiser's prophecy that the tide will eventually turn constitutes his own way of preserving a vision of nature and individualism even while recounting their demise. The development of his story, like that of Locke's, proceeds away from nature, in the direction of a state of affairs whose artificiality is explained and legitimated by the natural conditions that it destroys and supplants.

Money vs. Property

The Lockean story of the replacement of nature by artifice and of individuals by society appeared again and again in various forms during the Progressive Era. This obsessive repetition suggests that its tellers were attempting to come to grips less with the narrative itself than with the gaps in the narrative, and foremost among those gaps was its incomplete and problematic treatment of money. What happens to nature and property after the invention of money? Does the social contract endow money with the status of property, protecting it from all interference by the state? If so, what does that do to the concept of natural rights, since money is by definition artificial, unnatural, and dependent upon the tacit negotiations of social beings to imbue it with value? This unresolved tension in liberal theory had become especially acute by the turn of the century, as the most valuable assets seemed increasingly to be those that could not be seen. Moreover, beginning in the early 1890s, the American judiciary, led by the Supreme Court, had begun to treat all interests that had any value at all as property, thus removing them from state interference.[13] Although courts justified their laissez-faire rulings by recourse to liberal principles, progressives saw them as undermining rather than supporting the concept of ownership, since such rulings seemed to define "property" in a way that deprived it of its self-regulating qualities.

If progressives viewed themselves as the true descendants of Locke and Smith, however, their frequent resort to narratives with a nostalgic bent also implicitly acknowledged the cracks in liberal ideology. The new legal protections afforded to intangible interests had exacerbated those cracks, exposing the conflicts that Locke's narrative had both evoked and elided and that were part and parcel of the liberal tradition. As Benjamin Franklin's autobiography reveals, the sense that social constructs such as reputation could be more valuable than physical possessions had served as a disquieting reminder of liberalism's weaknesses even in pre-revolutionary America.[14] But Franklin's work also underscores the extent to which such tensions could be smoothed over within an economic system that was largely agrarian and artisanal—one in which physicalist conceptions of property made practical sense. By the end of the nineteenth century, of course, the economic climate was very different and the narrative fault lines more vexing. Arguments over how far the law could go in regulating business were really arguments about what counted as "property," and whether, in an age of corporate consolidation and high finance, that term still meant anything at all.[15]

Many progressive advocates of regulation assumed that "real" property possessed intrinsic value, while the value of "fake" property had to be maintained by appearances and tricks. To these individuals, money seemed governed by fictions whose authors often seemed to remain disturbingly concealed beneath layers of obscuring wealth. If there was an oligarchy, its members were not tyrants openly exposing their raw power to an awed populace, but clandestine artists able to dupe the public with self-serving representations and capitalize upon their exclusive access to the truth. Progressives perceived the very physicality of property as innately democratic, and they thus appealed to a natural state of affairs governed by the limitations inherent in material "things" rather than by the slippery and ever-changing standards of immaterial "interests." Implicit in these appeals, however, was the sense that a meaningful distinction between property and money was no longer possible, and that what had once been accomplished by protecting ownership must now be accomplished by other means.

Writing in 1924 of the "legal foundations of capitalism," the progressive economist John R. Commons noted the transition in the meaning of property that took place at the turn of the century: "Property, in the popular ordinary usage, the usage of the old common law and the one adhered to in the Slaughter House Cases and the Munn Case, meant any tangible thing owned. Property, in the later decisions, means any of the expected activities implied with regard to the thing owned. . . . One is Property, the other is Business. The one is property in the sense of Things owned, the other is property in the sense of exchange-value of things. One is physical objects, the other is marketable assets." Commons lamented this trend toward what he termed the "invisibility" of assets, noting that "These intangible and incorporeal properties are more valuable than all physical things" (18, 24). The transition he described is itself a narrative that is intimately related to narratives of the death of nature, and thus the story of the death of property appeared regularly during the Progressive Era. Walter Lippmann, for instance, in his book of social criticism entitled *Drift and Mastery* (1917), asserted that the shareholder of a corporation "may never see *his* property" or "know where his property is situated," and that as a result "the trusts are organizing private property out of existence, are altering its nature so radically that very little remains but the title and the ancient theory" (51). Asking "where in the name of sanity have all the courage, foresight, initiative gone to, what has happened to all the rugged virtues that are supposed to be inherent in the magic of property?" he answered his own query by arguing that "they have gone a-glimmering with the revolutionary change that the great industry has produced. Those personal virtues belong to an earlier age when men really had some personal contact with their property. But to-day the central condition of business is that capital shall be impersonal, 'liquid,' 'mobile.' The modern shareholder as a person is of no account whatever" (56). For Lippmann, the "revolutionary change" of industrialization had destroyed property and the individual along with it, leaving only impotent and ignorant shareholders. Yet this situation was not without its solution, and Lippmann's answer reveals the extent to which narratives of the death of property could authorize new ways to reconstitute its "magic." Since investors had become nothing more than a "scattered mob," he maintained, "the question of where money is to be applied is a matter for experts to answer. And so reform of the credit system does not consist in abolishing the financial expert. It consists in making him a public servant" (54). Progressives such as Lippmann and Commons frequently described a transition from a social order anchored by physical property to a state of "drift" dominated by the invisible values of business and money, but it was precisely this transition that authorized their arguments for legal intervention in the economic sphere. The "financial expert" would now serve the stabilizing role once served by the individual property owner, thus nostalgically preserving the "virtues" of property in a new social model based upon regulation. The "magic of property" would become the magic of professional regulation.

Lippmann's and Commons's anxiety over the "invisiblity" of the new forms of property echoed Harlan's concern in *Northern Securities* about the "disappearance" of railroad investors and their "reappearance" as shareholders of a holding company. For Harlan, a form of real ownership was being replaced by something fictitious, and fictions were manipulable by the powerful interests who controlled their mechanisms of production and dissemination.[16] The year after *Northern Securities* was decided, Thorstein Veblen expanded upon this perspective in his *Theory of Business Enterprise*, exposing the fictions by which the newly "invisible" forms of value operated. Noting that "the substantial foundation of the industrial corporation is its immaterial assets," he went on to explain how the value of such assets is created and maintained: "the men who have the management of such an industrial enterprise, capitalized and quotable on the market, will be able to induce a discrepancy between the putative and the actual earning-capacity, by expedients well known and approved for the purpose. Partial information, as well as misinformation, sagaciously given out at a critical juncture, will go far toward producing a favorable temporary discrepancy of this kind, and so enabling the managers to buy or sell the securities of the concern with advantage to themselves" (156–57). For Veblen, the primary asset of a corporation was its ability to manufacture discrepancies between the "actual" value of its business (reflected in its physical assets) and the "putative" value (reflected in its stock price). As a result, he asserted, "the fortunes of property owners are in large measure dependent on the discretion of others — the owners of intangible property" (175). The "misinformation" Veblen decries is akin to the "stories" that deprive Lily Bart of self-ownership in *The House of Mirth*; in both cases, forms of property are subjected to the control of storytellers who are able to manipulate the terms of reality itself. As Martha Banta notes, much of Veblen's work can be seen as a kind of literary criticism; he sought to identify (and debunk) the stories that underlay dominant structures of authority, and his identification of the fictions inherent in business practices formed part of that project. Yet he was also a storyteller in his own right, articulating "his belief in the eventual destruction of an increasingly outmoded business system and the emergence of the engineer — the unsentimental technocrat — as the leader of a reformed industrial age" (40). Like Lippmann's, Veblen's story suggests the possibility that the enlightened expert might dismantle the illusions that endow money with its power, and might help to destroy or redistribute the invisible value now accessible to only the privileged few.

Such hopeful projections reveal that progressive narratives of the decline of nature, property, and individuality and the rise of society, artifice, and money did not simply end there. The very movement they reflected — from a past grounded in values (both economic and moral) that were fixed and absolute to a present in which such values were being continually negotiated — implied the possibility of a happy ending, one in which artifice itself could be used to shape the present by looking back to a natural past. Even if property was dead, its spirit could live on through regulation.

In *The Financier* and *The Titan*, Cowperwood reflects both the physicality that progressives (following Locke) associated with nature and property, and the incorporeality that they linked with art and money. Cowperwood's acquisitiveness constitutes an attempt to extend the sphere of his ownership over as many objects and as much physical territory as possible, but at the same time he wants to transcend the material world of things. Dreiser thus emphasizes the extent to which finance can be seen as a "great art" and the financier as a kind of "poet" (*Financier* 11).[17] Most people, Dreiser proclaims, want money "for what it will buy in the way of simple comforts, whereas the financier wants it for what it will control — for what it will represent in the way of dignity, force, power" (*Financier* 182). The true financier wants things not for their inherent use value, but for their value as representations, as texts whose meanings are dependent upon a universe of readers. But Cowperwood is not necessarily a true financier; "things" continue to remain important to him. Thus, when his collusive relationship with the Philadelphia city treasurer, George Stener, allows him to build a large new house for himself, the origin of the capital that funds the construction seems to conflict with what the house itself (as material object) stands for: "The effect of a house of this character on its owner is unmistakeable. We think we are individual, separate, above houses and material objects generally; but there is a subtle connection which makes them reflect us quite as much as we reflect them. . . . Cut the thread, separate a man from that which is rightfully his own, characteristic of him, and you have a peculiar figure, half success, half failure, much as a spider without its web, which will never be its whole self again until all its dignities and emoluments are restored. The sight of his new house going up made Cowperwood feel of more weight in the world, and the possession of his suddenly achieved connection with the city treasurer was as though a wide door had been thrown open to the Elysian fields of opportunity." (*Financier* 97–98) Cowperwood feels more "whole" by virtue of his "connection" to his house, but that wholeness is also peculiarly related to his "possession" of a "connection" to Stener. When Cowperwood thinks about leaving his wife for Aileen Butler, he originally decides against it because he has "too many connections. . . . Too many social and . . . emotional as well as financial ties to bind him" (122). If ownership implies physicality, self-interest, and individuality, "connections" are its opposite. Yet "connections" — not property — are the true financier's medium; at the height of his prosperity in Philadelphia, Cowperwood imagines himself "surrounded and entangled" in "a splendid, glittering network of connections" (140). His success in finance is attributable less to nature than it is to artistry, and art, like money, gains value only through the invisible ties of social relations.

"Invisibility" would seem to be Cowperwood's stock-in-trade. He learns at a young age that "some stocks and bonds were not worth the paper they were written on, and that others were worth much more than their face value indicated," and this knowledge allows him to manipulate the city loan certificates that he is charged with selling at par value (11). The certificates are not actually "worth" their face value, since they would ordinarily be discounted to account for the possibility of default by the city, but Cowperwood is able to create a bull market for them by secretly buying certificates that he has just made available to the public. The control he exerts over the market value of these securities allows him to trade on them for his own personal benefit while at the same time fulfilling his obligations to the city of Philadelphia. His success is built upon duplicity — if others knew he was supporting the market for his own certificates, their value would plummet — and his financial prowess is thus at its core an ability to manipulate appearances.

This duplicity permeates his life, at least early in his career. In planning his future, he recognizes the need to "build up a seeming of virtue and dignity which would pass muster for the real thing," and he applies this principle both to his business dealings and to his relationships with his wives, Lillian and Aileen (121). As Cowperwood begins to have affairs in Chicago, for instance, Dreiser tells us that he "was so shrewd that he had the ability to simulate an affection . . . which he did not feel, or rather, that was not backed by real passion" (*Titan* 199). Cowperwood's skill at manipulating the value of assets not "backed" by anything substantive applies to marriage as much as to the market. Even after Aileen begins to suspect his infidelity, she is forced to "accept his excuses at face value" (201). The true financier, Dreiser suggests, never allows himself to be "long" on passion or property. A dealer in appearances, he must neither own things nor feel emotions, for both tend to limit his own fluidity — his own ability to assume the shape that best serves his interests.[18]

The concept of "face value" in the two novels implicates the very practices that, as Veblen noted, allowed for the creation and liquidation of immaterial assets; Cowperwood's face is a tangible asset that, like the loan certificates he trades, can be manipulated to realize the value of the intangible meanings it conceals. In the lobster and the squid episode, Dreiser emphasizes the unreadable quality of the predator — "you could not tell in which way his beady, black buttons of eyes were looking" — and Cowperwood's eyes partake of the same quality: "It was as though there were another pair of eyes behind those [people] saw, watching through thin, obscuring curtains. You could not tell what he was thinking" (*Financier* 7, 123). Yet it is precisely Cowperwood's face and eyes that attract people when they first meet him. Again and again, Dreiser emphasizes the "subtlety" of Cowperwood's expression — his eyes, we are told, "indicated much and revealed nothing" (75, 15). Cowperwood's appearance conveys its own unreadability, and thereby creates its own value by communicating the existence of secrecy and manipulation without exposing any details. The only asset that "backs" this "face value" is Cowperwood's ability to invent fictions — fictions that can endow any asset with value it would not otherwise possess.

Yet Cowperwood's dedication to appearances turns out to be incomplete, for Dreiser also presents him as frank (hence his name) and open about his self-interest — a quality that associates him more with the visibility of property than with the invisibility of money. And the downward trajectory of Dreiser's plot consigns Cowperwood's property-oriented perspective to the same dustbin in which it places his naturalness. Cowperwood becomes less and less deceptive as *The Financier* and *The Titan* progress and, at the same time, more and more wedded to property ownership. Although he regains his fortune at the end of *The Financier* by capitalizing on the failure of Jay Cooke, the turn of events prompts him to reevaluate his business. Such disasters, Dreiser tells us, "had cured him of all love of the stock exchange," and he decides to go west to invest in "street railways, land speculation, some great manufacturing project of some kind, even mining, on a legitimate basis" (444). Cowperwood decides to get out of the money business and into the property business. Although in Chicago he continues his ruthless and unscrupulous business practices, he also fails to court appearances as assiduously as he had in Philadelphia, and Dreiser points to this failure as the cause of his ultimate defeat: "How was it, he asked himself, that his path had almost constantly been strewn with stormy opposition and threatened calamity? . . . Was it not due to his inability to control without dominating personally — without standing out fully and clearly in the sight of all men? Sometimes he thought so. The humdrum conventional world could not brook his daring, his insouciance, his constant desire to call a spade a spade. . . . Dissembling enough, he was not sufficiently oily and make-believe" (*Titan* 438).

Yerkes himself had been famous for openly defending his bribery of public officials, and Dreiser implies that such openness is inconsistent with the monopolistic dreams Yerkes sought to realize.[19] Cowperwood, like Yerkes, becomes readable, and in so doing discards the artistic role of financier and assumes the natural one of property owner. What's more, Dreiser relates this development to the cessation of his sexual promiscuity; having fallen in love with Berenice Fleming, he woos her by stating, "My ideal has become fixed" (*Titan* 465). By the end of *The Titan*, Cowperwood's vaunted "subtlety" has vanished and his desire has largely been sated. His streetcar consolidation remains elusive, but the reason, Dreiser suggests, is that Cowperwood is not at heart a monopolist at all. Beginning his career as a dealer in stocks and bonds, he ends it (at the close of *The Titan*) as the sole proprietor of a thoroughly tangible streetcar business, and his failure to extend his franchises is due both to the brazen openness of his business methods and to the increasingly archaic quality of his ownership.[20]

And this is why he belongs to a previous era. Elevating nature over art and tangible things over intangible interests, Cowperwood goes down battling for principles that neither Dreiser nor his progressive counterparts actually believed in; he is heroic not in spite of his defeat, but *because* of it. Property, for Dreiser, no longer functions as a means of ordering human relations, and its invocation thus serves only to conceal social manipulations beneath a veneer of legitimacy. Cowperwood's trial, for instance, is conducted in the name of property; he is accused of larceny (a property crime), and the "corporation-minded judge" who presides over the trial "fairly revered property and power" (*Financier* 288). But the authority of property acts a shield for the collusive interests of Philadelphia's ruling "triumvirate" that the trial is really intended to protect. Although Dreiser criticizes the proceedings on the grounds of "the inutility of all law," he levels most of his critique at the application of an outmoded ideal of the sanctity of property to a set of circumstances arising from the conventionality of business practices and the fluctuating value of money (287). Law's "inutility" is a result of its adherence to a philosophy of essences, its extension of property rights into domains governed only by appearances and tacit negotiations. Before Cowperwood's sentencing, Dreiser describes the sentencing of an African American man accused of stealing a piece of pipe. The scene, on one level, provides a stereotypical account of a "shambling, illiterate, nebulous-minded black," who tells the judge that when he took the pipe he "didn' think 'twuz stealin' like zackly" (374). On another level, however, the black defendant's confusion is also Dreiser's. At a time when the most valuable assets are associated with the immaterial quality of public perceptions and expectations, the concept of stealing makes less and less sense as a principle by which conduct can be regulated. As one of the appellate judges in Cowperwood's case notes, Cowperwood's conviction would make the practices of most stock traders illegal. Dreiser's emphasis on the "inutility" of the law may not, at first glance, look progressive, but the terms of his criticism do. The trial is a sham because it fails to affirm the death of property; it assumes the concept can be applied to "business" and thus serves the interests of those who would endow the manipulable values of money with the legitimacy and inviolability accorded to ownership.[21]

Cowperwood's conviction in *The Financier* mirrors his ultimate defeat at the conclusion of *The Titan*. Such failures mark the boundary between an era of property and an era of money, and the establishment of that boundary on Dreiser's part is a political act that seeks to justify a new relation between the state and the market without disrupting the foundational tenets of liberalism. In the midst of his losing fight for the Chicago franchises, Cowperwood attempts to mollify his opposition by proposing a public service commission that would oversee streetcar fares and the corporate fees paid to the city. His proposal, though defeated, indicates the close connection between the rise of progressive regulation and the anachronistic ideals of individual ownership that served as progressivism's ideological base. While Cowperwood would have simply made the proposed commission a pawn under his own exclusive control, his defeat paves the way for the true public service commission — one founded on the triumph of artifice, yet heroically (and nostalgically) grounding the terms of its own regulation in the hallowed memory of nature, individualism, and property.

Authorizing Progressivism

Dreiser's conflicted efforts both to celebrate nature and to kill it complicate readings of naturalist authors that emphasize their collective belief in a transparent and representable reality. Recognizing the shortcomings of this perspective, recent critics such as Walter Benn Michaels, Philip Fisher, and Michael Davitt Bell have offered interpretations of Dreiser's works that focus on the gap between reality and representation that they implicitly convey. Bell, for instance, asserts that at the end of *Sister Carrie* "what remains is the longing, and it is as much the narrator's as Carrie's; for he is no more able than his heroine to believe in a separate order of 'essential things' that would render *his* representations truer than hers" (164). Reflecting a desire for the essentialism of a past that is now dead, Dreiser's nostalgia in *The Financier* and *The Titan* is evidence of such "longing." But it is also more than that, for Dreiser longs for something that he takes an active part in destroying. On the one hand, Dreiser's relegation of nature to the past would seem to discredit the mode of legal, political, and literary authority that requires nature's immanence and accessibility. On the other, however, his resort to nostalgia preserves nature's ghostly influence upon the present.

And this is precisely the fine line that progressivism walked in its attempt to reformulate the relation between public and private, the state and the market. Progressive reformers relied on an ideology of exposure to authorize their regulatory efforts, believing that if "the facts" behind corporate practices were uncovered and laid bare, then the invisible value now accessible to only the corporate insiders would dissipate or be redistributed. The trust, of course, was the very embodiment of such invisibility. Its stock price typically bore no relation to its tangible assets or its actual capitalization, thus enabling its promoters to extract wealth out of nothing more than the public perception of uninhibited power. This is what reformers meant when they referred to the stock of "trustified" corporations as "water-logged," and what Dreiser means when he cites the "fictitious value" created by consolidations and the "watery magnificence" of the trust form — the "water" in the trust's stock was the value not of its tangible assets, but of its apparent ability to dictate reality, to create fictions that could not be refuted (*Titan* 474, 399). Publicity, however, could do much to remedy this problem. In discussing possible ways to destroy what he called "the money trust" — the group of powerful investment bankers headed by J. P. Morgan that seemed to be involved in many corporate consolidations — Louis D. Brandeis emphasized the power of publicity to affect the profits reaped by the banking houses: "Among the most important facts to be learned for determining the real value of a security is the amount of water it contains. And any excessive amount paid to the banker for marketing a security is water. Require a full disclosure to the investor of the amount of commissions and profits paid; and not only will investors be put on their guard, but bankers' compensation will tend to adjust itself automatically to what is fair and reasonable" (*Other* 104). Brandeis's rather naive faith in the existence of a "real value" for securities underscores the extent to which progressive attempts to require disclosure were, in essence, efforts to apply a logic grounded in the certainties of nature and property to corporate practices that seemed remarkably resistant to it. One of the most touted achievements of Wilson's first term was the creation of the Federal Trade Commission, an agency designed specifically to expose secret anticompetitive practices and thus destroy their value. By publicizing the elements by which stock became "watered," reformers hoped to imbue the inherently intangible nature of modern business with the virtues of visibility. Yet the very need for regulation implied that what they were dealing with was not property at all — that the concept of "real value" no longer made sense — and that exposure would serve not so much to ferret out "reality" as to offer a different interpretation of "reality." "The expert" charged with uncovering corporate secrets would serve as a kind of editor, redistributing the intangible value now hidden within corporate fictions according to a new — more egalitarian — plot.

In spite of these implications, of course, progressive rhetoric (as evidenced by doctrinal pronouncements conceived of as "timeless" rather than by time-bound narratives) continued to insist upon the availability of reality, truth, and facts, just as it remained adamant about the possibility of restoring the vitality of nature and property. And Dreiser's novels, at least on one level, express similar sentiments. Cowperwood's "frankness" is clearly a progressive virtue; it bestows upon him the incidents of property — visibility, substance, reality — and operates as a foil to the illusion and insubstantiality of money, thereby defining him as a failed monopolist and a successful hero of progressive reform. Moreover, Dreiser's narration conforms to the same credo, probing into the details of Yerkes's financial transactions with all the zeal that Ida Tarbell exhibited in her muckraking articles on Standard Oil, but with none of the outrage. Like Howells and Hopkins had before him, Dreiser places his own narrative in opposition to those more sensationalistic journalistic accounts of reality, suggesting that literature might relate stories that were, in a sense, more "true." The objectivity and distance that characterize the description of Cowperwood's financial schemes are those of "the expert" charged with carefully explaining the hidden intricacies of business to an ignorant public and allowing the facts to speak for themselves. Citing *The Financier* and *The Titan* among other naturalistic novels of business, June Howard notes that the "political discussion" within such novels "opens a place for the reformer who wants to control the corporation and thus overcome the laws of force and achieve a rational and regulated society" (74). Such a goal required a belief in the innate rationality of the truth, and Dreiser's journalistic (but not sensationalistic) array of facts associates him with the logic that reformers such as Brandeis relied upon to undergird their regulatory agendas.

But Dreiser's novels are more willing to acknowledge the limitations of this ideology of exposure than were most progressives. Facts may dominate the narration in *The Financier* and *The Titan*, yet they are also strangely elusive, even for the ostensibly neutral narrator. During his hero's struggle to extricate himself from his legal and financial tangle in *The Financier*, Dreiser interrupts the progress of his narrative to interject a lamentation about the bounds of his own fiction, exclaiming "If only the great financial and political giants would for once accurately reveal the details of their lives!" (200). While his novels purport to do just that, they are also infused with an acute awareness that they are as fictional as the kind of "stories" that financiers sell to a gullible public. Dreiser's faith in exposure was troubled by an uncomfortable sense that "the expert" was actually nothing more than another storyteller. A similar sense of unease had pervaded Howells's explorations of the author's legal role in *A Modern Instance* and *The Quality of Mercy*, yet Howells nonetheless held out hope for literature's capacity to relate stories superior to those told by self-interested money-grubbers and pandering journalists. Similarly, Dreiser's sense of deficiency did not prevent him from offering his own version of the facts — to the contrary, one might say that it endowed his narrative voice with an authority that the "purely" legal voice of Brandeis did not possess. In an age dominated more by the fictions of money than by the realities of property, Dreiser suggests, it is the novelist — the "expert" at storytelling — who can best combat the anti-egalitarian effects of those fictions. If novelists possess no privileged access to nature, they nonetheless can affirm the significance of that concept by revealing the places in which it is absent. Dreiser's nostalgia locates "essence," "reality," and "nature" in the past, but it also keeps the meaning of such terms alive by emphasizing (diachronically) their lapsed vitality and (synchronically) their uncanny residues. His novels of business, therefore, fulfill Howells's vision by opening a place not only for the progressive reformer, but for the progressive author as well, whose "expertise" allows for insights into the fictions by which money operates. Money is not property, Dreiser insists, and if that assertion does not in itself cause money to disappear, it nonetheless suggests that the power of fictionality might be employed as effectively to limit the growth of corporate wealth as to enhance it.

At the end of *The Financier*, Dreiser imagines Cowperwood as Macbeth encountering the Weird Sisters. He surmises that, in addition to Cowperwood's riches and achievements, the witches would have foretold "sorrow, sorrow, sorrow," and the author concludes by asking, "What wise man might not read from such a beginning, such an end?" (448). Although Dreiser's lesson here is, in part, about the vanity of worldly success, it is also about the proposition that endings can always be seen as immanent in beginnings. As the founding narratives of liberalism indicate, the very decision to begin with "nature" foretells its transformation into "society," and the Progressive Era counterparts to such narratives point to the fact that, by the early twentieth century, the decision to begin with "property" implied the inevitable emergence of "business" and "money." Yet if Dreiser's ending has already been foretold, that fact does not render the story moot. Although convention has replaced essence and there are no longer any "real values" to assert, the very act of narrating this transition makes possible the past's continued influence upon the present, even if only as an object of desire.

And this, it turns out, is precisely the lesson of the lobster and the squid.

Although the lobster sits in the tank "apparently looking at nothing," he is in fact reading the movements of the squid. Each time he snatches a piece of the squid's body, the squid emits a "cloud of ink" that temporarily protects it (*Financier* 7, 8). Dreiser is both lobster and squid, killing nature, property, and the past, but simultaneously preserving them in his own "cloud of ink." Yet even more significantly, he is the young Cowperwood, standing outside of the fray and observing its progress. The squid dies at the hands of the lobster, but the lobster will die at the hands of humans — has already died, in fact, by virtue of being read and narrativized by the spectators. The whole "drama" is obsolete by the time it is observed, for the very existence of the observer establishes a new paradigm and makes the story of this "savage" struggle a story of the past (8). Consequently, by the end of *The Titan* the narrative of one individual triumphing over another has changed to one of "the mass" triumphing over "the individual." Commencing his own novel with a model of the state of nature, Dreiser proceeds to describe its displacement by a model of society — an ending implied in the very terms of his beginning. Yet unlike the shareholders of the Great Northern and Northern Pacific, nature does not "disappear"; it is preserved nostalgically in the person of the observer, the expert, the professional, and — it would seem — the author. What wise man might not read from such a beginning, such an end?

Postscript

Dreiser's version of progressive authorship stands at a crossroads that my own narrativization of this era identifies as both an end and a beginning. For if Dreiser shows how the author might be thought of as an "expert" — someone whose narratives function in a regulatory manner within a public sphere defined by storytelling — he also points toward the emergence of the "purely" literary expert — the writer whose professional expertise serves to distinguish the territory of literature from that of law, politics, and the messiness of public discourse (a figure best exemplified, as my introduction asserts, by T. S. Eliot). In other words, modernism's conception of authorship has a political and legal genealogy that an earlier generation of authors makes explicit. While those authors address a wide array of legal issues (many of which continue to vex us today), they are united by the fact that each envisions a public realm that is more than the sum of its disparate and warring parts — a realm traditionally bound together through the neutral mediation of an independent and autonomous legal sphere, but now re-visioned as a space composed of and guided (for better or worse) by narratives. As I hope to have made clear by now, the belief in a form of literary autonomy and purity expressed by Eliot and others in the post–World War I era can be seen as a reformulation of the legal ideals invoked by an earlier generation of authors; the politics of literary modernism (even the authoritarian bent of some of its practitioners) is rooted in the very principles of liberal democratic philosophy that underlie conceptions of property and the rule of law. The legal engagement I see in American fiction written between 1880 and 1920 is one manifestation of the nation's ongoing attempts to grapple with the porous nature of its own foundational ideals, and the modernists' turn toward literary professionalism and specialization should thus be viewed as the next chapter in this political, legal, and literary saga.

Although I find the legal and literary dialogue in these works compelling, I hope that my analysis has succeeded in raising issues more tangential to this relation as well. One of the implications of my analysis, for instance, is that literature possesses an institutional dimension implicit in the very term "literature" itself. While this may not be revelatory, it is worth noting nonetheless. Debates over the literary canon are often seen as "political," but to the extent that they are also about which narratives will be officially sanctioned as public guideposts, they should be viewed as "legal" as well. Such debates are ultimately about how real lives (those of students, teachers, readers, and even nonreaders) will be regulated by textual authority. Indeed, in an era in which the rise of cultural studies has suggested the obsolescence of "literature" as a subject of analysis, an understanding of literature's institutional dimension underscores not just the undesirability, but the impossibility of eliminating it as a meaningful cultural category. For when we deny works of literature the authority to which they lay claim, we inevitably construct another set of texts to replace them — texts that, if not termed "literature," nonetheless occupy the same public space. As I have argued above, authority can be transformed, but it cannot disappear.

Finally, I hope that my readings of these texts serve as reminders to those of us engaged in interdisciplinary pursuits that interdisciplinarity as a critical practice is independent of the tools afforded to us by contemporary critical theory. As helpful as theory is in pursuing such inquiries (and my readings have certainly been informed by it), that fact does not preclude the notion that being interdisciplinary might also have mattered greatly to earlier generations of writers and thinkers. Moreover, these works suggest that merging disciplinary perspectives is a time-honored method in the United States for asserting a public voice and a measure of institutional power — goals that might be said to lie beneath the current academic interest in interdisciplinarity as well.

In English departments, American literature written between the Civil War and World War I (certain "major" authors such as James and Twain excepted) often plays second or third fiddle to those periods and movements — American romanticism and literary modernism to be specific — regarded as more "successful." The "failure" of literary realists to achieve their own stated goals, for instance, has now become the conventional wisdom of much of Americanist scholarship. But when one looks beyond narrowly defined disciplinary categories regarding genres (political novel, historical romance) and movements (realism, naturalism) — in other words, when one approaches turn-of-the-century fiction in the interdisciplinary spirit in which much of it was written — one finds that it says things few romantic or modernist novels could. What's more, those things are intimately related to the very concerns many of us now have regarding the place of literature in the nation's political and social life. Let us accord a new respect for the spirit of this age, and look to its cultural productions for insight into our own desires for public voices and institutional power.

NOTES

Introduction

1 As Burton J. Bledstein notes, "the word 'amateur,' which earlier in the eighteenth century had simply referred to a person who pursued an activity for the love of it, increasingly acquired negative and pejorative references as the nineteenth century developed" (31). Emerson's "The Poet," published in the 1844 collection *Essays: Second Series*, was written while this more "pejorative" meaning was developing. In fact, Emerson contributes to that development.

The meanings attached to the words "profession" and "professional" are more complex. Bruce A. Kimball identifies "six 'moments' in the rhetoric of 'profession'":

First was the extension of "profession" from referring to a religious vow to denoting the group who made the vow, especially, the "secular" clergy. Second was the shift in reference from the clergy to dignified, non-religious occupations. Third was the introduction of the terms "learned professions" and "liberal professions," which identified certain dignified occupations. Fourth was the displacement of "professed" by "professional" as the adjective denoting "occupational" or "vocational." Fifth was the introduction of the noun "professional" to replace "professor," which was narrowed to the field of education. The sixth moment in the rhetoric of "profession" was the sloughing away of the terms "learned professions" and "liberal professions" in the early twentieth century, as "professions" began to refer to many vocations, just as it had in sixteenth-century English. (16)

Kimball's fourth "moment" is the point at which "professional" emerged as the opposite of "amateur."

2 Fish makes this explicit when he states to a hypothetical adversary, "you could persuade me that everything I want to preserve depends on a position other than the one I hold, and if you did that, your position would then be mine and I would believe what you believe; but until that happens I will argue for my position with all the confidence that attends belief even though I know that

under certain conditions at some time in the future I might believe something else" (*Is There* 369).

3 The idea that capitalist systems are now experiencing what Jürgen Habermas calls a "legitimation crisis" does not make sense unless we limit the meaning of "crisis" to refer to a particular institutional configuration. There can never be what Habermas calls a "legitimation deficit"; if one set of institutional beliefs and practices loses its authority, it can only be because another set has replaced it (Habermas 47). Authority can be transformed, but it cannot disappear.

4 Referring to legal systems employing a legal-rational model, Weber states that "the possibility of entering with others into contractual relations the content of which is entirely determined by individual agreement . . . has, as compared with the past, been immensely extended in modern law, at least in the spheres of exchange of goods and of personal work and services" (188). Weber is also quick to point out, however, that legal-rational systems do nothing to ensure that all can take advantage of this freedom of choice; those who have little or no property are just as constrained as they would be under a more overtly restrictive regime.

5 See especially Fish's critique of Habermas's "Universal Pragmatics" in the essay entitled "Critical Self-Consciousness, Or Can We Know What We're Doing?" (*Doing* 436–67).

6 See, for instance, James L. Battersby's attempt to undermine Fish's radical contextualism by pointing out that "the view that all our ideas are historically or professionally conditioned is itself not historically or professionally conditioned" (56). That is to say, if we accept Fish's premises, his argument becomes utterly unpersuasive because it is empty and self-refuting.

7 In addition to Bledstein and Kimball, Margali Sarfatti Larson has explored the "rise of professionalism" during this period. Both Bledstein and Larson emphasize the class-based nature of professional ideology. Bledstein maintains that professionalism "was a culture — a set of learned values and habitual responses — by which middle-class individuals shaped their emotional needs and measured their powers of intelligence" (x). Larson resists equating professionals with an identifiable class, but argues that "the very notion of profession is shaped by the relationships which these special occupations form with a type of society and a type of class structure" (xvi). Kimball's analysis traces the cultural history of professionalism back to its origins in the idea of "vocation."

8 Within the context of this argument, I view the terms "professional," "institutional," and "disciplinary" as roughly synonymous. As Laurence Veysey demonstrates in discussing the ways in which the humanities have diverged from standard models of professionalization, there are certainly particular in-

stances in which one would want to distinguish and complicate these terms (see Veysey 57–62). But since I am examining a particular epistemology and methodological model grounded in legal-rational authority — an element that extends across boundaries that would otherwise be meaningful — I treat these concepts as rooted in the same cultural development.

9 For a thorough discussion of the development of "legal science" in the nineteenth century, see Robert W. Gordon.

10 Holmes's metaphor of the story anticipates the description of the law provided by Robert Cover in his influential essay, "Nomos and Narrative." Cover argues that "law may be viewed as a system of tension or a bridge linking a concept of a reality to an imagined alternative" (*Narrative* 101). The notion that narratives can be a tool to assert alternatives that are, to some extent, already written into the law is one that the authors I discuss use in the construction of their own legal narratives.

11 The idea that stories form a central element in the operation of legal systems has motivated much of the interdisciplinary study of law and literature in recent years. Robert Cover articulated this connection when he argued that "no set of legal institutions or prescriptions exists apart from the narratives that locate it and give it meaning. For every constitution there is an epic, for each decalogue a scripture" (*Narrative* 95–96). This perspective underlies the collection of essays edited by Peter Brooks and Paul Gewirtz entitled *Law's Stories*, as well as literary histories that focus on the law such as Carl S. Smith's, John P. McWilliams Jr.'s, and Maxwell Bloomfield's *Law and American Literature: A Collection of Essays* and Brook Thomas's *Cross-Examinations of Law and Literature: Cooper, Hawthorne, Stowe, and Melville*.

A different perspective emerges in Wai Chee Dimock's *Residues of Justice: Literature, Law, Philosophy*. Dimock notes the ways in which literary texts embody a legal logic with respect to the definition and enforcement of justice, but she also demonstrates that such texts frequently undermine that logic by exposing its "residues." Her analysis implies that there is something inherently oppositional in narrative; something that resists the static equations embedded in legal conceptions of justice. Dimock's arguments are compelling and powerfully articulated, but I would nonetheless suggest that the narratives she cites as oppositional form part of a legal as well as literary process of defining justice — they offer perspectives that can be seen as no less "legal" than those the law currently valorizes.

12 Those who see Holmes as a defender of a narrow and technical version of the law often cite his famous 1897 address "The Path of the Law," in which he states "I often doubt whether it would not be a gain if every word of moral

significance could be banished from the law altogether, and other words adopted which should convey legal ideas uncolored by anything outside the law." Yet he also concludes this address with a call for lawyers to broaden their study of law to include its "remoter and more general aspects." "It is through them," he tells his legal audience, "that you not only become a great master in your calling, but connect your subject with the universe and catch an echo of the infinite, a glimpse of its unfathomable process, a hint of the universal law" (*Collected* 179, 202). Such language reveals the Emersonian idealism that lies behind Holmes's ostensibly constricted "legalism."

13 This in spite of the insistent assertions of legal scholars associated with the Critical Legal Studies movement that the rule of law is a myth. For a discussion of the attack on the rule of law as a concept, see Andrew Altman's *Critical Legal Studies: A Liberal Critique* (chap. 1). One could argue that the very despair conjured up by contemporary legal processes and institutions testifies to the power of the ideal against which they are being measured. Whether the target be the "politicization" of the judiciary, the lack of professional ethics among lawyers, or the "media circuses" surrounding high-profile trials, attacks on the state of the law either implicitly or explicitly invoke principles such as independence, objectivity, fairness, and moral integrity — the cornerstones of the rule of law.

14 Scholarly interest in the literary nature of the law began with the rise of the Critical Legal Studies movement in the 1980s. The model has since been employed by feminist legal scholars and those involved in Critical Race theory, who have used storytelling as a way to expose the gaps and the strategies of power underlying the law's formal rationality. See, for instance, Patricia Williams's *The Alchemy of Race and Rights* and Martha Minow's "Stories in Law" (in Brooks and Gewirtz 24–36).

Examples of readings that reflect a deterministic sense of law's effect on literature would be Walter Benn Michaels's treatment of Stowe and Hawthorne in *The Gold Standard and the Logic of Naturalism*, and Priscilla Wald's reading of Lydia Maria Child's *Hobomok* in *Constituting Americans*. Both critics compellingly analyze literary reflections of the law, but neither suggests the notion that literature might operate to help construct, and thus revise, legal formulations. A more romantic vision of literary resistance to the law is evidenced by Richard Weisberg's reading of Melville's *Billy Budd*. Weisberg argues that Melville calls "for a renewal of the old alliance of artistry with just action" and offers the hope that "literary art . . . may again join with a positive system of law to generate admirable language" (175, 176).

In a recent book analyzing literary and legal representations of accidents, Nan Goodman argues for a model of "law and literature" that emphasizes interdependence. Goodman asserts that "neither literary nor legal narratives in nineteenth-century America can be understood without the other" and that a "reciprocity" exists between law and literature (10, 9). But she also insists that the fields of law and literature need not be seen as "temporally or even topically related in order to profit from a comparison between them" (10). To the contrary, I maintain, like Robert Ferguson, that the two fields bear temporal and topical connections to one another in the United States, and that those historical connections helped shape the kind of literature produced in the late nineteenth and early twentieth centuries.

15 *Billy Budd* has inspired a number of analyses focusing on the legal themes it raises. John P. McWilliams Jr. compares Vere to Holmes, but concentrates on Holmes's views of the relationship between individual rights and social welfare. McWilliams leaves Melville on the fence with respect to this issue, caught between a belief in "timeless universal principles" and natural rights on one hand, and a Holmesian belief in the supremacy of public policy and the state on the other (Smith, McWilliams, and Bloomfield 81). Thomas reads the story as a comment on the antebellum decisions of Melville's father-in-law, Lemuel Shaw (who infamously upheld the law's form over its moral substance in enforcing the Fugitive Slave Act), and on the postbellum transformations in legal thought. He disagrees with McWilliams by noting that Vere's formalism embodies precisely the kind of static conception of law decried by Holmes. Thomas maintains that Melville wants his readers to see all claims to formal wholeness and integrity, whether legal or not, as exclusionary and authoritarian (*Cross-Examinations*). In a poorly reasoned argument, eminent legal scholar Richard Posner uses *Billy Budd* to demonstrate that legal and literary interpretation have nothing whatsoever to do with one another. In so doing, he takes a stand similar to that which I see Melville taking in the text; Melville, however, makes the case with a power entirely lacking in Posner's interpretation. For other readings focusing on the story's legal content, see Lawrence Douglas, Barbara Johnson, Charles A. Reich, and Richard Weisberg.

16 See E. L. Grant Watson, "Melville's Testament of Acceptance."

17 See especially the legally oriented readings offered by Thomas (*American*), Eric J. Sundquist, and Evan Carton.

18 Menand notes "the irony" inherent in Eliot's attempt to separate literary professionals from other professionals, such as businessmen: "the manner in which the modern artist tried to keep his ideological distance from the businessman,

to guard the autonomy of his work, was also one of the ways in which the artist and businessman were both, in spite of their self-conceptions, bound together" (Menand 100–101).

19 Bruce Robbins notes the symbiotic relationship between Eliot's aesthetic practices and professional literary critics of his era: "For would-be professionals in the first half of the century, struggling to displace the gentleman-scholar's tasteful, unhurried, independently funded appreciation of the finer things, Eliot's despair was enabling and invigorating. It declared in effect that their more rigorous and earnest professional activities were urgently required" (17).

The "Official" Narratives of William Dean Howells

1 Nathalia Wright finds the title more appropriate than Howells's original title for the novel — "The New Medea" — because the revised version draws more attention to "the administration of justice" (68). In fact, the discrepancy between the titles highlights the tension in the novel between absolute standards of justice (embodied in Greek tragedy) and the relative standards reflected in ever-changing social definitions of the concept.

2 See Story's dissent in *Proprietors of the Charles River Bridge v. Proprietors of the Warren Bridge.*

3 Alexander Hamilton articulated this principle in *The Federalist Papers*: "The independence of judges is equally requisite to guard the Constitution and the rights of individuals from the effects of those ill humors which the arts of designing men, or the influence of particular conjunctures, sometimes disseminate among the people themselves. . . ." (Federalist No. LXXVIII, 440).

4 Morton J. Horwitz notes that "the invocation of custom as a standard of justice was widespread in late nineteenth-century social thought," and he asserts that *The Common Law* fits within this tradition (Horwitz 125). And H. L. Pohlman maintains that the twentieth-century tendency to view Holmes as a radically original thinker obscures the extent to which his philosophy was "a product of nineteenth-century traditions of thought" (3).

5 Holmes's rejection of "logic" was, in part, a response to late nineteenth-century efforts to turn law into a kind of science. Christopher Langdell of Harvard Law School was the most prominent advocate of this position. For Holmes, Langdell's approach imposed an artificially rational structure on the law that, by emphasizing its internal consistency, ignored the outside forces that have shaped it.

6 Philip P. Wiener also notes this epistemological conflict. Although he locates Holmes within a "scientific" tradition that emphasized change, evolution, and skepticism, he asserts that "it cannot be said that Holmes's evolutionary and pragmatic conception of truth was consistently expressed. He oscillates, with equally brilliant eloquence at both extremes, between an individualist, subjective theory and a social, objective one" (187).

7 This model of legal authority bears comparison to that of contemporary legal philosopher Ronald Dworkin. In *Law's Empire* (1986), Dworkin argues that law is neither pure convention, wedded to previously articulated norms and meanings, nor simply an instrumental means of enacting politically interested goals. He formulates a model of "law as integrity," which "insists that legal claims are interpretive judgments and therefore combine backward- and forward-looking elements; they interpret contemporary legal practice seen as unfolding political narrative." Dworkin argues that deciding cases is like writing a chain novel — each judge charged with rendering a difficult judgment must invent a new chapter while nonetheless remaining true to the coherence of the overall project. Thus, he maintains, we can still talk about decisions that are "right" and "wrong" without being strict legal formalists (225).

8 In *Literary Friends and Acquaintance*, Howells attributed their lapsed friendship to their different backgrounds. He summed up his first meeting with Holmes and the course of their subsequent relationship in the following paragraph:

> I rent myself away from the Autocrat's presence as early as I could, and as my evening had been too full of happiness to sleep upon at once, I spent the rest of the night wandering about the streets and in the Common with a Harvard Senior whom I had met. He was a youth of like literary passions with myself, but of such different traditions in every possible way that his deeply schooled and definitely regulated life seemed as anomalous to me as my own desultory and self-found way must have seemed to him. We passed the time in the delight of trying to make ourselves known to each other, and in a promise to continue by letter the effort, which duly lapsed into silent patience with the necessarily insoluble problem. (*Literary* 46–47)

9 Edmund Wilson argues that Holmes's Civil War experience — which included being wounded twice — played a major role in the development of his legal philosophy, having led him to abandon his youthful idealism in favor of skepticism and legal pragmatism. He maintains that Holmes "lost in the war the high hopes of the Northern crusade" and fell back on "a Calvinist position which will not admit the realization of the Kingdom of God on earth" (794).

10 As John P. Diggins notes, Adams "held out hope for a 'Republic of Virtue,' an American nation in which the squalid but inescapable realities of ambition,

avarice, and resentment could be tempered and perhaps tamed by the higher ideals of virtue, benevolence, and duty" (35). But Adams's belief that a class of individuals might develop who would serve as guardians of the republic began to fade after the Revolution, and his insistence on a governmental system defined by checks and balances evidences his unwillingness to grant authority to any one element of the citizenry.

11 Thomas distinguishes the realists' adherence to a logic of contract from the legal philosophy articulated by Holmes. He asserts that "whereas the utopian promise of contract cannot do without a link between contract and promising, Holmes could not think of promising without transcendental sanctions." Yet Holmes's thought, he maintains, was not without its own transcendentalism. The "boundary thought" in which Holmes engaged "gave his theory of contract a moral foundation that his own antifoundationalism denied" (*American* 45, 46). Thomas perceptively notes the epistemological tension inherent in Holmes's model of the law — a tension that, I argue, was equally present in Howells's novels.

12 Warren Hedges maintains that the notice "appears in Howells's text in an artifactual fashion, almost as if it were an exhibit in a trial," and that it helps to "anchor the text to the public discourse of law and historical reference" (42, 43). Rather than anchoring the text, however, I believe that it upsets it. "The public discourse of law" proves inadequate to "anchor" the text.

13 George R. Uba discusses this aspect of the novel and relates it to Maine's argument in *Ancient Law* that the history of "progressive societies" has centered around "a movement *from Status to Contract*" (Maine, quoted in Uba 79).

14 Robert H. Wiebe notes that, "With the exception of bankers, no group late in the nineteenth century stood in lower public repute" (116).

15 Wiebe remarks upon the desire by journalists for professional status: Many journalists, "distressed by the stereotypes of crude inquisitor and callous purveyor of sensation . . . followed the usual route to professionalism, attempting an exact definition of the field and encouraging the development of separate technical schools" (120).

16 In "The Man of Letters as a Man of Business," Howells would remark that "the *entente cordiale* between the two professions [of journalism and literature] seems as great as ever" ("Man of Letters" 22).

17 Borus notes that some writers at the end of the nineteenth century attempted to establish literary analogues to legal bar associations. In 1882, for instance, a group of writers formed the Authors Club of New York City, which "aimed at reconstructing the exalted status of the writer." Borus remarks that "Professional demeanor, not literary merit, was the basis of the club's member-

ship" and that "Journalists and technical writers were expressly barred because
they could not measure up to the club's vision of disinterested and contem-
plative men who communed with their imaginations in the quiet of club quar-
ters" (149).

18 The name of the town comes from Matthew 23:7, in which Jesus condemns
the "scribes and Pharisees" as "hypocrites," stating, "ye are like unto whited
sepulchres, which indeed appear beautiful outward, but are within full of dead
men's bones, and of all uncleanness." The passage invokes the internal/external
dichotomy of the novel's legal concerns, but Howells does not indicate which,
if any, of his characters the image would apply to. If Bartley, it would run counter to much of Howells's depiction of him in the rest of the novel. Edwin H.
Cady asserts that the passage applies to Atherton, who is guilty of a kind of
"Pharisaical demonism" (Cady, "Introduction" xxii).

19 My reading contrasts with those that interpret Bartley's death and Atherton's
authoritative voice as evidence of Howells's need to hold on to the moral certainties of a previous era. Many critics who take this approach cite the breakdown that Howells suffered while writing the novel, maintaining that Bartley's
disappearance from the latter portion of the book, and his eventual murder,
constitute attempts by the author to restore a kind of mental order. Kenneth
S. Lynn, for instance, asserts that "Howells . . . had emerged from his breakdown with an urgent need to denounce the flight of Bartley" (254). I see the
ending as a coming to terms with the new order rather than a return to the
old; if Howells's breakdown affected the structure of his novel, it was to reconcile him to Bartley more than to Atherton.

20 Among Emerson's many references to "character" is his definition of it in his
essay of the same title: "Character is [a] moral order seen through the medium
of an individual nature" ("Character" 498).

21 Cady asserts that Atherton's "idealism" is "unmistakably Swedenborgian"
("Introduction" xix). Henry Nash Smith, on the other hand, maintains that
Atherton "blends elements from two intellectual traditions: Horace Bushnell's
doctrine of 'Christian nurture,' and the secular doctrine of progress that was
an integral part of the dominant American ideology" (100). But Atherton's
specific intellectual lineage is not fleshed out by Howells, and not important
for his purposes; he simply wishes us to see Atherton as an idealist who appeals
to a mode of authority that is no longer vital.

22 Alfred Habegger emphasizes Howells's antisentimentalism, noting that "one
of the nineteenth-century myths Howells scotched in [*A Modern Instance*] is
the redemptive function of the wife" (98). Joseph Allen Boone agrees that the
relationship between Bartley and Marcia is "the byproduct of sentimentally

fostered conceptions of romance," but he concludes that Howells is not successful at combating those conceptions (125).

23 Henry Nash Smith agrees that Atherton's moral terms "belong to the detritus of sentimental popular fiction" (98).

24 Lewis P. Simpson, in a chapter entitled "The Treason of William Dean Howells," emphasizes Howells's break with the "'ideal' New England literary order," which, for Howells, was embodied by the *Atlantic*'s original editor, James Russell Lowell (85). Atherton's standing in the legal community of Boston seems a reflection of that which Lowell possessed in the literary one.

25 Kaplan notes that Howells seems to identify Bartley's journalism with his own form of realism, but she concludes that Howells ultimately feels the need "to punish and thereby dissociate himself from Hubbard." Thus, she claims, the novel concludes by withdrawing "into the genteel world of polite conversation as Atherton's commentary presides over the narrative" (34, 35). While Howells is certainly uncomfortable with the Bartleyan aspects of his own writing, Atherton does not provide him with an acceptable alternative. As a result, he grudgingly adopts Bartley's Holmesian perspective as his own.

26 The novel is infrequently read now, and there is little critical commentary on it. Cady is one of the few scholars to address it at length. He maintains that Howells's exploration of business morality "places him at the beginning of a line which runs through Dreiser, Sherwood Anderson, Lewis, Fitzgerald, and Dos Passos to Cozzens and beyond." He also situates the novel at the end of Howells's period of artistic originality, stating "*The Quality of Mercy* marks the last true advance in the growth of Howells' mind" (*Realist* 176, 177).

27 Recent critics have tended to agree with Larzer Ziff's assessment that the tone Howells captures in the novel is of "the moral consciousness of the intelligent middle-class American" (39). Howells's focus, to be sure, is often on middle-class characters, but he tends to emphasize the failure of such characters to understand themselves or others, or to act decisively within their social environment. Northwick's middle-class status, for instance, does not provide him with the moral terms he needs to control his own actions. "Middle-class morality" is certainly an issue in Howells's novels, but it is often more problem than solution.

28 Maxwell would reappear in Howells's 1898 novel, *The Story of a Play*, in which he struggles to maintain his artistic integrity in the face of the theater's commercial demands.

29 John W. Crowley maintains that this passage links "Police Report" with Bartley's death in *A Modern Instance*, stating that "In both, a grim and violent 'jus-

tice' arose from Howells' need to repudiate acts of imaginative leniency that his acquaintance with sinners had produced" (123). While I do not reject the notion that Howells had a form of literary "justice" in mind in both works, I do not believe that he presents such a concept as an authoritative premise on which to ground either law or literature.

Helen Hunt Jackson and the Romance of Indian Nationhood

1 Valerie Sherer Mathes notes that "Jackson failed to create a sympathetic feeling for the Indians among many of her readers, who instead saw only a tender love story." She quotes one contemporary reviewer who described the novel as "'a little overweighted with misery,' but totally inadequate in presenting the Indian problem," and another who wrote that *Ramona* constituted "'no burning appeal, no crushing arraignment, no such book as *Uncle Tom's Cabin*'" (*Jackson* 82–83). Michele Moylan describes two dominant reactions to *Ramona*, stating that "Jackson's earliest readers often responded to the novel either by objecting to her portrayal of Indians, finding it romanticized and dangerous, or by reading *Ramona* as a call for continuing philanthropic efforts to 'civilize' the Indians" (229). Moylan believes Jackson's purpose in the work was to issue a call to action on behalf of Indian rights.

It is worth noting that one reviewer who did find the book effective as a work of reform was the lawyer and novelist Albion Tourgée. Calling *Ramona* "unquestionably the best novel yet produced by an American woman," Tourgée praised the book for its "strain of angry, tender, hopeless protest against wrong" and its critique of Americans as "a people as jealous of their own rights and privileges, as defined by their own laws and customs, as they are heedless of all other claims to consideration" ("Study" 251, 247). Perhaps Tourgée's legally oriented perspective enabled him to appreciate Jackson's approach to reform more than those readers expecting a work of pure moral suasion.

2 This assessment, of course is far from unanimous. Daneen Wardrop, for instance, argues that although Jackson "appropriates Indian and Chicano cultures," she does so "in order to advocate for them." Wardrop asserts that Jackson's advocacy works through establishing a "feminized landscape," challenging the "dominant male economies" that give rise to Indian dispossession (28, 34). And David Luis-Brown maintains that the novel contains both an overt plot and a "shadow plot," the former reinforcing a romantic racialism that confirms racial difference and the latter subverting that assumption by

"proposing cross-racial alliances" "establishing the personhood of Indians" (823, 828).

3 See William T. Hagan, Frederick E. Hoxie, and Loring Benson Priest for thorough discussions of the ideology of Indian reform in the late nineteenth and early twentieth centuries.

4 Cheryl Walker notes that Indians began to emerge as symbols for America in the eighteenth century: "As the new nation was established, it became clear that a new iconography was needed to construct and reinforce an idea of Americanness in a population not used to conceptualizing the thirteen colonies as a cultural and political unit." Consequently, "the figure of the Native American became central to national identity" (26). Susan Scheckel makes a similar point when she argues that "by claiming Indians . . . as part of their own national story, nineteenth-century Americans found a way to ground national identity in the distant, inaccessible, 'immemorial past'" (8).

5 For an analysis of the different ways in which the concept of "wardship" has been applied to Indians, see Felix S. Cohen's *Handbook of Federal Indian Law* (169–73). Joseph Burke, James E. Falkowski, and Francis Paul Prucha each provide thorough descriptions and analyses of the Cherokee Cases (see Falkowski 100–105; Prucha, *Great Father*, vol. 1, 208–13). For a discussion of the cases' current legal meaning, see Charles Wilkinson.

Priscilla Wald also analyzes the cases, asserting that Marshall's opinions were torn by the contradictions in Indian policy that created the specter of "persons" whom the law could not officially acknowledge. For Wald, the cases are essentially about "the incomprehensible hole in the map within the perimeters of Georgia" (26).

6 Thus, Priscilla Wald is only partly correct when she notes that a Cherokee nation "would challenge the integrity of the state and of the Union," imposing "an important symbolic threat" (28). This is true, but *not* acknowledging the Cherokee nation would also pose a symbolic threat, for it would disrupt the terms of difference that Americans relied upon to construct their own sense of national identity.

7 Quoted in Prucha, *Documents* 136. The prohibition was part of a rider attached to the Indian Appropriation Act.

8 The "plenary power" doctrine held that the Constitution had vested Congress with absolute authority to regulate Indian affairs — an authority that could not be circumscribed by a treaty. This principle would gradually develop strength in the nineteenth century and would culminate in the Supreme Court's decision in *Lone Wolf v. Hitchcock* (1903), which ruled explicitly that Congress had

the power to abrogate treaties with Indians. Called "the Indians' *Dred Scott* decision" in a later judicial opinion, *Lone Wolf* seemed to subject Congressional power to no judicial limitations whatsoever (Newton 221). Blue Clark provides a thorough analysis of *Lone Wolf* and its legacy. Russel Lawrence Barsh and James Youngblood Henderson argue that the "plenary power" doctrine is still alive in the law, "legitimating increasingly interventionist policies, and demeaning Indian citizenship" (Barsh and Henderson 63). See also Laurence M. Hauptman for an analysis of the doctrine's survival.

9 As Indian Commissioner Ely S. Parker (a Seneca Indian himself) argued in 1869, "The Indian tribes of the United States are not sovereign nations, capable of making treaties, as none of them have an organized government of such inherent strength as would secure a faithful obedience of its people in the observance of compacts of this character" (quoted in Prucha, *Documents* 134).

10 Sidney L. Harring also takes note of this element of the Court's opinion:

> What is remarkable about the *Crow Dog* decision's recognition of tribal law as an inherent attribute of sovereignty is not that the Supreme Court had any respect for Brule law or even knew anything substantive about it. Characterizing the case as one of "red man's revenge," the Court hardly bothered to conceal its contempt for tribal institutions. Yet at the same time, *Crow Dog* upheld Marshall's recognition of tribal sovereignty in *Worcester*, a significant statement given the heightened Indian-white conflict fifty years later. . . . The case is memorable for both its strength and its weakness, as well as for the Court's fundamental inability to come to terms with the complexity of Indian-white relations or with a legal strategy to give effect to tribal sovereignty. (129)

11 In a message to Congress delivered in 1870, President Grant described the new process of appointing Indian agents as a cornerstone of his peace policy. He noted that "the societies selected are allowed to name their own agents, subject to the approval of the Executive, and are expected to watch over them and aid them as missionaries, to Christianize and civilize the Indian, and to train him in the arts of peace" (quoted in Prucha, *Documents* 135).

12 See Thomas, *American* 11.

13 It is interesting to note that Alessandro and Felipe experience similar feelings of sibling connection that veer dangerously toward romantic love. Felipe realizes that he must support Ramona's decision to marry Alessandro, and thus willingly assumes the role of brother to Ramona and brother-in-law to Alessandro. But as David Luis-Brown points out, there are also homoerotic undertones to the relationship between Alessandro and Felipe. Noting how

Alessandro saves Felipe after he faints and then nurses him to health, Luis-Brown asserts that Alessandro provides Felipe with both "physical support" and "the healing caress of a loving mother," and that "Felipe alludes to the homoerotic character of their relationship when he remarks that when Alessandro sang, 'I thought the Virgin had reached down and put her hand on my head and cooled it'" (826).

14 Jackson made her position clear in *A Century of Dishonor*:

> The notion which seems to be growing more prevalent, that simply to make all Indians at once citizens of the United States would be a sovereign and instantaneous panacea for all their ills and all the Government's perplexities, is a very inconsiderate one. To administer complete citizenship of a sudden, all round, to all Indians, barbarous and civilized alike, would be as grotesque a blunder as to dose them all round with any one medicine, irrespective of the symptoms and needs of their diseases. It would kill more than it would cure. (340)

15 Paul W. Kahn summarizes the principle in this way: "The rule of law is ... the rule of no one. To be the rule of no one, it must appear to be the product of everyone. The choice, it seems, is between the freedom of the people and the freedom of individuals. The former produces law; the latter, oppression" (94).

16 This was especially evident in the Supreme Court's decision in *Crow Dog*, as Justice Matthews could see the issue only as one of the "white man's morality" versus the "red man's revenge." As Sidney L. Harring points out, however, the Brule Sioux did not allow the murder involved in that case to stand as an acceptable act of "revenge." Instead, a tribal council was convened and a settlement worked out with the victim's family — a method of conflict resolution that concentrated on reconciliation rather than adjudication. See Harring, 100–115.

17 Gutierrez-Jones reads the madness of Alessandro and the temporary incapacity of Ramona as evidence of Jackson's view that Indians lacked the kind of agency that would construct them as legal subjects. Stating that "for both characters, their ultimate submersion in legal issues — Alessandro's 'stealing' of a horse and Ramona's failure to testify about Alessandro's murder — is portrayed as a lack of intentionality," he argues that this lack of agency allows Jackson's characters to "be 'inhabited' by Anglo readers without requiring of them a significant effort at cultural translation" (64). But Gutierrez-Jones fails to note the way in which madness in the novel calls attention to the law's *erasure* of Indian agency; although the law considers madness a form of incapacity, Jackson uses madness to point to the law's own incapacity to recognize the sovereignty

of the Indian self. That failing renders the "local" law unauthoritative, not truly "national."

18 I thus take issue with Luis-Brown's assertion that the novel ultimately "undermines racial discourses of absolute difference" and that it dismantles "whiteness as a strategy of sectional reconciliation and racial and gender oppression" (830). Although Jackson does provide a mestiza character whose hybridity does not render her inferior, her "Indian" and "white" identities are ultimately connected more to culture and nationhood than to blood — and those cultural and national affiliations are kept separate but equal within her own consciousness.

19 The problem of the white man who seemed to "turn Injun" was faced directly by the Supreme Court in 1846, and with a response similar to the one Jackson offers. In *U.S. v. Rogers*, the Court was faced with deciding if a white man who had been adopted into the Cherokee nation and had been accused of a crime was subject to punishment by the state government. A treaty provided that the state would have no jurisdiction for crimes committed by one Indian against another, and the question thus became if a white man could ever "turn Injun." Chief Justice Roger Taney answered with a no, asserting that the treaty exception "does not speak of the members of a tribe, but of the race generally, — of the family of Indians" (*U.S. v. Rogers* 573). Taney's decision elevated race over nationality (Jackson does the opposite), but he came to a conclusion similar to Jackson's about the ability to be both Indian and American.

20 See Vine Deloria Jr. and Clifford M. Lytle for a thorough discussion of the genesis of and controversies surrounding the Indian Reorganization Act.

Narrating Citizenship in Pauline Hopkins's *Contending Forces*

1 Although Tate suggests that Hopkins's domestic representations of political concerns are authorized by a Victorian conception of the "complementary" nature of the public and private spheres, this complementarity nonetheless contained within it a separateness that her analysis seeks to deny.

2 The concept of "sentimental power" is Jane Tompkins's (Tompkins 122). Although it is a way of talking about the political relevance of sentimental narratives, it implicitly relies on a separation of public and private realms — a separation that, Tompkins maintains, women writers used to assert a form of moral authority.

3 In this sense, she employs a conception of literature similar to that articulated by Henry James in "The Art of Fiction." As I have discussed in the introduc-

tion, James saw fiction as a kind of history whose material was stored "in documents and records" (James 78). Both writers felt the need to locate literary practices in concrete texts and to emphasize the extent to which storytelling could be viewed as a disciplined and positivistic endeavor.

4 Carole McAlpine Watson notes that black women's novels at the turn of the century were infused with a sense of "racial corporateness" and that "the central concern of their stories is the welfare of the race as a group" (7). In the oppressive racial environment of the period, concerns about gender were subordinated to the overriding imperative of African American solidarity. I do not mean to suggest that gender-related issues are irrelevant to interpreting Hopkins's texts, but simply that underscoring gender distinctions did not constitute a central component of her political strategy.

5 See my discussion of Weber in the introduction.

6 Carla L. Peterson explores the way in which the novel conforms to and diverges from the genre of the historical romance. Noting its imperialist ideology at the turn of the century, she states that "Hopkins sought to turn this genre back against itself, to critique its nationalist and imperialist ideology from a black feminist perspective" (180).

7 My analysis of Wells's writing accords with Sandra Gunning's claim that "In texts such as *Southern Horrors*, Wells forced the collision of stereotypes about black and white women in order to construct, at the point of fragmentation, the traces of an alternative discourse on racial violence and women" (88). I am interested in the extent to which this "alternative discourse" was a legal one, and in Wells's and Hopkins's use of such a discourse to address violence against both black men and women.

8 Trudier Harris asserts that the obsession with rape as a justification for lynching indicates that the practice was, in part, a kind of "scapegoat ritual" by which white male psychosexual guilt was displaced onto black men (see Harris 11–19). Her analysis of the ceremonial aspects of lynchings is compelling, but writers such as Hopkins and Wells were especially concerned with the legal and political contexts of the violence.

9 Paul Laurence Dunbar's short story "The Lynching of Jube Benson" underscores the extent to which the "evidence" relied upon by lynch mobs fell short of legal standards. In the story, a white doctor regretfully recalls his participation in a lynching, detailing the circumstantial evidence that led the mob to accuse an honest and hardworking black man of rape and murder. After the man is hung, the doctor examines the body of the white female victim and discovers that the assailant's skin lodged beneath her fingernails is white rather

than black. The narrative expresses confidence that forensic methods of investigation can ultimately combat the narratives of black bestiality, as the doctor ends his account with the anguished statement, "Gentlemen, that was my last lynching" (240).

10 Although the novel does not mention it, manumission was actually illegal in North Carolina until 1830, a fact that further complicates the "legality" of Montfort's murder (see Cover 75).

11 For discussions of legal realism, see Laura Kalman and William W. Fisher III. Mark Kelman provides a good introduction to Critical Legal Studies, and James Boyle provides a representative sample from the movement. For a critique of Critical Legal Studies, see Andrew Altman.

12 Kenneth L. Karst has argued that citizenship encompasses more than an entitlement to certain rights — it also serves as a means by which the national community is defined. Karst uses the concept of "belonging" to show how application of different degrees of citizenship symbolically include or exclude specified groups from full membership in the nation. Hopkins's use of due process principles in her narration suggests that the neutrality she seeks from the law has symbolic value — it is a way of acknowledging the extent to which African Americans "belong" to America.

13 Lois Lamphere Brown argues that *Contending Forces* is "a striking, racialized sentimental narrative that is significantly different from previous African American sentimental novels. [Hopkins] utilizes only certain portions of the Anglo American form, and she does not adopt the racially reoriented tactics of sentimental empowerment introduced by her African American peers" (69). But while Brown points out some important ways in which the novel diverges from the genre—particularly with regard to Sappho's sexual background— the novel's family-oriented structure and the centrality of its marriage plot locate it firmly within the tradition. Hopkins does, however, reenvision that tradition as encompassing a kind of legal engagement in addition to its moral and religious idealism.

14 As Ann duCille notes, "Will Smith is a towering example of the positive black patriarch — supportive black sons, brothers, and husbands whose loving male lustlessness both complements and enables the female passionlessness that black women writers employed in their campaign to redefine black womanhood in positive cultural terms" (43).

15 Hopkins's sewing circle seems to invoke the growing club movement among African American women during this period, an association that ties it to the male-dominated anti-lynching meeting. As Wells notes in her autobiography,

the anti-lynching meeting for women held in New York in 1892, over which she presided, "was the real beginning of the club movement among the colored women in this country" (*Crusade* 81).

16 Adele Logan Alexander, for instance, describes an incident in which "four robed Warren County [Georgia] Klansmen gang-raped a young black girl, beat eleven other freedpeople, and shot and killed yet another, all in one bloody and frenzied Sunday night" (150).

17 Citing Sappho's name, Elizabeth Ammons reads her character as a figure for Hopkins and for black women writers in general. The fact that she ultimately divulges her secrets and survives her ordeals, Ammons asserts, reflects Hopkins's hope that "out of the violence and sexual outrage of the black woman's experience in America will come — despite the effort to silence her — great art" (*Conflicting* 80).

18 Tate also notes the difference in tone between Hopkins's first novel and her subsequent ones, which "marginalized their stories of courtship and development" and "depict growing racial frustration" (19).

19 In this respect, the novel resembles Twain's *Pudd'nhead Wilson*, in which the exposure of Tom Driscoll's criminality also results in the exposure of his black heritage and leads to his subsequent enslavement. Although Tom may, in some sense, deserve what he gets, Twain's resolution exposes the way in which race overrides legal ideals; Tom is punished not for his crime, but for being black.

20 The bill was drafted by the well-known constitutional lawyer Albert E. Pillsbury, and stated, in part, that "the putting to death of a citizen of the United States by a mob in default of protection of such citizen by the state or its officers, shall be deemed a denial to the citizen by the state of the equal protection of the laws" (Pillsbury 708). The bill targeted every member of such a mob and every state officer guilty of failing to provide protection. Although the bill did not pass, James M. McPherson notes that "the idea of a federal law did not die . . . and Pillsbury's proposal became the basis of the Dyer anti-lynching bill in the 1920s (which was filibustered to death in the Senate)" (309).

Charles Chestnutt's Fictions of Ownership

1 My reading of *Plessy* is indebted to Eva Saks's interpretation of miscegenation laws. Saks argues that such laws "attempted to stabilize property in race by investing white blood with value and arresting its circulation," thereby turning the question of an individual's race into "the equivalent of a title search" (49, 52).

2 Washington's public comments about constitutional rights did not always match his private actions. As Louis R. Harlan has shown, Washington secretly supported a legal challenge to the grandfather clause of the 1898 Louisiana constitution's voting provision. Not only did he raise much of the money for the court test, but he also took an active role in planning its strategy (297–98).

3 Chesnutt's series on "The Future American" appeared in the *Boston Evening Transcript* on 18 August 1900, 25 August 1900, and 1 September 1900. Chesnutt argues in the series that racial amalgamation is inevitable and that, if legal and social prohibitions against miscegenation were removed, "in three generations the pure whites would be entirely eliminated, and there would be no perceptible trace of the blacks left" (18 August). Although it is tempting to accept such language at face value and assume that Chesnutt genuinely believed in "pure white" blood, a close reading of his fiction indicates that he used such terms strategically. The law employs such concepts, and Chesnutt's nonfictional writings on race address the law on its own terms.

4 I will not continue to enclose the word "blood" in quotation marks. As used in this chapter, however, the term refers to the legal concept employed in defining racial distinctions and should therefore be viewed as a construct rather than a "natural" category.

5 Charles A. Lofgren, in *The Plessy Case: A Legal-Historical Interpretation*, maintains that Tourgée's property-based argument was "the most legally orthodox and easily grasped of the Fourteenth Amendment arguments" in *Plessy* (188). While it is true that by framing the issue of discrimination in terms of property rights Tourgée sought to make the issue of discrimination more concrete for the Court, the unstated implications of the argument were more far-reaching than either Tourgée's brief or the Court's opinion acknowledged. Chesnutt's fiction attempts to explore those implications.

6 The two lawyer-novelists maintained a correspondence throughout the 1890s. The year before the *Plessy* case, Tourgée had recruited Chesnutt for an associate editorship on a magazine he was helping to found called *The Basis, A Weekly Magazine of Citizenship*. Chesnutt turned the offer down (see Heermance 102).

7 W. E. B. DuBois would later join Chesnutt and Tourgée in remarking on the tangible value of whiteness. In *Black Reconstruction in America*, DuBois describes the rifts between black and white laborers in the South during Reconstruction by noting that "the white group of laborers, while they received a low wage, were compensated in part by a sort of public and psychological wage" in the form of "titles of courtesy," preferential legal treatment, superior schools, etc. (700).

8 It is worth noting that one of the novel's minor characters is named Plato. A young African American boy who is one of Rena's pupils, Plato is a character

out of black minstrelsy who still calls Tryon "Mars Geo'ge" and is willing to do anything for a fifty-cent piece. If the concept of "blood" partakes of Platonism, Chesnutt seems to imply, it is a distinctly white form of it. Plato represents a white "ideal" of black behavior, but hardly one that African Americans would endorse.

9 Chesnutt, like Mark Twain, was both fascinated and repulsed by the South's anachronistic celebration of feudal codes and ceremony, and both authors relate this aspect of Southern culture to the construction of blood. *The House behind the Cedars* owes a great deal to *Pudd'nhead Wilson*, but Chesnutt takes the idea of blood as title further than Twain by revealing how such a concept manifests itself in African American attempts to acquire other forms of property. For readings of property issues in Twain's novel, see Saks and Sundquist.

10 Chesnutt's belief in a labor theory of value is particularly evident in his short story "Po' Sandy," in which the white Northern narrator, John, wishes to build a new kitchen out of the lumber that constitutes the conjured body of a slave. Uncle Julius's story of Sandy prevents the appropriation of this tangible manifestation of the fruits of slavery, enabling it to be used for a black church. As Sundquist notes, "Julius has a right to the created property of slavery — produced by his own labor and that of his ancestors — while John does not" (376). John Warwick is but a version of John the narrator in *The Conjure Woman* stories. Both seek to profit from a system that, although postbellum, has its origins in slavery. Behind the material advantages of whiteness, "Po' Sandy" suggests, lies labor performed by blacks.

11 Morton Keller describes the devaluation of property in South Carolina: "South Carolina's property valuation of $400 million in 1860 shrank to $50 million in 1865. The state ranked third in the nation in per capita wealth in 1860; ten years later it was fortieth" (199).

12 The relation of rights to ownership, of course, was influentially articulated by Locke, whose philosophy of natural rights rested upon the idea that "every Man has a *Property* in his own *Person*" (328).

13 For the most influential discussion of "possessive individualism," see C. B. Macpherson. Brook Thomas, however, argues that analyses of nineteenth-century America have tended to rely too heavily upon Macpherson's ideas (Thomas, *American* 39–40).

14 The difficulty in separating rights from white privilege was reflected in the first major piece of civil rights legislation passed after the ratification of the Thirteenth Amendment. The Civil Rights Act of 1866 stated, in part, that all citizens "shall have the same right . . . to make and enforce contracts, to sue, be

parties, and give evidence, to inherit, purchase, lease, sell, hold, and convey real and personal property, and to full and equal benefit of all laws and proceedings for the security of person and property, as is enjoyed by white citizens." As the statute makes clear, rights (particularly property rights) could not be imagined without reference to whiteness itself, thereby incorporating a category of exclusion and privilege into legal efforts to eliminate such categories.

15 This is William L. Andrews's reading. Emphasizing the story's didacticism, he states that "through Wellington's chastened experience, misguided blacks were to learn that the important things in life are not the 'privileges' of close association with white people which theoretically the black man may share in the North. Instead, what really matters are the tangible benefits of life — marital devotion, financial security, careful planning, and restraining good sense — symbolized in Wellington's relationship to Milly" (91).

16 Tourgée's novel *Bricks Without Straw* also emphasizes this irony and, like Chesnutt's story, highlights the relation between ownership and power. Noting that in some states slaves were considered to be forms of realty and were therefore transferred by deed, he describes the purchase of a tract of land by the freedman Nimbus Ware from his former master, stating that "the recent *subject* of transfer by deed was elevated to the dignity of being a *party* thereto. The very instrument of his bondage became thereby the sceptre of his power" (*Bricks* 120). As in Chesnutt's story, however, the freedman's ownership is tenuous, as the Ku Klux Klan targets him for his success, and the validity of his title is later questioned. Andrews points out the similarities between Ben Davis and Nimbus Ware (see Andrews 97).

Lorne Fienberg remarks on the irony of Davis's conviction for stealing, stating that he "is convicted by the ideology which he once believed would protect his own efforts to prosper in a transformed southern economy" (235).

17 Fienberg notes that, "If Davis has not literally stolen the colonel's whip, then the white citizens of Patesville are surely correct that he has designs on the power of self-mastery that the whip represents" (234).

18 Gibson seems to modify this position in his introduction to the Penguin edition of the novel, in which he emphasizes the constraints on Warwick and Rena imposed by social definitions of race. Dickson D. Bruce Jr. also takes note of the novel's pessimism, but attributes it to the conflict between Chesnutt's "assimilationist ideals" and "the overarching reality of being black" (178). In my view, "assimilation" is a problematic term to use with Chesnutt because it implies black capitulation to whiteness. Chesnutt hoped for a raceless society in which black and white would lose all meaning, but in the meantime he criti-

cized those blacks who simply adopted white standards of appearance and behavior.

19 Sundquist asserts that "the law is a barrier to the free exercise of racism and therefore must be overridden" (430).

20 Brook Thomas explicitly distinguishes Chesnutt's fiction from that of the realists, but he also notes that it is not quite sentimental. Chesnutt, he maintains, posits "an enlightenment view of a moral universe" — one in which equitable principles grounded in natural law are accessible to individuals through the faculty of reason — and he asserts that this position is neither realistic nor sentimental (*American* 182). But the sharp division between these literary modes that Thomas, like Warren, insists upon is belied by Chesnutt's fiction. Rather than representing an alternative to realism and sentimentalism, Chesnutt's works reveal their convergences.

21 Fortune asserted in his 1884 book, *Black and White*, that "individual ownership in the land is a transgression of the common right of man, and a usurpation which produces nearly, if not all, the evils which result upon our civilization" (217). Chesnutt maintained a correspondence with Fortune.

22 Andrews reads "The Partners" as an essentially didactic lesson that "the march of progress for Afro-America could not become simply a competitive trampling lest in a moral sense the ultimate victory be a pyrrhic one" (85). This is certainly true, but the story's emphasis on the problem of black ownership significantly complicates this lesson. The narrative's subtext searches for the terms by which one can be both black and "titled" at the same time.

23 See Chesnutt, *Frederick Douglass* 66–72.

24 Darryl Hattenhaur also notes that the novel cannot be easily classified. He asserts that Chesnutt employs a "dialogic mixing of genres and narrative techniques" and that this "textual miscegenation" is central to his depiction of racial miscegenation (198).

25 Barton J. Bernstein discusses this influence, asserting that "sociological and psychological theories controlled the Court's decision" (198).

26 A version of Chesnutt's distinction between Warwick's self, grounded in rights, and Rena's, based in feeling, has appeared in contemporary legal debates. The Critical Legal Studies movement has taken a lead in critiquing legal discourse that relies upon the notion of rights, advocating instead the use of a discourse that valorizes needs. As Patricia Williams notes in *The Alchemy of Race and Rights*, however, many African Americans have been reluctant to abandon a concept that they see as a source of personal protection. She states that "where one's experience is rooted not just in a sense of illegitimacy but in *being* illegitimate, in being raped, and in the fear of being murdered, then the black ad-

herence to a scheme of both positive and negative rights — to the self, to the sanctity of one's own personal boundaries — makes sense" (154).

Privacy and Subjectivity in Wharton's *The House of Mirth*

1 Simone de Beauvoir influentially articulated the way in which "woman" and "object" have come to be synonymous, and the idea has formed a cornerstone of feminist theory ever since. But explorations of the connection between objectification and the unitary nature of the liberal subject are of more recent origin. Luce Irigaray, Julia Kristeva, and Judith Butler are among the theorists who have attempted to deconstruct the unity of consciousness in the interests of a feminism grounded in plurality. Butler, for instance, maintains that "the enabling conditions for an assertion of 'I' are provided by the structure of signification" and that, through subversive practices such as parody, it is possible to disrupt this structure (143). Mary E. Hawkesworth provides a sound overview of the various strands of feminist epistemology since Beauvoir.

2 My reading takes issue with Judith Fetterley's argument that Lily's payment of her debt to Gus Trenor constitutes "a final revelation of the 'real' Lily Bart." Although Fetterley interprets the novel as "a powerful denunciation of patriarchal culture," she fails to account for the gendered conception of "reality" that operates to limit Lily's options (Fetterley 210, 200).

3 For discussions of the right to privacy since Warren and Brandeis, see Morris L. Ernst (with Alan U. Schwartz) and J. Thomas McCarthy. For a critique of this right, see Richard A. Posner, "The Right of Privacy."

4 Michael Grossberg's examination of American family law in the eighteenth and nineteenth centuries indicates the public function that the home served in reconciling the tensions of republican ideology. He maintains that homes were charged with "the vital responsibility of molding the private virtue necessary for republicanism to flourish," and that "the home and the polity displayed some striking similarities," including "the equation of property rights with independence" and "a commitment to self-government" (7, 6).

5 In *Women and Economics*, for instance, Gilman argued for social changes that would develop a greater sense of individuality in women. Women, she maintained, "consider themselves mere fractions of families and incapable of any wholesome life of their own. The knowledge that peace and comfort may be theirs for life, even if they do not marry, — and may be still theirs for life, even if they do, — will develope (*sic*) a serenity and strength in women most beneficial to them and to the world" (300).

6 This position was a common one among "mugwump" intellectuals of the period. Henry Adams, for instance, in an 1876 address he titled "Primitive Rights of Women," argued that women's rights must be grounded in the family, as "the strongest and healthiest of all human fabrics," and that society's view of marriage had advanced beyond its early origins in property to a conception in which some measure of sexual equality was possible.

7 The home acted as a visible representation of what Michel Foucault has called "subjected sovereignty." He provides the following examples of this cultural construct: "the soul (ruling the body but subjected to God), consciousness (sovereign in a context of judgment, but subjected to the necessities of truth), the individual (a titular control of personal rights subjected to the laws of nature and society), basic freedom (sovereign within, but accepting the demands of an outside world and 'aligned with destiny')" (*Language* 221).

8 One commentator, writing in the *American Law Review*, asserts with some hyperbole: "this decision elicited much discussion all over the world." He also wryly notes that "the newspaper press, apparently unmindful of its own delinquencies, in respect to a decent regard for the private rights of individuals, has almost unanimously disapproved of the decision" (Elbridge Adams 45).

9 Elaine Showalter, on the other hand, reads the novel as a rejection of the aristocratic assumptions behind the concept of the "lady novelist." Agreeing with Elizabeth Ammons's assertion that the end of the novel foresees "a union of the leisure and working classes," she maintains that Lily's death envisions "a world in which women like Gerty Farish and Nettie Struther will struggle hopefully and courageously. Lily dies — the lady dies — so that these women may live and grow" (Ammons, *Edith* 43; Showalter 101). But these interpretations align Wharton with a liberal ideology (Gerty, like Selden, has her own flat), which the novel seems to struggle against.

10 Cynthia Griffin Wolff, however, reads the story as if Alice really is what Waythorn believes her to be — "a unique perversion of the human condition" (Wolff 105). She views Alice as a victim of a "pernicious form of femininity" in which female selfhood is subordinated to the demands of men, but she fails to see the irony in Wharton's depiction of Waythorn's judgments.

11 *Lochner* has never been explicitly overruled, but it is now largely vilified as an example of a rigid judicial formalism that usurps the public's right to enact social legislation. For discussions of "substantive due process" and the conservative tenor of the Supreme Court at the turn of the century, see Morton J. Horwitz and Arnold M. Paul.

It is noteworthy that, even though Louis Brandeis sought judicial recognition of a right to privacy, he was one of the most fervent crusaders against the

Supreme Court's formalistic definition of rights. As a result, he took on the *Lochner* decision a few years later when he agreed to argue for a maximum hours law in *Muller v. Oregon* (1908). The law applied only to women, and the Court upheld it without overruling *Lochner*. Brandeis presented the Court with a plethora of data indicating the damage done to women and to families from working extended hours; he thus employed an appeal to the justices' own senses of domestic proprieties and their bias about female capabilities.

12 In an argument grounded in feminist legal scholarship that elevates relational over adversarial styles of negotiation, Elaine N. Orr asserts that Wharton affirms a world "not of discrete individuals and objects but of relationships" (70). She perceptively notes the novel's concern with the nature of boundaries and with the problem of unity, but her reliance upon the concepts of "community" and "relationships" overlooks Wharton's equal if not greater concern with privacy and subjectivity. For Wharton, privacy involves separation from others and is therefore not a communitarian value. But it also makes possible a subjectivity that recognizes the presence of others within it, that acknowledges its existence as a composite rather than a unitary entity.

Invoking Warren and Brandeis in his reading of Henry James's *The Bostonians*, Brook Thomas argues that James "presents a self that is defined by the exchanges into which it enters," thus constructing an intersubjective rather than autonomous version of selfhood (*American* 71). But Thomas also maintains that, for James, interpersonal exchanges create "a space between" individuals — "a space that both constructs and — so long as it exists — helps to maintain a private self" (*American* 72). Thus, Wharton's version of privacy, as I see it, differs from that which Thomas finds articulated in *The Bostonians*. Wharton exposes the duality and uncertainty that lies at the core of privacy and thereby places Thomas's "space" within the subject rather than between subjects. If James ultimately affirms the existence of a "private self" (even one that emerges only through interpersonal exchanges), Wharton reveals how the unitary nature of such a self incorporates the same power imbalances that underlie the unity of the home.

13 Wharton's insistence on showing us the hostility of the law and of society to affirmations of uncertainty may account for Emily Miller Budick's assertion that a "nonskepticist philosophy of art" informs the novel. Budick argues that, while "Wharton and the people she represents are willing to take risks within the realm of big business and commercial enterprise," they are not "prepared to question the existence of the world itself or the relation between the real and the unreal. In particular, they will not risk the venture of skepticism" (127). On the contrary, Wharton's novel asserts a radical skepticism about the

nature of "reality," yet it also indicates the extent to which dominant conceptions of individuality are tied to an epistemology grounded in absolutes.

14 The scene in which Lily burns the letters is but one instance of Wharton's narrative shifts. Another occurs as Lily is leaving the Trenors' house after Gus has attempted to take advantage of her. Wharton juxtaposes Lily's distress with Selden's "objective" observation of her, highlighting the different versions of "reality" that result.

15 In *The Common Law*, Holmes defined rights positivistically: "A legal right is nothing but a permission to exercise certain natural powers, and upon certain conditions to obtain protection, restitution, or compensation by the aid of the public force. Just so far as the aid of the public force is given a man, he has a legal right, and this right is the same whether his claim is founded in righteousness or iniquity" (214).

16 Wolff reads the ending as Wharton's questioning of the "set piece in American literature" presenting "the death of a beautiful woman as seen through the eyes of her lover." Asserting that we must "condemn Selden for savoring the resonances of Lily's death," she places that death on a par with Lily's portrayal of Mrs. Lloyd in the tableau vivant scene — both perfect her status as an idealized object. It is true that Selden seems to reconcile himself to Lily's death a bit too easily, but he also transforms the terms in which he thinks of "the real Lily Bart," suggesting a similar transformation within himself.

17 Amy Kaplan reaches a similar conclusion with respect to Lily's death. She argues that Wharton "refuses to treat writing as the retrieval of knowledge from the wastebasket of intimacy; but in burning those letters she replaces them with Lily, who ends her life 'thrown out into the rubbish heap'" (103).

18 Wolff argues that Archer's "final act affirms the coherence of his own identity, and in this assertion of 'self,' [he] achieves genuine maturity" (325). But maturity, for Wharton, is not necessarily the same as "identity" or "self"; in fact, her novel complicates such integral concepts, describing instead a process of maturation that involves disintegration.

Dreiser's Progressive Nostalgia

1 *A Hoosier Holiday* is filled with passages that use nature to distinguish a previous time from the current one, but that also indicate the past's residues in the present. In a similar description of the era of the "great financiers," Dreiser asserts, "Those were great days in the capitalistic struggle for control in Amer-

ica. The sword fish were among the blue fish slaying and the sharks were after the sword fish. Tremendous battles were on, with Morgan and Rockefeller and Harriman and Gould after Morse and Heinze and Hill and the lesser fry. We all saw the end in the panic of 1907. Posterity will long remember this time" (58–59).

2 Many readers have noted that Dreiser's treatment of Cowperwood is conflicted and seemingly at odds with itself. Richard Lehan, for instance, asserts that in *The Financier* and *The Titan* "Dreiser both extolled the rugged individualist and attacked the vested interests of the robber barons. . . . Better than any other American novelist, Dreiser in these works revealed the dynamics of American political and social life — not only the battle between tycoon and tycoon, but between the tycoon and the public, a battle that warred within his own heart" (100).

3 Although these two novels were conceived by Dreiser as part of a trilogy on the life of Yerkes (which he titled *A Trilogy of Desire*), the third installment, *The Stoic*, was not published until 1947 and does not engage the same issues as the first two. *The Stoic* reflects the turn toward communism and Eastern mysticism that Dreiser took toward the end of his career, and it thus functions less as part of a trilogy than as a wholly separate novel.

4 Like Locke, Smith articulated a labor theory of property, and this foundation arises from the very physicality of the body. He thus asserted that "the property which every man has in his labour, as it is the original foundation of all other property, so it is the most sacred and inviolable. The patrimony of a poor man lies in the strength and dexterity of his hands; and to hinder him from employing this strength and dexterity in what manner he thinks proper without out injury to his neighbor is a plain violation of this most sacred property" (*Wealth* 110).

5 As Alfred D. Chandler Jr. notes, before New Jersey modified its corporation law in 1889, it took a special act of a state legislature to incorporate a company that could hold stock in other companies. Thus, the trust emerged as a way to avoid this requirement. After the change in New Jersey law and the passage of the Sherman Act, however, "the 'New Jersey holding company' took the place of the trust as the legal form used to merge a number of single-unit enterprises operating facilities in several states into a single, large consolidated enterprise" (319–20).

6 Henry Adams described Roosevelt's reaction to Holmes's dissent by asserting that Roosevelt "went wild about it." Roosevelt later wrote in a letter to Henry Cabot Lodge that "Holmes should have been an ideal man on the bench. As a

matter of fact he has been a bitter disappointment" (quoted in G. Edward White 307).

7 Louis D. Brandeis offered a similar reading of Carnegie's career. He asserted that "the main purpose in forming [the Steel Trust] was to eliminate from the steel business the most efficient manufacturer the world has ever known — Andrew Carnegie," and that the trust's intent was "not the purchase of a mill, but the retirement of a man" ("Trusts" 201–2).

8 Martin J. Sklar notes the prominent role played by Wilson in what he terms the "corporate reconstruction of American capitalism." He asserts that, "in a time of conflict between an ascending corporate capitalism and a receding competitive capitalism, Wilson . . . appealed to partisans of both. He thereby personified the transition from the competitive stage to the corporate stage of capitalism" (384). Although Sklar does not address the role that Wilson's nostalgia played in this process, he does emphasize Wilson's admiration for Frederick Jackson Turner's frontier thesis — a nostalgic response to the demise of "the West" that served as a model for much of Wilson's political and economic thought.

9 Sklar and Gabriel Kolko have been two of the most forceful exponents of this interpretation of progressivism. Kolko argues that "Progressivism was initially a movement for the political rationalization of business and industrial conditions, a movement that operated on the assumption that the general welfare of the community could be best served by satisfying the concrete needs of business" (2–3).

10 Philip Gerber similarly asserts that "Perhaps the critical element tipping the balance to favor Dreiser's selection of Yerkes for the prototype *genus financier* was the streetcar king's ultimate failure" (113).

11 Dreiser would deal with this portion of Yerkes's life in *The Stoic* — a novel that, even more than the previous two installments in the trilogy, emphasizes failure. It relates not only Cowperwood's death but the raiding of his estate by his creditors and the complete erasure of his financial and artistic legacy.

12 Richard Lingeman notes that Cowperwood's individualism is contrary to the kind of cooperation that Yerkes's career exhibited: "Yerkes acted in league with other prominent Philadelphia financiers, but in [*The Financier*], and to serve Dreiser's heroic conception of him, he is a lone wolf" (64).

13 Morton J. Horwitz asserts that, at the turn of the century, "American courts came as close as they ever had to saying that one had a property right to an unchanging world" (151).

14 Dreiser's decision to use Yerkes as his model for Cowperwood was undoubtedly influenced, in part, by a desire to invoke the spirit of Franklin, another

Philadelphia financier. Cowperwood's first name also seems to evidence a connection.

15 Wesley Hohfeld, for instance, wondered whether the term "property" could be used in any intelligible sense. In an article published in 1913 that was to become one of the most influential legal analyses of property, he noted the "ambiguity" inherent in much legal terminology and asserted that

> the word "property" furnishes a striking example. Both with lawyers and laymen this term has no definite or stable connotation. Sometimes it is employed to indicate the physical object to which various legal rights, privileges, etc., relate; then again — with far greater discrimination and accuracy — the word is used to denote the legal interest (or aggregate of legal relations) appertaining to such physical object. Frequently there is a rapid and fallacious shift from the one meaning to the other. At times, also, the term is used in such a "blended" sense as to convey no definite meaning whatever. (21–22)

Hohfeld's concern has been articulated more recently by Thomas C. Grey in an essay entitled "The Disintegration of Property." Grey asserts that "the theory of property rights held by the modern specialist tends both to dissolve the notion of ownership and to eliminate any necessary connection between property rights and things." For Grey, "The substitution of a bundle-of-rights for a thing-ownership conception of property has the ultimate consequence that property ceases to be an important category in legal and political theory" (69, 81).

16 Holmes, on the other hand, was much less concerned with the fictionality inherent in corporate practices. He openly acknowledged what Harlan, Commons, and Lippmann would only tacitly suggest — namely, that property itself was a kind of legal fiction. While progressive narratives implied this when they located property in the past, their authors steadfastly refused to admit telling "stories." For Holmes, of course, the law was itself a "story." Holmes both was and was not a progressive. He worked with many of the same assumptions that progressives such as Commons and Lippmann did, but his openness about the contingency of those assumptions was decidedly unprogressive.

17 This accounts for why Dreiser turned to Eugene Witla, an artist, in his next work, *The Genius* (1915). Dreiser actually wrote most of *The Genius* before he published his novels of business, and it is thus reasonable to read Cowperwood and Witla as kindred spirits.

18 Howard Horwitz also underscores this aspect of financiering, but argues that Cowperwood's fluidity constitutes his attempt to escape from the forces of the market by escaping from the self. For Horwitz, Cowperwood's "hypotheca-

tory art secures the self by exploding . . . the representationality of value and property." Because it is precisely "the visibility and materiality of value's lineage that subjects it and its attendant self to vicissitude," he maintains, Cowperwood tries to remain "endlessly plastic, finally unaccountable" (H. Horwitz 199). Horwitz's interpretation perceptively highlights the conflict between material property and immaterial "values" that lies behind Dreiser's depiction of Cowperwood. Nonetheless, it stops short of identifying the political nature of Dreiser's resolution. Horwitz notes that Cowperwood finally comes to stand more for a "conventional individualism" grounded in essence than for a fluctuating "deindividualization," but for him this fact represents a liberal residue at odds with Dreiser's more radical impulse to reject liberal ideology. I maintain, on the other hand, that Dreiser emphasizes Cowperwood's individualism only to relegate it to extinction. Ultimately, the novels affirm the fluctuating values of the market, and seek to revise liberal narratives to authorize a more equitable and orderly distribution of those values.

19 During his fight for the franchise extensions, Yerkes admitted in an address at Chicago's Sunset Club, "So far as monopoly is concerned, I admit that we want a monopoly of the streets of this city . . . we do not want the eternal sandbagger after us all the time. When they say there is bribery in the City Council, why not give us the fifty year franchise we ask for and thus stop the bribery?" (quoted in Gerber 114).

20 Noting that one of the things that makes Cowperwood "heroic" is his "increasingly open acknowledgement of self-interest," Pizer argues that this quality sets Cowperwood apart from those reformers who "profess a concern for the public good" (*Novels* 177). But while Dreiser does distinguish Cowperwood from the "dreamers" who work for socially idealistic ends, he also ties his protagonist to them by virtue of the innately egalitarian nature of Cowperwood's openness. This is especially clear in *The Titan* when Cowperwood bluntly and unreservedly attempts to bribe Governor Swanson; Dreiser emphasizes the "understanding sympathy" between the two men (490).

21 This is exactly what progressives accused the Supreme Court of doing in its rulings involving "liberty of contract" and "substantive due process," and what gave rise to the legal movement known as "sociological jurisprudence." Although Brandeis and Holmes were each (in their own ways) participants, its best representative is probably Roscoe Pound, who defined it as "a movement for pragmatism as a philosophy of law; for the adjustment of principles and doctrines to the human conditions they are to govern rather than to assume first principles; for putting the human factor in the central place and relegat-

ing logic to its true position as an instrument" (quoted in Commager 376). In a series of articles published in the first two decades of the twentieth century, Pound attacked the Court's "mechanical jurisprudence" and argued that concepts such as "property" and "rights" be treated as socially malleable rather than as rigid and formalistic.

BIBLIOGRAPHY

Adams, Elbridge L. "The Right of Privacy, and its Relation to the Law of Libel." *American Law Review* 39 (January/February 1905): 37–58.

Adams, Henry. "Primitive Rights of Women." In *The Great Secession Winter of 1860–61 and Other Essays*, edited by George Hochfield, 333–60. New York: Sagamore, 1958.

Alexander, Adele Logan. *Ambiguous Lives: Free Women of Color in Rural Georgia, 1789–1879*. Fayetteville: University of Arkansas Press, 1991.

Altman, Andrew. *Critical Legal Studies: A Liberal Critique*. Princeton, N.J.: Princeton University Press, 1990.

Ammons, Elizabeth. *Conflicting Stories: American Women Writers at the Turn into the Twentieth Century*. New York: Oxford University Press, 1991.

———. *Edith Wharton's Argument with America*. Athens, Ga.: University of Georgia Press, 1980.

Anderson, Benedict. *Imagined Communities: Reflections on the Origin and Spread of Nationalism*. London: Verso, 1991.

Andrews, William. *The Literary Career of Charles W. Chesnutt*. Baton Rouge: Louisiana State University Press, 1980.

Arendt, Hannah. *Between Past and Future: Eight Exercises in Political Thought*. New York: Viking, 1968.

Ayers, Edward L. *Vengeance and Justice: Crime and Punishment in the 19th-Century American South*. New York: Oxford University Press, 1984.

Banta, Martha. *Taylored Lives: Narrative Productions in the Age of Taylor, Veblen, and Ford*. Chicago: University of Chicago Press, 1993.

Barsh, Russel Lawrence, and James Youngblood Henderson. *The Road: Indian Tribes and Political Liberty*. Berkeley: University of California Press, 1980.

Battersby, James L. "Professionalism, Relativism, and Rationality." *PMLA* 107 (1992): 51–64.

Bederman, Gail. *Manliness and Civilization: A Cultural History of Gender and Race in the United States, 1880–1917*. Chicago: University of Chicago Press, 1995.

Bell, Michael Davitt. *The Problem of American Realism: Studies in the Cultural History of a Literary Idea*. Chicago: University of Chicago Press, 1993.

Bender, Thomas. *Intellect and Public Life: Essays on the Social History of Academic Intellectuals in the United States*. Baltimore: Johns Hopkins University Press, 1993.

Berkhofer, Robert F., Jr. *The White Man's Indian: Images of the American Indian from Columbus to the Present*. New York: Knopf, 1978.

Bernstein, Barton J. "Plessy v. Ferguson: Conservative Sociological Jurisprudence." *Journal of Negro History* 48 (1963): 196–205.

Berry, Mary Frances. *Black Resistance/White Law: A History of Constitutional Racism in America*. New York: Penguin, 1994.

Bhabha, Homi K. *The Location of Culture*. London: Routledge, 1994.

Bledstein, Burton J. *The Culture of Professionalism: The Middle Class and the Development of Higher Education in America*. New York: Norton, 1976.

Boone, Joseph Allen. *Tradition Counter Tradition: Love and the Form of Fiction*. Chicago: University of Chicago Press, 1987.

Borus, Daniel H. *Writing Realism: Howells, James, and Norris in the Mass Market*. Chapel Hill: University of North Carolina Press, 1989.

Bourdieu, Pierre. "The Force of Law: Toward a Sociology of the Juridical Field." Translated by Richard Terdiman. *Hastings Law Journal* 38 (July 1995): 805–53.

———. *In Other Words: Essays Toward a Reflexive Sociology*. Translated by Matthew Adamson. Palo Alto, Calif.: Stanford University Press, 1990.

Boyle, James, ed. *Critical Legal Studies*. New York: New York University Press, 1992.

Brandeis, Louis D. *Other People's Money, And How the Bankers Use It*. New York: Frederick A. Stokes, 1914.

———. "Trusts and Efficiency." In *Business — A Profession*. Boston: Small, Maynard, 1914.

Brodhead, Richard. *The School of Hawthorne*. New York: Oxford University Press, 1986.

Brooks, Peter, and Paul Gewirtz, eds. *Law's Stories: Narrative and Rhetoric in the Law*. New Haven, Conn.: Yale University Press, 1996.

Brown, Gillian. *Domestic Individualism: Imagining Self in Nineteenth-Century America*. Berkeley: University of California Press, 1990.

Brown, Lois Lamphere. "'To Allow No Tragic End': Defensive Postures in Pauline Hopkins's *Contending Forces*." In *The Unruly Voice: Rediscovering Pauline Elizabeth Hopkins*, edited by John Cullen Gruesser, 50–70. Urbana: University of Illinois Press, 1996.

Bruce, Dickson D., Jr. *Black American Writing from the Nadir: The Evolution of a Literary Tradition, 1877–1915*. Baton Rouge: Louisiana State University Press, 1989.

Brundage, W. Fitzhugh. *Lynching in the New South: Georgia and Virginia, 1880–1930*. Urbana: University of Illinois Press, 1993.

Budick, Emily Miller. *Engendering Romance: Women Writers and the Hawthorne Tradition, 1850–1990*. New Haven, Conn.: Yale University Press, 1994.

Burke, Joseph. "The Cherokee Cases: A Study in Law, Politics, and Morality." *Stanford Law Review* 21 (1969): 500–531.

Butler, Judith. *Gender Trouble: Feminism and the Subversion of Identity*. New York: Routledge, 1990.

Cady, Edwin H. Introduction to *A Modern Instance*, by William Dean Howells. New York: Penguin, 1984.

———. *The Realist at War: The Mature Years of William Dean Howells*. Syracuse, N.Y.: Syracuse University Press, 1958.

Carby, Hazel V. *Reconstructing Womanhood: The Emergence of the Afro-American Woman Novelist*. New York: Oxford University Press, 1987.

Carton, Evan. "*Pudd'nhead Wilson* and the Fiction of Law and Custom." In *American Literary Realism*, edited by Eric J. Sundquist, 82–94. Baltimore: Johns Hopkins University Press, 1982.

Chandler, Alfred D., Jr. *The Visible Hand: The Managerial Revolution in American Business*. Cambridge, Mass.: Harvard University Press, Belknap Press, 1977.

Cherokee Nation v. State of Georgia, 30 U.S. 1 (1831)

Chesnutt, Charles W. *The Colonel's Dream*. New York: Doubleday, 1905.

———. *Frederick Douglass*. Boston: Small, Maynard, 1899.

———. *The House behind the Cedars*. New York: Penguin, 1993.

———. *The Marrow of Tradition*. Ann Arbor: University of Michigan Press, 1969.

———. "The Partners." In *The Short Fiction of Charles W. Chesnutt*, edited by Sylvia Lyons Render. Washington, D.C.: Howard University Press, 1981.

———. "Po' Sandy." In *The Conjure Woman*. Ann Arbor: University of Michigan Press, 1969.

———. "The Sway-Backed House." In *The Short Fiction of Charles W. Chesnutt*, edited by Sylvia Lyons Render. Washington, D.C.: Howard University Press, 1981.

———. "Uncle Wellington's Wives." In *The Wife of His Youth and Other Stories of the Color Line*. Ann Arbor: University of Michigan Press, 1968.

———. "The Web of Circumstance." In *Wife of His Youth and Other Stories of the Color Line*. Ann Arbor: University of Michigan Press, 1968.

———. "What is a White Man?" *New York Independent*, 30 May 1889, pp. 5–6.

Chesnutt, Helen M. *Charles Waddell Chesnutt: Pioneer of the Color Line*. Chapel Hill: University of North Carolina Press, 1952.

Chopin, Kate. *The Awakening*. New York: Penguin, 1976.

Clark, Blue. *"Lone Wolf v. Hitchcock": Treaty Rights and Indian Law at the End of the Nineteenth Century*. Lincoln: University of Nebraska Press, 1994.

Clark, Walter. "The True Remedy for Lynch Law." *American Law Review* 28 (1894): 801–7.

Cohen, Felix S. *Handbook of Federal Indian Law*. Washington, D.C.: United States Government Printing Office, 1945.

Colored American Magazine (specific articles cited in text).

Commager, Henry Steele. *The American Mind: An Interpretation of American Thought and Character Since the 1880's*. New Haven, Conn.: Yale University Press, 1950.

Commons, John R. *Legal Foundations of Capitalism*. New York: Macmillan, 1924.

Cooper, Anna Julia. *A Voice from the South*. New York: Negro Universities Press, 1969.

Cover, Robert M. *Justice Accused: Antislavery and the Judicial Process*. New Haven, Conn.: Yale University Press, 1975.

———. *Narrative, Violence, and the Law: The Essays of Robert Cover*, edited by Martha Minow, Michael Ryan, and Austin Sarat. Ann Arbor: University of Michigan Press, 1992.

Crowley, John W. *The Black Heart's Truth: The Early Career of W. D. Howells*. Chapel Hill: University of North Carolina Press, 1985.

Deloria, Vine, Jr., and Clifford M. Lytle. *The Nations Within: The Past and Future of American Indian Sovereignty*. New York: Pantheon Books, 1984.

Diggins, John P. "The Three Faces of Authority in American History." In *The Problem of Authority in America*, edited by John P. Diggins and Mark E. Kann, 17–39. Philadelphia: Temple University Press, 1981.

Dike, Samuel W. "The Effect of Lax Divorce Legislation Upon the Stability of American Institutions." *Journal of Social Science* 14 (November 1881): 152–63.

Dimock, Wai Chee. "Debasing Exchange: Edith Wharton's *The House of Mirth*." *PMLA* 100 (1985): 783–92.

———. *Residues of Justice: Literature, Law, Philosophy*. Berkeley: University of California Press, 1996.

Dixon, Thomas, Jr. *The Leopard's Spots: A Romance of the White Man's Burden, 1865–1900*. New York: Grosset and Dunlap, 1902.

Doreski, C. K. "Inherited Rhetoric and Authentic History: Pauline Hopkins at the *Colored American Magazine*." In *The Unruly Voice: Rediscovering Pauline Elizabeth Hopkins*, edited by John Cullen Gruesser, 71–97. Urbana: University of Illinois Press, 1996.

Dorris, Michael. Introduction to *Ramona*, by Helen Hunt Jackson. New York: Penguin, 1988.

Douglas, Lawrence. "Discursive Limits: Narrative and Judgment in *Billy Budd*." *Mosaic* 27 (December 1994): 141–60.

Dreiser, Theodore. *The Financier*. New York: Penguin, 1940.

———. *A Hoosier Holiday*. New York: John Lane, 1916.

———. *The Titan*. Cleveland: World Publishing, 1946.

DuBois, William E. B. *Black Reconstruction in America*. New York: Atheneum, 1973.

DuCille, Ann. *The Coupling Convention: Sex, Text, and Tradition in Black Women's Fiction*. New York: Oxford University Press, 1993.

Dunbar, Paul Laurence. "The Lynching of Jube Benson." In *The Heart of Happy Hollow*, 223–42. New York: Negro Universities Press, 1969.

Dworkin, Ronald. *Law's Empire*. Cambridge, Mass.: Harvard University Press, Belknap Press, 1986.

Eliot, T. S. "Professionalism, Or . . . ." *The Egoist* 5 (April 1918): 61.

———. "Tradition and the Individual Talent." In *The Sacred Wood*, 47–59. London: Methuen, 1950.

Elk v. Wilkins, 112 U.S. 94 (1884).

Ely, James W., Jr., and David J. Bodenhamer. "Regionalism and the Legal History of the South." In *Ambivalent Legacy: A Legal History of the South*, edited by Bodenhamer and Ely, 3–29. Jackson, Miss.: University Press of Mississippi, 1984.

Emerson, Ralph Waldo. "'Address to the Citizens of Concord' on the Fugitive Slave Law." In *Emerson's Antislavery Writings*, edited by Len Gougeon and Joel Myerson, 53–72. New Haven, Conn.: Yale University Press, 1995.

———. "Character." In *Emerson: Essays and Lectures*, edited by Joel Porte, 495–509. New York: Library of America, 1983.

———. "The Divinity School Address." In *Emerson: Essays and Lectures*, edited by Joel Porte, 75–92. New York: Library of America, 1983.

———. "The Poet." In *Emerson: Essays and Lectures*, edited by Joel Porte, 447–68. New York: Library of America, 1983.

Ernst, Morris L., and Alan U. Schwartz. *Privacy: The Right to Be Let Alone*. New York: Macmillan, 1962.

Ex Parte Crow Dog, 109 U.S. 556 (1883).

Falkowski, James E. *Indian Law/Race Law: A Five-Hundred-Year History*. New York: Praeger, 1992.

The Federalist Papers. Edited by Isaac Kramnick. New York: Penguin, 1987.

Ferguson, Robert A. *Law and Letters in American Culture*. Cambridge, Mass.: Harvard University Press, 1984.

Ferguson, SallyAnn H. "Rena Walden: Chesnutt's Failed 'Future American.'" *Southern Literary Journal* 15 (1982): 74–82.

Fetterley, Judith. "'The Temptation to be a Beautiful Object': Double Standard and Double Bind in *The House of Mirth*." *Studies in American Fiction* 5 (1977): 199–211.

Fienberg, Lorne. "Charles W. Chesnutt's *The Wife of His Youth*: The Unveiling of the Black Storyteller." *ATQ* 4 (1988): 219–37.

Fish, Stanley. *Doing What Comes Naturally: Change, Rhetoric, and the Practice of Theory in Literary and Legal Studies*. Durham, N.C.: Duke University Press, 1989.

———. *Is There a Text in This Class? The Authority of Interpretive Communities*. Cambridge, Mass.: Harvard University Press, 1980.

———. *There's No Such Thing as Free Speech and It's a Good Thing, Too*. New York: Oxford University Press, 1994.

Fisher, Philip. *Hard Facts: Setting and Form in the American Novel*. New York: Oxford University Press, 1985.

Fisher, William W., III, Morton J. Horwitz, and Thomas Reed, eds. *American Legal Realism*. New York: Oxford University Press, 1993.

Foner, Eric. *Reconstruction: America's Unfinished Revolution, 1863–1877*. New York: Harper, 1988.

Fortune, Timothy Thomas. *Black and White: Land, Labor and Politics in the South*. New York: Arno Press, 1968.

Foucault, Michel. *Discipline and Punish: The Birth of the Prison*. Translated by Alan Sheridan. New York: Vintage, 1979.

———. *Language, Counter-Memory, Practice: Selected Essays and Interviews*, edited by Donald F. Bouchard. Ithaca, N.Y.: Cornell University Press, 1977.

Gerber, Philip L. "The Financier Himself: Dreiser and C. T. Yerkes." *PMLA* 8 (1973): 112–21.

Gibson, Donald B. Introduction to *The House behind the Cedars*, by Charles W. Chesnutt. New York: Penguin, 1993.

———. *The Politics of Literary Expression: A Study of Major Black Writers*. Westport, Conn.: Greenwood Press, 1981.

Gillman, Susan. "The Mulatto, Tragic or Triumphant? The Nineteenth-

Century American Race Melodrama." In *The Culture of Sentiment: Race, Gender, and Sentimentality in Nineteenth-Century America*, edited by Shirley Samuels, 221–43. New York: Oxford University Press, 1992.

Gilman, Charlotte Perkins. *The Home.* 1903. Urbana: University of Illinois Press, 1972.

———. *Women and Economics: A Study of the Economic Relation Between Men and Women as a Factor in Social Evolution.* Boston: Small, Maynard, 1899.

Godkin, E. L. "The Rights of the Citizen: IV. To His Own Reputation." *Scribner's Magazine* 8 (1890): 59–67.

Goodman, Nan. *Shifting the Blame: Literature, Law, and the Theory of Accidents in Nineteenth-Century America.* Princeton, N.J.: Princeton University Press, 1998.

Gordon, Robert W. "Legal Thought and Legal Practice in the Age of American Enterprise, 1870–1920." In *Professions and Professional Ideologies in America*, edited by Gerald L. Geison, 70–110. Chapel Hill: University of North Carolina Press, 1983.

Grey, Thomas C. "The Disintegration of Property." In *Property*, edited by J. Roland Pennock and John W. Chapman, 69–85. New York: New York University Press, 1980.

Grossberg, Michael. *Governing the Hearth: Law and the Family in Nineteenth-Century America.* Chapel Hill: University of North Carolina Press, 1985.

Gunning, Sandra. *Race, Rape, and Lynching: The Red Record of American Literature, 1890–1912.* New York: Oxford University Press, 1996.

Gutierrez-Jones, Carl. *Rethinking the Borderlands: Between Chicano Culture and Legal Discourse.* Berkeley: University of California Press, 1995.

Habegger, Alfred. *Gender, Fantasy, and Realism in American Literature.* New York: Columbia University Press, 1982.

Habermas, Jürgen. *Legitimation Crisis.* Translated by Thomas McCarthy. Boston: Beacon Press, 1973.

Hagan, William T. *The Indian Rights Association: The Herbert Welsh Years, 1882–1904.* Tucson: University of Arizona Press, 1985.

Harlan, Louis R. *Booker T. Washington: The Making of a Black Leader, 1856–1901.* London: Oxford University Press, 1972.

Harring, Sidney L. *Crow Dog's Case: American Indian Sovereignty, Tribal Law, and United States Law in the Nineteenth Century.* Cambridge: Cambridge University Press, 1994.

Harris, Cheryl I. "Whiteness as Property." *Harvard Law Review* 106 (1993): 1709–91.

Harris, Trudier. *Exorcising Blackness: Historical and Literary Lynching and Burning Rituals*. Bloomington: Indiana University Press, 1984.

Harsha, William Justin. "Law for the Indians." *North American Review* 134 (1882): 272–92.

Hattenhaur, Darryl. "Racial and Textual Miscegenation in Chesnutt's *The House behind the Cedars*." *Mississippi Quarterly* 47 (1993): 27–48.

Hauptman, Laurence M. "Congress, Plenary Power, and the American Indian, 1870 to 1992." In *Exiled in the Land of the Free: Democracy, Indian Nations, and the U.S. Constitution*, chap. 8. Santa Fe, N.M.: Clear Light, 1992.

Hawkesworth, Mary E. "Knowers, Knowing, Known: Feminist Theory and Claims of Truth." *Signs* 14 (1989): 533–57.

Hedges, Warren. "Howells's 'Wretched Fetishes': Character, Realism, and Other Modern Instances." *Texas Studies in Literature and Language* 38 (1996): 26–50.

Heermance, J. Noel. *Charles W. Chesnutt: America's First Great Black Novelist*. Hamden, Conn.: Archon Books, 1974.

Hegel, Georg Wilhelm Friedrich. *The Philosophy of History*. New York: Dover, 1956.

Hobbes, Thomas. *Leviathan*. Edited by Michael Oakeshott. New York: Macmillan, 1962.

Hofstadter, Richard. *The Age of Reform: From Bryan to F.D.R.* New York: Knopf, 1963.

Hohfeld, Wesley Newcomb. "Some Fundamental Legal Conceptions as Applied in Judicial Reasoning." *Yale Law Journal* 23 (1913–14): 16–59.

Holmes, Oliver Wendell, Jr. *The Common Law*. Boston: Little, Brown, 1938.

———. "The Law." In *Collected Legal Papers*, 25–28. New York: Harcourt, Brace, 1921.

———. "The Path of the Law." In *Collected Legal Papers*, 167–202. New York: Harcourt, Brace, 1921.

Hopkins, Pauline Elizabeth. *Contending Forces: A Romance Illustrative of Negro Life North and South*. New York: Oxford University Press, 1988.

———. *Hagar's Daughter: A Story of Southern Caste Prejudice*. In *The Magazine Novels of Pauline Hopkins*, 3–284. New York: Oxford University Press, 1988.

———. *Of One Blood: Or, The Hidden Self*. In *The Magazine Novels of Pauline Hopkins*, 285–437. New York: Oxford University Press, 1988.

———. *Primer of Facts Pertaining to the Early Greatness of the African Race*. N.p., 1905.

———. *Winona: A Tale of Negro Life in the South and Southwest*. In *The Magazine Novels of Pauline Hopkins*, 439–621. New York: Oxford University Press, 1988.

Horwitz, Howard. *By the Law of Nature: Form and Value in Nineteenth-Century America*. New York: Oxford University Press, 1991.

Horwitz, Morton J. *The Transformation of American Law, 1870–1960: The Crisis of Legal Orthodoxy*. New York: Oxford University Press, 1992.

Howard, June. *Form and History in American Literary Naturalism*. Chapel Hill: University of North Carolina Press, 1985.

Howells, William Dean. *Criticism and Fiction and Other Essays*. New York: New York University Press, 1965.

———. *Literary Friends and Acquaintance: A Personal Retrospect of American Authorship*. New York: Harper, 1901.

———. "The Man of Letters as a Man of Business." In *Literature and Life*, 1–35. New York: Harper, 1902.

———. *A Modern Instance*. New York: Penguin, 1984.

———. "Police Report." *Atlantic Monthly* 49 (January 1882): 1–16.

———. *The Quality of Mercy*. Bloomington: Indiana University Press, 1979.

———. *Selected Letters, Volume 3: 1882–1891*. Edited by Robert C. Leitz III. Boston: Twayne, 1980.

Hoxie, Frederick E. *A Final Promise: The Campaign to Assimilate the Indians, 1880–1920*. Lincoln: University of Nebraska Press, 1984.

———. *International News Service v. The Associated Press*, 248 U.S. 215 (1918).

Jackson, Helen Hunt. *A Century of Dishonor: A Sketch of the United States Government's Dealings with some of the Indian Tribes*. Norman, Okla.: University of Oklahoma Press, 1995.

———. *Ramona*. New York: Penguin, 1988.

Jackson, Helen Hunt, and Abbot Kinney. *Report on the Condition and Needs of the Mission Indians of California, Made by Special Agents Helen Hunt Jackson and Abbot Kinney, to the Commissioner of Indian Affairs*. Appendix XV to Helen Hunt Jackson, *A Century of Dishonor*. Norman, Okla.: University of Oklahoma Press, 1995.

James, Henry. "The Art of Fiction." In *Partial Portraits*. London, Macmillan, 1919.

Johnson, Barbara. *The Critical Difference: Essays in the Contemporary Rhetoric of Reading*. Baltimore: Johns Hopkins University Press, 1980.

Kahn, Paul W. *The Reign of Law: "Marbury v. Madison" and the Construction of America*. New Haven, Conn.: Yale University Press, 1997.

Kalman, Laura. *Legal Realism at Yale, 1927–1960*. Chapel Hill: University of North Carolina Press, 1986.

Kammen, Michael. *Sovereignty and Liberty: Constitutional Discourse in American Culture*. Madison: University of Wisconsin Press, 1988.

Kaplan, Amy. *The Social Construction of American Realism*. Chicago: University of Chicago Press, 1988.

Karst, Kenneth L. *Belonging to America: Equal Citizenship and the Constitution*. New Haven, Conn.: Yale University Press, 1989.

Keller, Morton J. *Affairs of State: Public Life in Late Nineteenth Century America*. Cambridge, Mass.: Harvard University Press, Belknap Press, 1977.

Kelman, Mark. *A Guide to Critical Legal Studies*. Cambridge, Mass.: Harvard University Press, 1987.

Kimball, Bruce A. *The "True Professional Ideal" in America: A History*. Cambridge: Blackwell, 1992.

King, Alexander C. "Lynching as a Penalty." In *Race Problems of the South: Report of the Proceedings of the First Annual Conference Held Under the Auspices of the Southern Society for the Promotion of the Study of Race Conditions and Problems in the South*. New York: Negro Universities Press, 1969.

Kolko, Gabriel. *The Triumph of Conservatism: A Reinterpretation of American History, 1900–1916*. New York: Macmillan, 1963.

Kronman, Anthony T. *Max Weber*. Stanford, Calif.: Stanford University Press, 1983.

Kurland, Philip B., and Gerhard Casper, eds. *Landmark Briefs and Arguments of the Supreme Court of the United States: Constitutional Law*. Vol. 13. Arlington, Va.: University Publications of America, 1975.

Larson, Magali Sarfatti. *The Rise of Professionalism: A Sociological Analysis*. Berkeley: University of California Press, 1977.

Lehan, Richard. *Theodore Dreiser: His World and His Novels*. Carbondale: Southern Illinois University Press, 1974.

Lingeman, Richard. *Theodore Dreiser: An American Journey, 1908–1945*. New York: Putnam, 1990.

Lippmann, Walter. *Drift and Mastery: An Attempt to Diagnose the Current Unrest*. New York: Henry Holt, 1917.

Lochner v. New York, 198 U.S. 45 (1905).

Locke, John. *Two Treatises of Government*. Cambridge: Cambridge University Press, 1963.

Lofgren, Charles A. *The Plessy Case: A Legal-Historical Interpretation*. New York: Oxford University Press, 1987.

Luis-Brown, David. "'White Slaves' and the 'Arrogant *Mestiza*': Reconfiguring Whiteness in *The Squatter and the Don* and *Ramona*." *American Literature* 69 (1997): 813–39.

Lynn, Kenneth S. *William Dean Howells: An American Life*. New York: Harcourt, 1971.

Macpherson, C. B. *The Political Theory of Possessive Individualism: Hobbes to Locke.* Oxford: Oxford University Press, 1962.

Maine, Henry Sumner. *Ancient Law.* Dorset, 1986.

Marbury v. Madison, 5 U.S. 137 (1803).

Marzolf, Marion Tuttle. *Civilizing Voices: American Press Criticism, 1880–1950.* New York: Longman, 1991.

Mathes, Valerie Sherer. *Helen Hunt Jackson and Her Indian Reform Legacy.* Austin: University of Texas Press, 1990.

———, ed. *The Indian Reform Letters of Helen Hunt Jackson, 1879–1885.* Norman, Okla.: University of Oklahoma Press, 1998.

McCarthy, J. Thomas. *The Rights of Publicity and Privacy.* New York: C. Boardman, 1987.

McPherson, James M. *The Abolitionist Legacy: From Reconstruction to the NAACP.* Princeton, N.J.: Princeton University Press, 1975.

Meier, August. *Negro Thought in America, 1880–1915: Radical Ideologies in the Age of Booker T. Washington.* Ann Arbor: University of Michigan Press, 1966.

Melville, Herman. *Billy Budd, Sailor (An Inside Narrative).* Edited by Harrison Hayford and Merton M. Sealts Jr. Chicago: University of Chicago Press, 1962.

Menand, Louis. *Discovering Modernism: T. S. Eliot and His Context.* New York: Oxford University Press, 1987.

Michaels, Walter Benn. *The Gold Standard and the Logic of Naturalism: American Literature at the Turn of the Century.* Berkeley: University of California Press, 1987.

Milder, Robert. *Critical Essays on Melville's Billy Budd, Sailor.* Boston: C. K. Hall, 1989.

Miller, J. Hillis. *Topographies.* Stanford, Calif.: Stanford University Press, 1995.

Minow, Martha. "Stories in Law." In *Law's Stories: Narrative and Rhetoric in the Law,* edited by Peter Brooks and Paul Gewirtz, 24–36. New Haven, Conn.: Yale University Press, 1996.

Moylan, Michele. "Materiality as Performance: The Forming of Helen Hunt Jackson's *Ramona.*" In *Reading Books: Essays of the Material Text and Literature in America,* edited by Michele Moylan and Lane Stiles, 223–47. Amherst: University of Massachusetts Press, 1996.

Newton, Nell Jessup. "Federal Power Over Indians: Its Sources, Scope, and Limitations." *University of Pennsylvania Law Review* 132 (1984): 195–288.

Northern Securities Co. v. United States, 193 U.S. 197 (1904).

Olsen, Rodney D. *Dancing in Chains: The Youth of William Dean Howells.* New York: New York University Press, 1991.

Orr, Elaine N. "Contractual Law, Relational Whisper: A Reading of Edith
Wharton's *The House of Mirth*." *Modern Language Quarterly* 52 (1991):
53–70.

Paul, Arnold M. *Conservative Crisis and the Rule of Law: Attitudes of Bar and
Bench, 1887–1895*. Ithaca, N.Y.: Cornell University Press, 1960.

Peterson, Carla L. "Unsettled Frontiers: Race, History, and Romance in
Pauline Hopkins's *Contending Forces*." In *Famous Last Words: Changes in
Gender and Narrative Closure*, edited by Alison Booth, 177–96.
Charlottesville: University Press of Virginia, 1993.

Pillsbury, Albert E. "A Brief Inquiry into a Federal Remedy for Lynching."
Harvard Law Review 15 (1902): 707–13.

Pizer, Donald. *The Novels of Theodore Dreiser: A Critical Study*. Minneapolis:
University of Minnesota Press, 1976.

———. *Realism and Naturalism in Nineteenth-Century American Literature*.
Carbondale: Southern Illinois University Press, 1984.

Plessy v. Ferguson, 163 U.S. 537 (1896).

Pohlman, H. L. *Justice Oliver Wendell Holmes and Utilitarian Jurisprudence*.
Cambridge, Mass.: Harvard University Press, 1984.

Posner, Richard A. *Law and Literature: A Misunderstood Relation*. Cambridge,
Mass.: Harvard University Press, 1988.

———. "The Right of Privacy." *Georgia Law Review* 12 (1978): 393–428.

Priest, Loring Benson. *Uncle Sam's Stepchildren: The Reformation of United States
Indian Policy, 1865–1887*. New Brunswick, N.J.: Rutgers University Press,
1942.

Proprietors of the Charles River Bridge v. Proprietors of the Warren Bridge,
11 Pet. 420 (1837).

Prucha, Francis Paul, ed. *Documents of United States Indian Policy*. Lincoln:
University of Nebraska Press, 1975.

———. *The Great Father: The United States Government and the American
Indians*. Vol. 1. Lincoln: University of Nebraska Press, 1984.

Reich, Charles A. "The Tragedy of Justice in *Billy Budd*." In *Critical Essays on
Melville's Billy Budd, Sailor*, edited by Robert Milder, 127–42. Boston:
C. K. Hall, 1989.

Robbins, Bruce. *Secular Vocations: Intellectuals, Professionalism, Culture*. London:
Verso, 1993.

Roberson v. Rochester Folding Box Co., 64 N.E. 442 (1902).

Rosaldo, Renato. *Culture and Truth: The Remaking of Social Analysis*. Boston:
Beacon Press, 1989.

Rose, Carol M. *Property and Persuasion: Essays on the History, Theory, and Rhetoric of Ownership*. Boulder, Colo.: Westview Press, 1994.

Saks, Eva. "Representing Miscegenation Law." *Raritan* 8 (1988): 39–70.

Scheckel, Susan. *The Insistence of the Indian: Race and Nationalism in Nineteenth-Century American Literature*. Princeton, N.J.: Princeton University Press, 1998.

Sedlack, Robert P. "The Evolution of Charles Chesnutt's *The House behind the Cedars*." *CLA Journal* 19 (1975): 125–35.

Showalter, Elaine. *Sister's Choice: Tradition and Change in American Women's Writing*. Oxford: Clarendon Press, 1991.

Simpson, Lewis P. *The Man of Letters in New England and the South: Essays on the History of the Literary Vocation in America*. Baton Rouge: Louisiana State University Press, 1973.

Sklar, Martin J. *The Corporate Reconstruction of American Capitalism, 1890–1916: The Market, the Law, and Politics*. Cambridge: Cambridge University Press, 1988.

Smith, Adam. *The Wealth of Nations*. Vol. 1. London: J. M. Dent, 1950.

Smith, Carl S., John P. McWilliams Jr., and Maxwell Bloomfield. *Law and American Literature: A Collection of Essays*. New York: Knopf, 1983.

Smith, Henry Nash. *Democracy and the Novel: Popular Resistance to Classic American Writers*. New York: Oxford University Press, 1978.

Stanton, Elizabeth Cady. "Solitude of Self." In *The Concise History of Woman Suffrage: Selections from the Classic Work of Stanton, Anthony, Gage, and Harper*, edited by Mari Jo Buhle and Paul Buhle. Urbana: University of Illinois Press, 1979.

State v. Vinson J. Cantey, 2 Hill 614 (S.C., 1835).

Sumner, William Graham. "The Mores of the Present and the Future." In *Essays of William Graham Sumner*, edited by Albert Galloway Keller and Maurice R. Davie. Vol. 1, 73–88. New Haven, Conn.: Yale University Press, 1934.

Sundquist, Eric J. *To Wake the Nations: Race in the Making of American Literature*. Cambridge: Harvard University Press, Belknap Press, 1993.

Tate, Claudia. *Domestic Allegories of Political Desire: The Black Heroine's Text at the Turn of the Century*. New York: Oxford University Press, 1992.

Thomas, Brook. *American Literary Realism and the Failed Promise of Contract*. Berkeley: University of California Press, 1997.

———. *Cross-Examinations of Law and Literature: Cooper, Hawthorne, Stowe, and Melville*. Cambridge: Cambridge University Press, 1987.

Tompkins, Jane. *Sensational Designs: The Cultural Work of American Fiction, 1790–1860*. New York: Oxford University Press, 1985.

Tourgée, Albion W. *Bricks Without Straw*. New York: Fords, Howard, and Hulbert, 1880.

———. "Study in Civilization." *North American Review* 143 (1886): 246–61.

Twain, Mark. *Pudd'nhead Wilson*. Oxford: Oxford University Press, 1992.

Uba, George R. "*Status* and *Contract*: The Divorce Dispute of the 'Eighties and Howells' *A Modern Instance*. *Colby Library Quarterly* 19 (1983): 78–89.

U.S. v. Kagama, 118 U.S. 375 (1886).

U.S. v. Rogers, 45 U.S. 567 (1846).

Veblen, Thorstein. *The Theory of Business Enterprise*. New York: Scribner's, 1904.

Veysey, Laurence. "The Plural Organized Worlds of the Humanities." In *The Organization of Knowledge in Modern America, 1860–1920*, edited by Alexandra Oleson and John Voss, 51–106. Baltimore: Johns Hopkins University Press, 1979.

Wald, Priscilla. *Constituting Americans: Cultural Anxiety and Narrative Form*. Durham, N.C.: Duke University Press, 1995.

Walker, Cheryl. *Indian Nation: Native American Literature and Nineteenth-Century Nationalisms*. Durham, N.C.: Duke University Press, 1997.

Wardrop, Daneen. "The *Jouissant* Politics of Helen Hunt Jackson's *Ramona*: The Ground That Is 'Mother's Lap.'" In *Speaking the Other Self: American Women Writers*, edited by Jeanne Campbell Reesman, 27–38. Athens, Ga.: University of Georgia Press, 1997.

Warner, Charles Dudley. *The American Newspaper*. Boston: James R. Osgood, 1881.

Warren, Kenneth W. *Black and White Strangers: Race and American Literary Realism*. Chicago: University of Chicago Press, 1993.

Warren, Samuel D., and Louis D. Brandeis. "The Right to Privacy." *Harvard Law Review* 4 (1890): 193–220.

Washington, Booker T. *The Future of the American Negro*. Boston: Small, Maynard, 1899.

Watson, Carole McAlpine. *Prologue: The Novels of Black American Women, 1891–1965*. Westport, Conn.: Greenwood Press, 1985.

Watson, E. L. Grant. "Melville's Testament of Acceptance." In *Critical Essays on Melville's Billy Budd, Sailor*, edited by Robert Milder, 41–45. Boston: C. K. Hall, 1989

Weber, Max. *Max Weber on Law in Economy and Society*. Edited by Max Rheinstein. Cambridge, Mass.: Harvard University Press, 1954.

Weisberg, Richard. *The Failure of the Word: The Protagonist as Lawyer in Modern Fiction.* New Haven, Conn.: Yale University Press, 1984.

Wells, Ida B. *Crusade for Justice: The Autobiography of Ida B. Wells.* Edited by Alfreda M. Duster. Chicago: University of Chicago Press, 1970.

———. *Southern Horrors: Lynch Law in All Its Phases.* In *Selected Works of Ida B. Wells-Barnett,* edited by Trudier Harris, 14–45. 1892. New York: Oxford University Press, 1991.

Wharton, Edith. *The Age of Innocence.* New York: Collier, 1948.

———. *A Backward Glance.* New York: Appleton-Century, 1934.

———. *The House of Mirth.* New York: Penguin, 1985.

———. "The Other Two." In *The Collected Short Stories of Edith Wharton,* edited by R. W. B. Lewis, Vol. 1., 380–96. New York: Scribner's, 1968.

———. *The Touchstone.* In *Madame de Treymes and Three Novellas.* New York: Macmillan, 1987.

White, G. Edward. *Justice Oliver Wendell Holmes: Law and the Inner Self.* New York: Oxford University Press, 1993.

White, Hayden. "The Value of Narrativity in the Representation of Reality." In *On Narrative,* edited by W. J. T. Mitchell, 1–23. Chicago: University of Chicago Press, 1981.

Wiebe, Robert H. *The Search for Order, 1877–1920.* New York: Hill and Wang, 1967.

Wiener, Philip P. *Evolution and the Founders of Pragmatism.* Cambridge: Harvard University Press, 1949.

Wilkinson, Charles. *American Indians, Time, and the Law.* New Haven, Conn.: Yale University Press, 1987.

Williams, George Washington. *History of the Negro Race in America, 1619–1880.* New York: Arno Press, 1968.

Williams, Patricia J. *The Alchemy of Race and Rights.* Cambridge: Harvard University Press, 1991.

Williamson, Joel. *The Crucible of Race: Black-White Relations in the American South since Emancipation.* New York: Oxford University Press, 1984.

Wilson, Edmund. *Patriotic Gore: Studies in the Literature of the American Civil War.* New York: Oxford University Press, 1966.

Wilson, Woodrow. *The New Freedom: A Call for the Emancipation of the Generous Energies of a People.* New York: Doubleday, 1913.

Wolff, Cynthia Griffin. *A Feast of Words: The Triumph of Edith Wharton.* New York: Oxford University Press, 1995.

Worcester v. Georgia, 31 U.S. 515 (1832).

Wright, Nathalia. "The Significance of the Legal Profession in *A Modern Instance*." In *From Irving to Steinbeck: Studies of American Literature*, edited by Motley Deakin and Peter Lisca, 57–70. Gainesville, Fla.: University of Florida Press, 1972.

Yeazell, Ruth Bernard. "The Conspicuous Wasting of Lily Bart." *ELH* 59 (1992): 713–34.

Ziff, Larzer. *The American 1890's: Life and Times of a Lost Generation*. New York: Viking, 1966.

INDEX